P9-AFT-324

Santa Clara County Free Library

REFERENCE

5816

Santa Clara County Free Library

California

Alum Rock	Milpitas { Calaveras / Community Center / Sunnyhills
Campbell	
Cupertino	Morgan Hill
Gilroy	Saratoga { Community / Village
Los Altos { Main / Woodland	Stanford-Escondido

Research Center-Cupertino

For Bookmobile Service, request schedule

A Personal Name Index to Orton's "Records of California Men in the War of the Rebellion, 1861 to 1867"

GALE GENEALOGY AND LOCAL HISTORY SERIES

Series Editor: J. Carlyle Parker, Head of Public Services and Assistant Library Director, California State College, Stanislaus; and Founder and Librarian Volunteer, Modesto California Branch Genealogical Library of the Genealogical Department of the Church of Jesus Christ of Latter-day Saints, Salt Lake City, Utah

Also in this series:

AMERICAN INDIAN GENEALOGICAL RESEARCH—*Edited by Jimmy B. Parker and Noel R. Barton**

BLACK GENESIS—*Edited by James Rose and Alice Eichholz*

BLACKS IN THE FEDERAL CENSUS—*Edited by James Rose and Alice Eichholz**

CITY COUNTY INDEX TO 1850 CENSUS SCHEDULES—*Edited by J. Carlyle Parker**

COMPENDIUMS OF QUAKER GENEALOGICAL RESEARCH—*Edited by Willard Heiss**

GENEALOGICAL HISTORICAL GUIDE TO LATIN AMERICA—*Edited by Lyman De Platt**

GENEALOGICAL RECORDS OF BLACKS IN SOUTHEASTERN CONNECTICUT, 1650-1900—*Edited by James Rose and Barbara Brown**

GENEALOGICAL RESEARCH FOR CZECH AND SLOVAK AMERICANS—*Edited by Olga K. Miller*

LIBRARY SERVICE FOR GENEALOGISTS—*Edited by J. Carlyle Parker**

MENNONITE GENEALOGICAL RESEARCH—*Edited by Delbert Gratz**

MONTANA'S GENEALOGICAL RECORDS—*Edited by Dennis L. Richards**

A SURVEY OF AMERICAN GENEALOGICAL PERIODICALS AND PERIODICAL INDEXES—*Edited by Kip Sperry*

WESTERN CANADIAN GENEALOGICAL RESEARCH—*Edited by Jimmy B. Parker and Noel R. Barton**

*in preparation

General Editor: Paul Wasserman, Professor and former Dean, School of Library and Information Services, University of Maryland

Managing Editor: Denise Allard Adzigian, Gale Research Company

A Personal Name Index to Orton's "Records of California Men in the War of the Rebellion, 1861 to 1867"

Volume 5 in the Gale Genealogy and Local History Series

Index
Compiled by

J. Carlyle Parker

Head of Public Services and Assistant Library Director
California State College, Stanislaus
and
Founder and Librarian Volunteer
Modesto California Branch Genealogical Library of the
Genealogical Department of the Church of Jesus Christ of
Latter-day Saints
Salt Lake City, Utah

179687

Gale Research Company
Book Tower, Detroit, Michigan 48226

Bibliographical Note

The material in this volume indexes personal name references in "Records of California Men in the War of the Rebellion, 1861 to 1867," compiled by Brigadier-General Richard H. Orton, Adjutant-General of California, and published by J. D. Young, Superintendent of State Printing, Sacramento, 1890.

"Records of California Men in the War of the Rebellion, 1861-1867" is available in a clothbound reprint from the Gale Research Company.

Library of Congress Cataloging in Publication Data

Parker, J   Carlyle.
    A personal name index to Records of California men in the War of the Rebellion, 1861 to 1867, compiled by Brig.-Gen. Richard H. Orton ...

    (Gale genealogy and local history series ; v. 5)
    1. California. Adjutant General's Office. Records of California men in the War of the Rebellion, 1861 to 1867—Indexes. 2. California—Militia—Indexes. 3. United States—History—Civil War, 1861-1865—Regimental histories—California—Indexes. 4. United States—History—Civil War, 1861-1865—Registers, lists, etc.—Indexes. I. Title.
E497.3.C162P37   016.9737'494   78-15674
ISBN 0-8103-1402-9

To
Janet

VITA

J. Carlyle Parker is head of public services and assistant library director at California State College, Stanislaus. He also founded and is the volunteer librarian of the Modesto California Branch Genealogical Library of the Genealogical Department of the Church of Jesus Christ of Latter-day Saints, Salt Lake City. He received his B.A. in history from Brigham Young University and M.L.S. from the University of California, Berkeley.

Parker has authored numerous articles and reviews for library and genealogical journals, and compiled and edited several bibliographies, indexes, and union catalogs. He also has conducted oral history interviews and is an instructor and lecturer on genealogical, historical, and oral history research.

CONTENTS

INTRODUCTION

Over a century and a decade have passed since the first incomplete Register of California Volunteers was published in 1865. In an effort to include volunteers who served until 1867 and correct numerous omissions and errors, the State Legislature, in 1889, authorized preparation and publication of a new list. Adjutant-General Orton compiled and published the second list in 1890. General Orton admitted that he was not able to prepare a complete list and history of volunteers, as the records in his office were incomplete. Except for the California Hundred and the California Cavalry Battalion, Californians that went East and joined other states' units were not included in Orton's work.

Orton's list includes two cavalry regiments, one cavalry battalion, eight infantry regiments, and three infantry battalions. The volume also includes a list of deceased officers and enlisted men, brief histories of each unit, and an incomplete list of the stations occupied. The entry for each name includes the full name; rank; place of enrollment; date of enlistment; date of muster; and remarks that include the place and date of, and the reason for, mustering out; desertion; reenlistment; transfer; promotion; discharge; death; and wounds. Each company's commissioned and noncommissioned officers are listed by rank. The names of enlisted men or privates are in alphabetical order by company; and, since there were 126 companies of California volunteers, this made Orton's list extremely difficult to use.

When I was first introduced to Orton's list of Civil War volunteers, I was very disappointed to learn that it did not have an index. Desperation drives many librarians, historians, and genealogists to index research materials that are impossible to use. Thus I was driven to prepare a sane approach to Orton's list.

This index includes 14,445 names in one alphabetical order. The alphabetical order generally follows the filing rules used for the lists of privates in Orton's list. Names that begin with M', Mac, and Mc are filed as spelled to conform to Orton's list. Abbreviations have been alphabetized as if spelled out. Misspelled names have not been corrected. Rank designations have been excluded except when no given name is printed. Some names also appear more than once on a page and no attempt has been made to identify them. It is

common for names to appear more than once in the historical narrative and among the lists of commissioned and noncommissioned officers.

Also included in the index are the names of Confederate and Union political and military leaders mentioned in some of the historical narratives. A duplicate list of volunteers identified as blacks is included at the end of the index for the convenience of researchers interested in black genealogy and/or history.

Researchers interested in obtaining copies of the Compiled Service Records of a person named in this index should request a copy of GSA Form 6751 from Military Service Records (NNCC), National Archives (GSA), Washington, D. C. 20408. To complete this form the researcher needs to consult Orton to determine the company and regiment of the volunteer and record this information on it. The "Military" box under "1. Check Record Desired" should be checked to obtain the Compiled Service Records.

The Compiled Service Records contain a multitude of data relating to the military service of individuals. The genealogical data given is the volunteer's name, place of birth, age, and occupation.

The "Pension" box should also be checked, as the pension records also contain some genealogical data, namely certificates of birth and marriage. Widows' applications include a death certificate as well. A family data questionnaire and dependents' personal histories may be included in some files.

The papers of the companies of the California Volunteers are housed in the California State Archives in Sacramento as a part of the Military Records Group. These papers do not include the service records of volunteers. They contain less biographical information than Orton's list and virtually no genealogical information. These records are unindexed and are also difficult to search.

Another source that may need to be consulted by researchers of California Volunteers is the National Archives Microfilm Publications, Microcopy No. 533, INDEX TO COMPILED SERVICE RECORDS OF VOLUNTEER UNION SOLDIERS WHO SERVED IN ORGANIZATIONS FROM THE STATE OF CALIFORNIA, published by the National Archives of the National Archives and Records Service, General Services Administration, Washington, D. C., 1964. This index is contained on seven reels of microfilm and may be obtained on interlibrary loan from the Federal Archives and Records Center, 1000 Commodore Drive, San Bruno, California 94066. It may also be purchased from the National Archives, Washington, D. C. Its contents are as follows: Roll or reel 1, A-Cl; 2, Co-Fos; 3, Fot-I; 4, J-McD; 5, McE-P; 6, Q-St; and 7, Su-Z.

In comparing the first 200 entries of the Orton index with the above National Archives index, it was found that the Orton index contained 15 (7 1/2 percent) names not found in the National Archives index. Eight (4 percent) of the names were of volunteers in the California Hundred and/or California Cavalry

Battalion that joined the Second Massachusetts Cavalry. One name was of a civilian mentioned in part of Orton's narrative. The National Archives index contained 10 (5 percent) names that were not included in Orton. It also contained references to 4 (2 percent) names of service men from other states that were temporarily attached to California units. Their service records would be filed in the state to which their organization belonged.

The National Archives index also contains numerous see references or "Reference Cards" from variable spellings of surnames to the surname under which a volunteer's records are filed. There are also some differences between the two indexes in the surname spellings and in the middle initials.

As a result of these differences, it may be wise for some researchers to use both indexes. However, as a general rule, the Orton index should be adequate for most research needs. Because of its easier use, accessibility, and lower cost, it will, of course, receive the most use. Nevertheless, the National Archives index must not be forgotten; and, in some cases, it will be essential to consult it.

Some useful and interesting aspects of Civil War history that researchers should consider are mentioned in the following book:

Groene, Bertram H. TRACING YOUR CIVIL WAR ANCESTOR. Winston-Salem, North Carolina: J.F. Blair, 1973.

As a general rule, the place of enrollment given in Orton was at or near the home of each enlistee and would probably have been his county of residence. As a result, this work will be of value to genealogists and historians as a state wide index or locality finding aid to identify previously unknown places of residence. It can also be used as an index to the Compiled Service Records and Pension Records of the National Archives, wherein genealogists and historians can obtain the birth date and place; marriage date and place; perhaps death date and place; and other historical data concerning their volunteer ancestors by submitting GSA Form 6751.

I am grateful to Denise Parker, who typed the manuscript, and to Mary E. Schell, Government Publications Section, California State Library, for supplying a copy of Orton's nineteenth-century work. David L. Snyder of the California State Archives provided information concerning the present status of California Civil War records. James D. Walker, research consultant and genealogy and local history specialist of the National Archives, and JoAnn Williamson, chief archivist of the San Bruno Federal Archives and Records Center, were very helpful with information concerning the records available at the National Archives and the San Bruno Center. Gratitude is also expressed for the patience of my librarian, faculty, and church colleagues who tolerated my indexing during countless administrative meetings and conventions.

May every researcher find his or her veteran; may they enjoy the search; and

may they treasure the smallest bit of information they discover concerning him.

J. Carlyle Parker
Turlock, California

A PERSONAL NAME INDEX TO ORTON'S
"RECORDS OF CALIFORNIA MEN IN THE WAR OF
THE REBELLION, 1861 TO 1867"

A

Abbey, Volney 260
Abbott, Augustine M. 760
Abbott, Benjamin 727
Abbott, Chandler C. 671, 713
Abbott, Charles 750
Abbott, Ira 526, 544, 566
Abbott, John 87, 136, 147, 286
Abbott, Otis F. 631
Abbott, William H. 244
Abby, Samuel 864
Abeley, Frederick 652
Abil, Francisco 318
Abila, Santos 318
Abler, Louis 556
Abrams, Evans 492
Abrams, Francis 610, 618
Acker, Edward M. 664
Ackerman, Charles H. 854
Ackerman, Herman 449
Ackerman, James B. 854
Ackerman, Joseph 664
Ackley, James E. 610
Acton, John 526, 576
Acton, William 808
Actors, William H. P. 645
Adair, James A. 691
Adams, Alexander 337
Adams, Alfred 835
Adams, Augustus 736
Adams, Benjamin F. 245
Adams, Charles 252, 545, 576, 845
Adams, Charles D. 252
Adams, Charles E. 243

Adams, Charles H. 118
Adams, David 800
Adams, Emanuel 162
Adams, George 756
Adams, George W. 785, 871
Adams, Green 800
Adams, Henry 805
Adams, James L. 88, 252
Adams, John 236, 458, 816, 871
Adams, John M. 142
Adams, John O. 732
Adams, John Q. 618
Adams, John W. 220
Adams, Jonathan 610
Adams, Jos. L. 143
Adams, Nelson E. 211
Adams, Robert 590
Adams, Weston 787
Adams, William 203, 269
Adams, William H. 286
Adams, William R. 526, 576
Adams, Zebdiel B. 850, 864
Adamson, Luther J. 747
Addee, Daniel 478
Addis, Samuel 269
Addison, Thomas J. 124
Adelsdorfer, Isaac 441
Adle, Oliver 355
Adler, Louis 727
Admire, William P. 252
Adney, John W. 373
Adolphe, Reige G. 742
Adrian, Louis 774
Adshed, William 657
Agan, Hugh 603

Agan, Patrick 500
Agard, Edwin 773
Aguayo, Antonio 318
Aguiar, Rafael 318
Ahern, James 413, 682
Ahern, William 342, 390
Aherns, Carl 726
Ahlquist, John 400
Aikens, Nicholas M. 871
Ainsworth, William 545, 810
Aitken, James 753
Aitken, William 760
Akers, Thomas 682
Akers, William 844
Akey, David B. 147, 200, 234, 420
Akins, Nicholas M. 699
Akins, Thomas 277
Albans, Michael 311
Albee, Charles P. 395, 409, 713
Alber, John 478
Albers, Conrad 526
Albert, Henry 92, 100
Albert, James W. 770
Albert, John S.H. 464
Alberton, Edwin 395, 409, 717
Albrecht, Adam 442
Albro, Thomas J. 269
Albus, Conrad 434
Alcott, Jachies D. 478
Aldrich, Julius 800
Ales, William H. 386, 390
Alexander, Andrew H. 258
Alexander, Chas. 138
Alexander, Daniel 639, 664
Alexander, Franklin J. 803
Alexander, Frederick 526
Alexander, John 485, 500
Alexander, John D. 839
Alexander, Marcus 434
Alexander, Morin 526, 576
Alexander, Thomas 363
Algie, Hugh 867
Algyer, John 124, 202
Alison, Warren 433
Allan, Albert 252
Allander, William 844
Allen, Pvt. 187
Allen, Ai. W. 359
Allen, Alfred 773
Allen, Alma H. 252

Allen, Charles 458, 854
Allen, Charles P. 545, 571
Allen, Cornelius C. 355
Allen, David H. 269
Allen, E. Henry 854
Allen, Edgar H. 203
Allen, Edward L. 813
Allen, George H. 857
Allen, Henry 638
Allen, Henry Lew 790
Allen, Henry S. 600, 609
Allen, Henry W. 854
Allen, Hiram H. 471
Allen, Isaac P. 236
Allen, James 153, 252, 566
Allen, John 395, 687
Allen, John A. 800
Allen, John C. 526
Allen, John E. 457
Allen, John H. 269
Allen, Lee 776
Allen, Lindley H. 753
Allen, Noah 760
Allen, Samuel E. 536, 556
Allen, Thomas 90, 209
Allen, Walter A. 153
Allen, William B. 373
Allen, William H. 603, 618
Allen, William L. 500
Allen, William N. 543
Allendorff, John C. 143
Alley, James D. 203
Alleyn, Charles I. 709
Allis, Richard 220
Allison, James 203, 645
Allison, John 203
Allison, William L. 845
Allkire, Henry J. 819
Allman, John 179
Allman, John H. 260, 286
Alloway, John 691
Allsopp, John B. 464
Allwell, Andrew 867
Allymann, Thomas 833
Allyne, Samuel H. 73, 89, 124, 871
Alpeter, Henry 220
Alquist, Johan 691
Alsover, James P. 525
Altamirano, Isidro 318

Altenkirch, Jacob 220
Alvarado, Estevan 318
Alvord, Gen. 510
Alvord, William 28
Alyea, Joseph 347, 774
Amador, Trinidad 92
Amaro, Juan 311
Amer, Crannell 226
Ames, Everett 227
Ames, Harry S. 235
Ames, John G. 220
Ames, Seneca G. 163
Ames, William 377
Ameson, Nelson 100
Ammerman, Andrew J. 652
Ammon, Charles G. 840
Anatole, Warsaw 413
Anatole, Warsew 704
Andel, Charles W. 773
Anderson, Parson 179
Anderson, Allen L. 796, 799
Anderson, Andrew 760
Anderson, Anthony 337
Anderson, Buckner 101
Anderson, Charles 566, 736
Anderson, Christian 492
Anderson, Edward 790
Anderson, Frank 603
Anderson, Fred 347
Anderson, Frederick 727
Anderson, George 735, 854
Anderson, J. 179
Anderson, James 220, 269, 442,
  449, 556, 631, 691, 736, 871
Anderson, James B. 395, 695
Anderson, Jasper N. 736
Anderson, Jeremiah S. 785
Anderson, John 228, 464, 717, 864
Anderson, John, 2d 864
Anderson, John G. 742
Anderson, John W. 236, 252
Anderson, Joseph 553, 556
Anderson, Joseph S. 153, 871
Anderson, Larz 821
Anderson, Lewis 178, 277, 871
Anderson, Martin 713
Anderson, Neils 536, 545
Anderson, Nicholas 471
Anderson, Ole 845
Anderson, Peter 619, 782
Anderson, Richard R. 600, 610, 652

Anderson, Robert H. 449
Anderson, Samuel 682, 871
Anderson, Thomas 118, 210
Anderson, Walter B. 767
Anderson, William 458, 844
Anderson, William H. 713
Anderson, Wilson 434
Anderson, Wilson P. 219
Andress, James M. 652
Andrew, George 296
Andrews, Bvt. Maj. 36
Andrews, Gov. 848
Andrews, Alexander 788
Andrews, Benjamin F. 458
Andrews, Charles 347
Andrews, David P. 98, 122
Andrews, George 619
Andrews, George W. 286
Andrews, Henry 449, 478
Andrews, John Y. 555, 566
Andrews, Joseph 337
Andrews, Louis 377
Andrews, Stiles B. 337, 386
Andrews, Theodore R. 464, 492
Andrews, Thomas C. 442
Andrus, Isaac 639
Angel, Charles W. 570
Angel, Joseph 158, 774
Angelo, Raomage 639
Angels, Richard W. 269
Angle, Armatus L. 484
Anhisir, William B. 458
Anks, William 756
Annan, William 111
Ansen, Ole 603
Ansley, Stogdel 277
Anson, Peter C. 236
Antes, Ramon 774
Anthony, Asa 286, 871
Anthony, Frank G. 787
Anthony, Henry K. 218
Anthony, Lewis R. 442
Anthony, Matthew J. 824
Anthony, Stephen 871
Anthony, William G. 854
Anthony, William P. 449, 458
Anthony, Wright 101, 111
Antilotto, Joseph 355
Antonia, Carlos 311
Antonio, Reyes José 318
Anwater, Charles 571
Anwater, John 571

Aper, Herman 770
Apgar, Richard M. 781
Applebury, William S. 790, 793
Appleby, William 631
Applegate, David C. 871
Applegate, William C. 367, 390, 409
Appleget, David C. 404, 709
Appleton, George 433, 871
Appleton, Jonathan R. 682, 871
Aramento, Thomas 318
Arbonville, Francois 458
Archer, Andrew J. 785
Archer, Isaac 359
Archibald, James P. 750
Arcola, Andrew 645
Arden, Horace 355
Arendt, James H. 652
Areya, Marcos 307
Argo, Henry C. 111, 871
Argust, Benjamin M. 324, 363
Arillanes, J. de la Luz 315
Arillanes, J. Vicente 315
Aristido, Corquret 310
Arling, Isaac S. 664
Arloff, Charles W. 203
Armitage, John 525, 543, 554, 581
Armor, Robert H. 871
Armour, Robert H. 449
Armstrong, David 603
Armstrong, George 571
Armstrong, Hugh 854
Armstrong, John 252, 603
Armstrong, Monroe 871
Armstrong, Munroe 153
Armstrong, Nelson 709
Armstrong, Thomas T. 603
Armstrong, William 395, 699, 871
Armstrong, Wm. H. 372
Armstrong, William O. 260
Arneson, Nelson 111
Arnett, Frank C. 390, 409, 713
Arnett, John 793
Arnette, Frank C. 409, 713
Arnhold, Ferdinand 235
Arnold, David E. 153
Arnold, Edwin L. 368
Arnold, George W. 136, 147, 162, 244
Arnold, Granville S. 124, 413

Arnold, Philip 664, 756
Arnold, Vincent 788
Arnold, Wales 359
Aroyers, George 203
Arthur, Augustus 779
Arthur, John 534
Arthur, William 227
Artois, Gaston d' 732, 742, 802
Arzaga, Lauriano 318
Ash, David 404, 710
Ash, James M. 603
Ash, Lewis 625
Ash, Michael 704
Ash, Thomas P. 788
Ashbrook, James 458
Ashbrook, Truman 808
Ashburn, Joseph 603
Ashbury, John 713
Ashby, Charles H. 346
Ashby, Rice M. 645
Ashim, Lewis 220
Ashley, Joseph B. 808
Ashley, Lyman W. 245
Ashman, Wells D. 790
Ashmead, John S. 98, 101
Ashurst, George C. 771
Asken, James 790
Askew, William P. 269
Aspell, Samuel Hancock 354, 871
Assedo, Victor 311
Astell, James E. 610
Astill, Richard 400
Astorga, Ramon 307
Atchison, Charles 656
Atchison, Hiram 657
Atchison, James M. 800, 871
Athan, Franklin 582
Atherton, Henry L. 245
Atkins, Jesse 478
Atkins, Thomas 296
Atkinson, Charles 492, 810
Atkinson, Edward W. 566
Atkinson, James 567
Atkinson, James P. 269
Atkinson, John G. 359
Atkinson, William C. 324, 364
Atley, Henry 111, 717
Atmore, Matthew 179, 277
Attara, Antonio 492
Atwood, Charles W. 821

Atwood, Elijah A. 210, 871
Atwood, John W. 395, 404, 699
Aufenanger, John 337
Augustin, Abram 337
Augustine, Antoine 111
Auld, Samuel 464
Aulls, William 259
Ausley, S. 179
Auspeck, Henry F. 790
Austin, Adoniram J. 178, 534, 554, 585, 590
Austin, Charles 187, 228, 543, 554, 586, 871
Austin, George 610, 782
Austin, Jacob 662
Austin, James 611, 619
Austin, John 350, 739
Austin, Josephus 434
Austin, W. 35, 38, 39
Anwater, Charles 434
Avalos, Bruno 308
Averill, Evander 245
Aversch, John A. 710
Avert, Charles 742
Avery, Abel 760
Avery, Charles S. 269
Avery, Joseph D. 779
Avet, Julien 545
Axford, John 805
Axin, Titus 526, 576
Axtell, Hiram K. 699
Ayala, Abram 315
Ayala, Fermin 311
Ayala, Jesus 318
Ayala, Ramon 315
Ayer, Edward E. 122
Ayer, Osborn 864
Ayers, Gideon 101, 118
Ayers, John 118

B

Baade, Augustus F. 442
Baades, Ferdinand 478
Babbit, Horace E. 810
Babbit, Horace F. 811
Babcock 28
Babcock, Samuel W. 864
Babcock, Silas B. 867
Babin, Arthur 308

Babin, Louis 603
Bablett, Samuel M. 639
Bacharach, Charles 449
Bacigalupo, Charles 750
Backer, Charles 575-76
Backer, John L. 143
Backus 28
Backus, Samuel W. 242, 864
Bacon, Charles H. 567, 818
Bacon, Henry 148
Bacon, J. S. 28
Bacon, Joseph N. 492
Bacon, T. H. 28
Baddo, Israel 631
Bader, Ferdinand 442
Bader, William 449
Badger, Erwin M. 699
Badger, Frank C. 259
Badger, Samuel 368
Badger, William H. 732
Badillo, F. de Jesus 315
Badillo, Felipe 315
Baer, Charles 603
Bailey, Aldis L. 179, 536, 590
Bailey, Augustus 277
Bailey, Henry 478
Bailey, James 556
Bailey, John 311, 464
Bailey, Joshua E. 638
Bailey, Levi B. 619
Bailey, Sanford 162
Bailey, William 536, 545
Bain, John F. 872
Bainbridge, Robert 471
Baine, John F. 157
Baines, Henry 813
Bair, Joseph W. 111, 717
Baird, Charles L. 625
Baird, Robert 831, 845
Baker 28
Baker, Lt. 18-19
Baker, A. Frank 855
Baker, Abram 657
Baker, Andrew 464
Baker, Artemus D. 220
Baker, Bernard 409, 713
Baker, Bernhard 404
Baker, Charles 526
Baker, Charles A. 742
Baker, Charles O. 449

Baker, Chauncey E. 359
Baker, Frederick 203, 286
Baker, Henry C. 138
Baker, Hiram 793
Baker, James 631, 790
Baker, James H. 132
Baker, John 143, 311, 526, 619, 691
Baker, John A. 590
Baker, John E. 178
Baker, Nelson J. 124, 857
Baker, Ossian 373
Baker, Peter Y. 449, 477
Baker, Rolla 245
Baker, Simeon 805
Baker, Thomas 776
Baker, Wentworth 625
Baker, William 210, 434, 493, 526, 545
Baker, William A. 845
Baker, William R. 210
Balavia, Eugene 727
Balcom, Darnly O. 854
Baldais, José 143
Balderamos, Hermegildo 311
Baldes, Candido 308
Baldes, Joaquin 308, 872
Baldridge, John H. 790
Baldwin, Charles H. 576
Baldwin, Delos 434
Baldwin, Edward 611, 871
Baldwin, Ephraim C. 58, 61, 86, 98, 117, 122
Baldwin, George E. 864
Baldwin, J.A. 178
Baldwin, James W. 203, 803
Baldwin, James W., or H. 871
Baldwin, Josiah A. 864
Baldwin, Marcus T. 373
Baldwin, William H. 242
Bale, Edward 305, 310 317
Balencia, Francisco 308, 872
Balencia, Manuel 308
Balke, Charles 855
Ball, Charles H. 637
Ball, Eldridge B. 782
Ball, George 603
Ball, Isaac H. 651
Ball, James 377
Ball, James M. 736

Ball, John H. 260
Ball, John S. 227
Ball, Joseph H. 449
Ballard, Ephraim 756
Ballard, John B. 779
Ballenboch, William 805
Ballentack, William 872
Balletto, Billi 611
Balling, Anthony 576
Ballinger, Joseph P. 840
Balluff, John 603, 631
Bamford, William 603, 631
Bammann, Charles 805
Banan, John 793
Bancroft, Forrest H. 252
Bancroft, Horatio 73, 118
Bancroft, John 148
Bancroft, Levant 645
Band, George 442
Bandonado, Ygnacio 308
Bandorf, Charles G. 277
Bane, Thomas 535
Baneher, Patrick 252
Banks, Albert 808
Banks, David P. 774
Banks, George 243
Banks, George F. 368
Banks, John 687
Banks, John F. 844
Banks, Robert W. 434, 556, 586
Banman, Charles 458
Bannaghan, Michael 337, 386
Bannister, James 619
Banthem, William 360
Bantle, Frederick 471
Baptiste, Chertane 124
Baptiste, Juan M. 111
Baranowski, Henry 526, 545
Barber, Amos 779
Barber, Charles 148, 872
Barber, Edward E. 138
Barber, George W. 251
Barbey, J.L. 73
Barbour, John 373, 871
Barcafer, Thaddeus 178, 296
Barclay, Alexander F. 652
Barclay, Alexander J. 526
Barclay, William W. 91
Bard, James 864
Barden, George 788

Bardenwerper, Albert 260
Bardwell, James 555, 576
Barkell, Lt. 74
Barker, Geo. M. 464
Barker, Greenlief G. 590
Barker, Potts 816
Barker, Thomas 225, 250
Barlow, Frank 861
Barman, John 277
Barmes, Auguste H. 308
Barmetler, Jacob 236
Barncastle, John D. 695
Barnes, Augustus M. 124
Barnes, George 867
Barnes, George W. 749
Barnes, James 805
Barnes, James B. 872
Barnes, James H. 760
Barnes, John 864
Barnes, John D. 872
Barnes, Joseph H. 286
Barnes, Lafayette 364
Barnes, Richard T. 836
Barnes, Samuel D. 835
Barnes, Walter S. 695, 849, 857
Barnes, William B. 485, 742, 760
Barnes, William R. 132
Barnett, Garrett 625
Barnett, Henry 111, 364, 872
Barnett, John L. 203
Barnett, William S. 704
Barney, Chester L. 833
Barney, George W. 750
Barney, Loring N. 236
Barns, James N. 785, 873
Barnstead, Thomas D. 854
Barnum, Edward K. 813
Barnwell, John S. 739
Barnwell, Thomas F. 816
Bars, Henry F. 652
Baron, James 449
Barr, Edward S. 464
Barr, George W. 545, 582, 861
Barr, John 286, 327, 350
Barr, John L. 485
Barr, Samuel R. 603, 781
Barrett, Enos 824
Barrett, James 47, 69, 89, 872
Barrett, John 610, 664
Barrett, John B. 252

Barrett, Joseph 819
Barrett, Martin H. 691, 727
Barrett, Richard S. 335, 341, 372
Barrett, Thomas 727, 872
Barrett, Willis H. 245
Barrevas, Julian 318
Barron, Francis E. 864
Barron, Michael 556, 582
Barron, William 545, 556, 567, 590
Barrow, William H. 695
Barrow, James B. 556, 567
Barrows, Frederick R. 163
Barrows, James E. 782
Barry, Christian 788
Barry, James 91, 101, 360, 545, 566, 810
Barry, John 259
Barry, Luther M. 110
Barry, Michael 442
Barry, Michael J. 687, 808
Barry, Robert 220, 464, 664
Barry, William 458
Barstow, Joseph 153, 434
Barstow, Joseph G. 760
Bartel, David 260
Bartells, Carston 500
Barth, Charles H. 431, 476
Barthelow, Jasper M. 796, 805
Bartholomew, Andrew J. 611
Barthrop, Edward 236
Bartlett, Charles 491
Bartlett, Charles H. 678
Bartlett, Frederick 774
Bartlett, John 478, 603
Bartlett, Lawrence 236
Bartlett, Nathaniel 201, 260
Bartlett, Nehemiah 630
Bartlett, Simon H. 774
Bartlett, Thomas T. 69-70, 98, 110
Barton, Andrew 773
Barton, Benjamin F. 458
Barton, Charles A. 252
Barton, Charles E. 110
Barton, Charles W. 747
Barton, David 179, 277, 296
Barton, Edward E. 458
Barton, Henry 377, 412, 703
Barton, John 793
Barwell, John 759

Basch, Julius 471
Bascom, Darius N. 203
Bascom, Dicius 252
Bascom, Ray 148
Basford, William H. 277
Baskin, John C. 228
Bass, John H. 478, 747
Bassett, Frank 805
Bassett, Thomas 92
Bassignano, Victor 464
Baston, McLean 545, 582
Basye, Thomas H. 803
Batchelder, Joseph K. 252
Batcher, Richard 750
Bateman, Aaron L. 523, 585
Bateman, Alfred 664
Bates, Mr. 420
Bates, Adomian J. 813
Bates, Andrew S. 286
Bates, Henry 311
Bates, James M. 251
Bates, John R. 802
Bates, Joseph N. 277
Bates, Philip 101, 124
Bates, Richard 286
Bates, William 736
Bates, William H. B. 203
Bates, Wyndham R. 376
Batie, Ezra W. 785
Batteos, Sabine 111
Batti, Alexander 808
Battle, Joseph 756
Battles, Anthony 350
Baty, George W. 556
Baty, William 842
Bauer, Charles 148
Bauer, George 158
Bauer, John 132
Baugh, John 92
Baumgarten, William 682
Bauney, Henry 819
Baxter, David H. 813
Baxter, James 571, 727
Baxter, Marshall L. 163
Baxter, Thomas 355, 386
Baxter, Thomas B. 133
Baxter, Turner P. 526, 544, 571
Bay, Jacob 324, 350, 872
Bay, John W. 211
Bayard, Joseph O. 802

Bayle, Thomas 342
Bayley, Benjamin F. 716
Baylis, William A. 400, 687
Baylor, John R. 15, 22, 30, 42, 43, 69, 669
Bayly, Charles 727
Beach, Charles E. 836
Beach, Charles S. 360
Beach, John F. 434
Beach, Nathan A. 855
Beach, W. M. 179
Beach, William L. 275
Beal, Houston 226
Beal, John M. 143
Beal, Merrill C. 867
Beale, Mr. 24
Bealenberg, John 153
Beam, Jacob McL. 603
Beamis, James 567
Bean, Enos 355
Bean, James M. 543, 576
Bean, William H. 788
Bear Hunter 172-73, 175
Bearce, James C. 92
Beard, John 202
Beard, John S. 790
Beard, Michael 545
Beardsley, Joseph 611
Beardsley, Lewis 236
Beasely, Charles C. 493
Beatty, Samuel H. 124, 819
Beauregard, John 351
Beauregard, John T. 220
Beaver, Henry 337, 386
Beaver, James W. 805
Beaver, John 645
Bechster, Frederick W. 228
Bechter, William 252
Beck, John 645, 871
Beck, Levi 776
Beck, Peter N. 645
Becker, Franklin 611
Becker, Frederick W. 179, 199, 277
Becker, John 793
Becker, Samuel E. W. 522, 576, 611, 872
Becker, Valentine 500
Becker, Walter F. 286
Beckham, Henry 163, 227
Beckley, Benson D. 767

Beckweth, Ezra 658
Beckwith, Charles 199
Beckwith, Charles D. 296, 556
Beckwith, Leonard C. 832
Beckwith, William 785
Bedell, Tobias W. 158
Bedford, George M. 753
Bedford, Henry H. 695
Bedford, John 603, 631
Beebe, Sgt. 182
Beebe, Aaron M. 756
Beebe, George 133
Beebee, Alanson 285
Beebee, Samuel J., Jr. 864
Beech, Charles S. 111
Beem, Benjamin F. 774
Beers, George W. 464, 526
Beers, Richard 756
Beerup, Thomas 556
Beeth, Benjamin F. 861
Beggins, Bernard 203, 286
Behan, Peter 576
Behl, Edward 750
Behm, Nicholas 252
Behn, Ferdinand 652, 872
Behrens, Dierich 747
Beighel, Thomas 556
Beilen, Nicholas 742
Beinkoskey, Alexander 576
Beirnes, Terrence 245
Belardos, Deciderio 307
Belden, John W. 603, 631
Belderrain, Guillermo 315
Beler, Frank J. 395, 409, 695
Belknap, Thomas 100
Belknap, William D. 867
Bell, Alfred C. 203
Bell, Charles 619
Bell, Edmund 219
Bell, George 245
Bell, George A. 771
Bell, George T. 790
Bell, James 556
Bell, Jesse 163, 872
Bell, John 310, 776
Bell, Joseph E. 111
Bell, Marion 148
Bell, Nicholas J. 478
Bell, Robert 630
Bell, Robert W. 124

Bell, Roland H. 351
Bell, Thomas 695
Bell, Timothy C. 819
Bell, William 868
Bellafranca, Augustine 311
Bellegarde, Adolph S. 212
Bellinger, John 747
Bellman, Oliver P. 245, 813
Bellmer, John H. C. 458
Bellou, Francis 476, 491, 726, 749
Bellows, Edward W. 351
Belmyre, James H. 343, 351, 368, 391
Belta, Pvt. 187
Belter, Charles B. 571
Belto, Frank 228
Belvail, Joseph 131
Beman, Truman 732
Beman, William W. 678
Bement, Elmore 252
Bemis, Zeolotio 664
Benadom, George A. 788
Benchley, L. B., & Co. 28
Bender, Charles 442
Bender, Damian 779, 873
Bendle, George H. 678
Bendle, William 816
Benedict, Cornelius 143
Benedict, Cornelius W. 260
Benedict, George B. 750
Benedict, Homer H. 111
Benedict, Walker F. 220
Benham, William F. 400, 691
Benjamin, Charles E. 854
Benjamin, Jerome D. 732
Benkes, Michael 603
Bennett, Alexander 756
Bennett, Byron R. 526
Bennett, Clarence 68
Bennett, Clarence E. 87
Bennett, Ephraim R. 556, 571
Bennett, George 163
Bennett, George W. 753, 790
Bennett, Hamilton 652, 695
Bennett, James 753
Bennett, James P. 209
Bennett, John 219
Bennett, Joseph F. 335, 363, 372
Bennett, Lewis 500
Bennett, Mark 111

Bennett, Marks 343
Bennett, Miguel 318
Bennett, Obediah S. 824
Bennett, Orrin 590
Bennett, Patrick 442
Bennett, Richard 556, 571, 813
Bennett, Thomas 203, 294, 842, 867
Bennett, W.A. 179
Bennett, William 525, 576, 658
Bennett, William A. 534
Benninger, Irwin J. 867
Benninger, Samuel W.B. 602
Benny, Henry 337, 386
Benscater, Robert 556
Bense, Henry 709
Bensel, Royal A. 625
Benson, Henry M. 359, 372, 599
Benson, John 464
Benson, Oliver 846
Benson, Otto 234
Bentley, Alonzo J. 404, 710
Bentley, George W. 143
Benton, Frank 611
Berdan, Dixon 220
Berg, Joseph 101
Bergand, Alexis 713
Bergen, Charles E. 367
Bergen, Julius 485
Berger, William 471
Bergin, Christopher 747
Bergue, Mark 819
Bering, James 210, 212
Bermudes, Pedro 307
Bernan, Charles D. 111
Bernard, Heinimann 739
Bernard, John 567
Bernard, John A. 526, 571
Bernard, John P. 771
Bernare, Francis 611
Berney, Capt. 76
Bernhert, John M. 337, 377, 386
Bernico, Joseph 545
Berniker, Joseph 576
Berringer, Ferdinand 377
Berry, Christian 788
Berry, David 373
Berry, David J. 178, 200, 234, 284, 872
Berry, George E. 360
Berry, Henry 400, 687

Berry, James 645, 750
Berry, John 742
Berry, John J. 377
Berry, Joseph 158
Berry, Michael 732
Berry, Parker S. 767
Berry, Robert 493, 639
Berry, Samuel 124
Berry, Thomas J. 260
Berry, Tilford G. 556, 577
Berry, William 836
Berry, William P. 604
Berryessei, Gaudaloupe 805
Berryhill, John R. 236
Berryman, James 813
Berthet, Andre 586
Berthet, Andrew 545
Bess, Charles H. 391
Bess, William M. 286
Bessert, Peter A. 788
Bessi, Peter 442
Bessy, Avery M. 536
Best, Andrew R. 782
Best, John N. 652
Best, John T. 832-33
Best, Oliver W. 753
Best, Richard 760
Bethel, James N. 732
Better, Charles B. 526
Betts, George 368
Bevans, Edward 449
Bevert, William L. 807
Bevington, William 228, 442
Bewley, Allen H. 258
Bey, August 556
Beyer, Christopher C. 821
Biastock, Charles 710
Bibby, John 604
Bice, Aaron J. 409, 717
Bicensino, Caribo 819
Bick, Frederick 664
Bick, Henry 276
Bickett, William 651
Bickford, Thomas M. 201
Bickford, William A. 236
Bickle, John 277
Bickmore, J.D. 315
Bicknell, Freeman 123
Bicmore, Thomas 800
Bierman, Ernest 485

Bigelow, Barton B. 179, 535, 555, 590
Bigelow, Henry M. 373
Bigelow, Stephen F. 631
Bigers, Jonas 158
Biggs, Adam 639
Biggs, Daniel R. 713
Biggs, Marion F. 710, 873
Bigham, William 143
Biglan, Edward 732
Bigley, John 163
Billado, William H. 611
Billian, Francis 101
Billiard, Joseph 619, 871
Billig, Charles 524, 554, 589
Billing, Joseph 441
Billings, Horace 652
Billings, James J. 75, 77-79, 86, 142, 162, 242
Billings, Lucius A. 527, 545, 556
Billingsley, James F. 203
Bingham, Calvin H. 245
Bingham, George 286
Bingham, Powell 142
Bingham, Ralph P. 142
Binning, John 449
Birar, George W. 582
Birch, William 639, 846
Birchfield, Frederick F. 92
Bird, James 296, 464
Bird, Thompson J. 253
Bird, William B. 220, 236
Biringer, Ferdinand 260
Birt, William L. 736
Bisch, Alvis 158
Bishop, Francis M. 294
Bishop, George 857
Bishop, James 631
Bishop, Solomon S. 571, 871
Bishop, Thomas F. 713, 736
Biso, Joseph 750
Bispham, Henry 269
Bissel, Henry 92
Bissell, Edward 639
Bissell, Henry 871
Biswell, Cpl. 187
Bitschnaw, Joseph 824
Bixby, Charles H. 785
Bixby, Levi R. 788
Bixby, Samuel S. 868

Bizet, Robert 485
Black, Alexander 259
Black, David 464, 581
Black, Henry M. 720-21, 725
Black, Joseph F. 409, 687
Black, Nelson S. 478
Black Rock Tom 186
Black, Thomas G. 857
Blackburn, Cornelius 442
Blackburn, John 18
Blacker, Charles E. 808
Blackford, Robert A. 138, 872
Blackman, Jas. T. 277
Blackwood, John H. 664
Blain, Oren 771
Blair, Andrew M. 717
Blair, Francis 158
Blair, John 774
Blair, Robert 137
Blaisdell, Alonzo G. 664
Blaisdell, Guy 742
Blake, Benjamin 244
Blake, Bowers 92
Blake, Charles W. 111, 123, 354, 404, 678
Blake, Edward B. 630
Blake, Geo. A. H. 18
Blake, John 434
Blake, John G. 600, 604, 624, 630, 644
Blake, Josephus 855
Blake, Leo C. 92
Blakeney, Thomas J. 75, 87
Blakeslee, George H. 253
Blakesley, James H. 269
Blakley, George W. 164
Blanc, Louis 212
Blanchard, Francis R. 363
Blanchard, Henry R. 846
Blanchard, Oscar 858
Blanchard, Richard H. 142
Blanchard, William E. 868
Blanche, Edgar N. 858
Blancheon, Ilan 464
Blanchmain, Louis G. de 819
Blanco, Henry 153
Blane, Lewis 124
Blank, Gotlieb 296
Blankenship, Benson 360
Blansfield, Richard 664

Blattner, Gottliep 816
Blaynay, Chad. Walladee 833
Blechschmidt, Leopold 726, 747
Blechschmidt, Leopote 441
Blessing, William H. 742
Blethen, Dexter W. 372
Bleye, John 471
Blineo, Thomas F. 268
Bliss, Edward C. 413, 717
Bliss, Lysander C. 525
Bliss, William Y. 92
Block, Charles 434
Bloid, Charles B. 736
Bloom, Charles 811
Bloomfield, Martin 805
Blosser, William H. 700
Bluett, Joseph 867
Bluff, Charles K. 432, 442, 500
Blum, John 545, 586, 840, 872
Blume, Henry 753
Blundell, Joseph T. 639
Blush, Charles 611, 704
Boardman, David 664
Boardman, John 164
Boarland, J. 179
Boas, Patrick 449
Bobenmeyer, Charles 360
Bock, Francisco 287
Bodell, Lewis F. 582, 818
Boden, Edward 500
Boden, William C. 861
Bodi, Frederick 844
Bodine, Barton 111
Boedy, Andrew 619
Bogenhover, Christian 203
Boggs, Daniel W. 864
Boggs, Ezekiel W. 251
Boggs, Franklin 119
Boggs, Jackson 163
Bogle, Lewis 821
Bohall, Henry 836
Bohrer, John 556
Bojorguez, Luis 318
Boland, Andrew 577
Boland, John 750
Boland, Patrick 220
Boland, William 143
Bolander, John 785
Boles, Charles L. 124
Boley, Anthony 536

Boling, Patrick 536
Bolle, John 691
Bollinger, William 212
Bolten, John 793
Bolton, James 833
Bolton, James A. 477
Bolton, Samuel S. 347, 645
Bolze, Daniel 269
Bomer, James W. 602
Bond 28
Bond, George W. 351, 639
Bond, Newton 556, 590
Bond, Samuel 747
Bonds, George 228
Bonehard, John 153
Bonfanti, Antonio 434
Bonham, Andrew J. 790
Bonham, Calvin 604
Bonham, John S. 153
Bonnard, Gustave 311
Bonner, John 813
Bonner, Michael H. 252
Bonnifield, James T. 781
Bonsell, Peter 148
Bonticon, David 631
Bonton, Edwin H. 203
Boon, Garrit E. 236
Boon, William 604
Boone, Elias W. 346
Bootes, Gilbert M. 138
Booth, David E. 294
Booth, Richmond H. 638
Booth, Sylvester H. 228
Booz, Robert G. 824
Bopp, Francis J. 220
Borass, F.L. 179
Borbon, Romaldo 318
Border, Peter 101, 119
Borel, Theodore 138
Boren, John A. 143
Borgues, Ramon 308
Boring, Jacob 846
Boring, William J. 736
Borland, John 555, 590
Borland, John G. 260
Borman, Henry 485
Bornie, Joseph 220
Boronda, Francisco 311
Bortle, Geo. 245
Bosford, William H. 770

16

Bosha, Peter 211
Boskirk, Abraham Van 556
Bosqui, Maurice L. 836
Bossel, George W. 760
Bosser, Henry E. 631
Bossert, John 203
Bossu, Henry E. 611
Bossuot, John D. 604
Bost, James W. 727
Bost, John 727
Bostock, John 739
Boston, Angel 747
Bostwick, Ebenezer 571, 811
Boswell, John H. 857
Boswell, Levi 800
Bosworth, Nathaniel C. 646
Bother, Joseph 611
Botkin, Richard 148
Botsford, James 69, 90, 98, 109
Bottger, Martin 138
Botts, George W. 119
Boudier, Peter J. 736
Bourasso, Francis L. 590, 824
Bourke, Patrick 442
Bourke, Thomas 478, 646, 872
Bourland, James 395, 409, 713
Bourne, Thomas 277
Bourse, Thomas 760
Bouton, Pierce 632
Bovee, George 260
Boverdez, Casimira 308
Bovyer, Robert L. 760
Boween, Franklin B. 813
Boweiman, George J. 836
Bowen, Gardner C. 432
Bowen, Thomas 750
Bower, Ludivigio 311
Bowers, Joseph 840
Bowers, Thomas J. 153
Bowie, Cyrus 373
Bowie, George W. 9, 22, 38–39, 47, 418, 668, 676
Bowl, Anthony 833
Bowland, Wm. 100
Bowler, William M. 727
Bowles, Benjamin 611
Bowling, Samuel F. 158
Bowman, Alexander 682
Bowman, Elijah 138, 377
Bowman, James P. 219

Bowman, John 261
Bowman, John H. 619, 782
Bowman, Pierce 364, 395
Bowman, William 101
Bownes, George 268
Bowser, Henry W. 253
Box, James 269
Boyce, George 556
Boyd, Archibald M. 808
Boyd, James 632
Boyd, John 556, 571
Boyd, John, alias Joseph Williams 286, 619
Boyd, Othias B. 782
Boyd, Patrick 148, 871
Boyd, Thomas 582
Boyd, William 148, 399, 687
Boyd, William R. 611, 652
Boyden, David W. 368
Boyer, David 270
Boyer, James R. 413, 704
Boyes, Enoch 131, 872
Boyington, Robert 368
Boylan, Thomas 364
Boylan, William 90
Boyle, Anthony 618, 821
Boyle, George 604
Boyle, George P. 864
Boyle, Henry 337
Boyle, John 253, 478, 567, 577, 658, 735
Boyle, Michael 458
Boyle, Solomon 153, 872
Boyles, James 347, 646
Boyles, Thomas 449
Bracey, Demetrius W. 258
Bracken, Michael 228
Brackett, A. G. 187
Brackett, Geo. O. 836
Brackett, Horatio S. 771
Brackett, Samuel M. 449
Bracy, Demetrius W. 268
Bradburn, Joseph 148
Braddock, James 632
Bradford, Brant J. 368, 413, 704
Bradford, Caleb 268
Bradford, George L. 785
Bradford, Joseph L. 861
Bradford, William 833
Bradish, David 717, 872

Bradley, George 311
Bradley, George S. 575, 577
Bradley, James 250, 258, 284, 872
Bradley, John 736
Bradley, John B. 687
Bradley, John H. 779
Bradley, Michael 92, 493, 556, 617
Bradley, Peter 111, 410, 713
Bradley, Thomas 179, 261, 296
Bradley, William 449
Bradley, William F. 363
Bradley, William H. 704
Bradshaw, Henry 413, 704
Bradstin, Nicholas 471
Bradwell, Thomas 691
Brady 178
Brady, Albert 260
Brady, Edward 277
Brady, Eugene J. 277, 296
Brady, Frederick 492
Brady, James 101
Brady, John 351, 779
Brady, John H. 463
Brady, Michael 803
Brady, Patrick 337, 386, 404, 681
Brady, Thomas 478
Brady, William 632, 658, 750
Brady, William H. 458
Bragara, Louis 458
Bragasie, Joseph 434
Bragg, Augustus 261
Bragg, Charles 143
Bragg, Geo. F. 28
Brainard, William 821
Brakebill, Charles 99, 119
Braman, Benjamin D. 235
Brambilla, John 125
Bramhall, Martin L. 245
Bramlet, George 619
Branch, Charles W. 111
Branch, Frank W. 179, 590
Brand, George 756
Brandall, John 619
Brander, Alexander 776
Brandes, George 88, 101, 119
Brandon, Amberson 162
Brandon, James 687
Brandon, John 268
Brandon, John P. 687
Brandon, John R. 858

Brandon, Myson P. 785
Brannan, Ausbern W. 843
Brannan, Charles 203, 212
Brannan, Daniel 434
Brannan, Edward 687, 872
Brannan, George G. 226
Brannan, John 557, 803
Branson, Noah C. 819
Brant, Charles 526, 544, 555, 571
Brareton, John R. 200
Bras, Franciscus 458
Brasel, John 118
Brates, Francis F. 92
Braun, Frank 125
Braun, John 442
Bray, Charles 523, 556
Bray, William B. 816
Bray, William F. 471
Bray, William H. 700
Brazetton, James F. 253
Breed, Elias 611
Breed, Sylvanus 619
Breedlove, Ambrose 270
Breese, Riley 732
Brehmer, John W. 678, 872
Breman, James 691
Bremeo, Louis 143
Brennan, David 500
Brennan, Michael 228
Brennen, William 632, 639
Brents, William H. 236
Bresson, James 805
Bretzke, Albert 236
Brewer, Hiram 227
Brewer, Jacob M. 220
Brewer, John S. 373
Brewer, William 710, 872
Brewster 28
Brewster, Albert 732
Brewster, R.E. 28
Briant, Clark L. 158
Brickley, Michael 811
Brickley, Richard T. 857
Bridge, Thomas 536, 557
Bridges, Frank M. 449
Bridges, Gilford 840
Bridges, John 813
Bridges, Joseph H. 253
Bridges, Thomas S. 534
Brien, John 493, 873

Brier, Christopher 125
Briggs, Albert 727
Briggs, Charles P. 855
Briggs, George B. 434
Briggs, Henry 270
Briggs, John K. 178, 261, 871
Briggs, Laurin 212
Briggs, Lawrence 355
Briggs, Nicholas 285
Briggs, Theodore 101
Briggs, Thomas 75
Briggs, William O. 771
Brigham, Charles M. 449
Bright, Christopher 759
Bright, John L. 245
Brightenstein, William 125
Brighton, Anson F. 732
Brill, Frederick 347, 871
Brill, Frederick G. 355, 405, 710
Brink, Henry 143
Brinkley, James 658
Brison, John B. 664
Briston, Warrick A. 270
Bristow, John 277, 294
Britnell, John 732
Britschnerder, John A. 771
Britt, James 261
Britt, Thomas 610
Brittain, Eleana 806
Brittain, Joseph 485
Brittan, Charles 582
Brittan, J.W. 28
Brittan, Jesse S. 463
Britz, Mathias 458
Broach, Robert 351
Broad, William H. 779
Broadbeck, John A. 395, 410, 713
Broadbent, John 493
Broatch, Robert 844
Brobst, James S. 771
Brocher, Joseph 434
Brock, George C. 777
Brock, John 844
Brock, John W. 203
Brocker, Joseph 500
Brocket, Enoch 632
Brockway, John 639
Brockway, John P. 395, 695
Brockway, William H. 618
Brodt, Henreich 611

Brodthagen, Martin 632
Broeck, P.G.S. Ten 720
Broggan, Frank 226
Bromley, Eli 360
Bronk, Andrew G. 228
Bronson, Egbert 449
Bronson, George W. 687
Brook, Abram 158
Brook, Edward 611
Brookfield, James 609
Brooks 28
Brooks, Amos R. 739
Brooks, Charles S. 651
Brooks, Chas. W. 28
Brooks, Elisha 807-8
Brooks, Franklin 760
Brooks, Franklin K. 872
Brooks, George H. 367
Brooks, Geo. J. 28
Brooks, Jacob 777
Brooks, John A. 567, 586
Brooks, Justus 700
Brooks, Lorance 733
Brooks, M.B. 871
Brooks, Melancthon B. 478
Brooks, William V. 756
Brophy, Edwin 441
Brophy, John 441
Brophy, Michael 441
Brosius, William L. 253
Brossamer, Charles A. 857
Brosso, Moses 619
Brothers, Frank 477
Brothers, Michael 727, 872
Brothers, William 750
Brott, Col. 34
Brower, Celsus 725, 760
Brower, Henry J. 678
Brown, Adam 836
Brown, Albert 196, 284
Brown, Alexander 287, 871
Brown, Alexander H. 645
Brown, Alfred 123
Brown, Alfred E. 833
Brown, Alfred H. 760
Brown, Alonzo 557
Brown, Andrew 470
Brown, Anton 465
Brown, Arthur M. 109, 872
Brown, Benjamin 864

Brown, Benjamin P. 203, 296
Brown, Charles 74, 153, 377, 409, 449, 571, 577, 611, 646, 652, 716, 813, 872
Brown, Charles A. 133
Brown, Charles C. 771
Brown, Charles F. 235
Brown, Charles H. 777
Brown, Crocker 413, 682
Brown, Curtis M. 779
Brown, Cyrus J. 811
Brown, Daniel 771, 805
Brown, Daniel W. 148, 779
Brown, David 465, 793
Brown, Edward 260
Brown, Edwin 687
Brown, Edwin F. 395
Brown, Elijah S. 678
Brown, George 109, 111, 133, 212, 236, 527, 545
Brown, George A. 244
Brown, George C. 485
Brown, George F. 360
Brown, George H. 435
Brown, George L. 609, 663
Brown, George P. 782
Brown, George W. 545, 554, 570
Brown, Gilman 821
Brown, Green H. 833
Brown, Harmon R. 202
Brown, Henry 391, 435
Brown, Henry C. 678
Brown, Henry F. 846
Brown, Isaac 92, 457
Brown, Isaac F. 788
Brown, Isaac W. 522
Brown, Jacob 277
Brown, James 212, 236, 261, 435, 465, 625, 861
Brown, James B. 484
Brown, James E. 471
Brown, James F. 632
Brown, James S. 717
Brown, James W. 253
Brown, Jerry 119
Brown, John 101, 110, 119, 148, 364, 368, 391, 527, 571, 652, 840, 872
Brown, John, 1st 471
Brown, John, 2nd 471

Brown, John A. 228
Brown, John C. 844
Brown, John R. 220
Brown, Jonathan W. 816
Brown, Joseph 803, 816
Brown, Lewis C. 212
Brown, Luther C. 770
Brown, Martin 442
Brown, Oscar M. 68, 75, 76, 87, 381
Brown, Patrick 458
Brown, Robert 478, 536, 545
Brown, Samuel S. 557
Brown, Stephen S. 713
Brown, Stuart R. 465
Brown, Theodore H. 261
Brown, Thomas 582
Brown, Thomas A. 457
Brown, Thomas C. 813
Brown, Thomas S. 682
Brown, William 101, 111, 251, 270, 342, 350, 368, 390, 625, 639, 687, 771, 805, 844
Brown, William A. 677, 682, 691
Brown, William H. 133, 619, 658, 821, 872
Brown, William J. 782
Brown, William R. 97
Brown, Wilmer 198, 261, 284
Browner, Peter S. 646
Browning, Robert 727
Brownlie, Robert W. 152
Brownlow, John H. 101, 368, 872
Bruce, George 824
Bruce, Marshall 700
Bruce, Washington 742, 752
Bruce, William A. 442
Bruen, John 710
Brum, John 873
Bruman, Aaron 112
Brune, Deidrich 442
Bruner, Edward D. 864
Brunow, Albert 118
Bruns, John 811
Brush, Ellsworth H. 787
Brusle, Washington 767
Bryan, Edward 557, 586, 813
Bryan, James 743
Bryant, Arthur B. 811
Bryant, Jesse J. 750

Bryant, John P. 611
Bryant, Joseph 244
Bryant, Nathan R. 713, 813
Bryant, Richard 604
Bryant, William 611, 619
Bryant, Wm. T. 277
Bryant, Zachariah 639
Bryden, James W. 123
Bryfogle, Jacob B. 203
Brymer, Colin 536, 803
Buchanan, Allen 351, 413
Buchanan, Harrison M. 808
Buchanan, Ira M. 285, 525
Buchanan, R. C. 33, 36
Buchholz, Henry 756
Buchold, Paul 220
Buck, Charles E. 824
Buck, Charles G. 112
Buck, Charles H. 747
Buck, Charles O. 373, 871
Buck, Gardner C. 779
Buck, George H. 360
Buck, Lorin W. 373
Buck, Walter 112
Buckard, George F. 813
Buckingham, Daniel W. 465
Buckins, Henry H. 92
Bucklam, Warren 813
Buckland, Henry 360, 733
Buckley 18, 28
Buckley, Alexander 131
Buckley, Cornelius 351
Buckley, Edward 805
Buckley, John 133
Buckley, Michael 157
Buckley, Richard B. 813
Buckley, Thomas 677, 712, 735
Bucklin, Henry 867
Buckly, Patrick 742
Buckman, Henry R. 836
Buckman, Joseph 557, 571
Buckner, Charles 811
Buckner, William 112
Buckner, William O. 625
Budd, Charles K. 351
Budd, Charles R. 632
Budeweg, Charles 442
Budson, Alexander 112
Buell, D. C. 16, 18
Buelna, Teodocio 318

Buffum, Edwin R. 793
Buffum, Ira 250
Bugbe, J. Westley 337
Bugbee, Luther B. 486
Bugbee, Luther H. 458
Bugner, John 803
Bugue, Victor 846
Buhla, Augustus 664
Buhler, John 619
Buhn, Zacharias 158
Buhole, Ambrose 148
Buhrer, George N. 857
Bujanda, Jesus 318
Bulger, Reece R. 394, 699
Bulin, Lanklain 413, 704
Bull, William A. 793
Bullard, Hugh D. 405, 710
Bullard, Osgood 566
Bullen, William 112
Bulware, Madison 766
Bumgardner, William H.H. 855
Bump, Ark 236
Bunch, Lambert 125, 143
Bungan, John 527
Bunk, Valentine 785
Bunke, Thomas F. 149
Bunker, Benjamin B. 235
Bunkoff, Frederic 153
Bunn, Charles 861
Bunnell, Hiram 524, 571
Bunyan, John 493
Burbes, Christian 373
Burbus, Charles 782
Burch, Homer A. 774
Burch, Lambert 112
Burd, James 733
Burdick, Joseph B. 848, 854
Burdin, Henry 203, 287
Burge, Frederick M. 819
Burgean, James 658
Burgee, Harry 203
Burgess, Malachi D. 766
Burgess, Malichi D. 774
Burget, Ira 625
Burgher, Jacob 567, 871
Burgher, Jacob H. 760
Burk, John 611, 619, 658
Burk, Michael B. 739
Burk, Thomas 619
Burkard, George F. 695

Burke, George 813
Burke, Henry 664
Burke, James 747
Burke, Jeffery 368
Burke, Jeffrey 101
Burke, John J. 691
Burke, Joseph H. 868
Burke, Michael 125, 212, 228
Burke, Patrick 373, 632
Burke, Thomas 287
Burke, Thomas F. 143
Burke, Timothy 632
Burke, William 465
Burkett, George A. 409, 412, 670-71, 699, 712
Burkhardt, Frank 441-42
Burkholder, Robert 753
Burkie, John 756
Burkman, Nicholas 750
Burley, Pillitiah B. 663
Burlingham, Henry G. 854
Burlingham, Nathan D. 275
Burlkey, William 536, 590
Burnam, William 652
Burnap, Oscar 857
Burnell, William 793
Burner, Jacob W. 486, 493
Burner, John W. 471
Burnes, Rodman 591
Burnet, Alfred 626
Burnet, John 682
Burnett, David H. 586, 591
Burnett, George 664
Burnett, Henry A. 242, 275
Burnett, Henry R. 458
Burnett, Isaac T. 800
Burnett, John T. 716
Burnett, Robert B. 788
Burnett, Stephen D. 733
Burnham, Benjamin 158
Burnham, Edward 545
Burnham, Luther C. 260
Burnley, Samuel 808
Burns, Andrew 727
Burns, Barney 811
Burns, Charles V. 646
Burns, Daniel M. 610, 618
Burns, David 179, 277, 296
Burns, Edward 858
Burns, George 619

Burns, Harry A. 73, 91
Burns, Henry 471
Burns, Jacob 717
Burns, James 138, 471, 567, 582
Burns, John 226, 261, 296, 435, 449, 536, 727
Burns, John 2d 158
Burns, John 3d 158
Burns, John C. 245
Burns, John H. 782
Burns, Michael 747
Burns, Michael E. 470
Burns, Miles B. 545, 577
Burns, Patrick 435
Burns, Patrick A. 582
Burns, Peter L. 788
Burns, Robert 586, 864
Burns, Thomas 212, 284
Burns, William 212, 270
Burrell, Presto 581
Burres, James 836
Burrill, Judson 639
Burrow, James R. 449
Burrows, David J. 545
Burrows, John 442
Burt, Cyrus 760
Burt, Ellory J. 212
Burtnett, Obediah L. 203
Burton, Beverly B. 793
Burton, Charles 577
Burton, Daniel 567
Burton, Francis 119
Burton, George 835
Burton, H. S. 16, 35, 38, 39
Burton, Henry 733
Burton, James 709
Burton, James C. 872
Burton, John 236, 413, 682
Burton, Sheldon 797
Burton, Thomas 582
Bury, George O. 478
Bush, Charles 800
Bush, Henry 736
Bush, James 377
Bush, John 261
Bush, Joseph H. 143
Bush, Michael 404, 682
Bush, Silas C. 178, 277, 285
Bushnell, Adrian D. 212
Bushnell, William 499

Bushong, John 442
Buster, Thos. S. 297
Butcher, Marion 296, 591
Butcher, William T. 656, 858
Butherford, James F. 873
Butler, Albert B. 842
Butler, James A. 536
Butler, John J. 527, 545
Butler, Michael I. 464
Butler, Oliver 153
Butler, Peter D. 285
Butler, Samuel 619
Butler, Thomas 617
Butler, Thomas S. 277
Butter, Asa 833
Butter, John H. 664
Butterfield, Henry A. 158
Button, Levi L. 287
Butts, George 646
Buxton, Charles M. 555
Buxton, George H. 813
Buxton, Jarvis 554, 570
Buzaird, Alvin H. 203
Buzelmier, Francis 442
Bye, James W. 767, 773
Byers, John 790, 793
Byler, John 486
Byrne, Felix O. 799
Byrne, John 571
Byrne, Matthew 793
Byrne, Patrick 727
Byrne, Thomas 535, 577, 586
Byrnes, Andrew L. 158
Byrnes, Dennis 639
Byrnes, Joel 619
Byrnes, Michael J. 843
Byron, Moses M. 164
Bywaters, Joseph 836

C

Cadwallader, Isaac D. 536
Cady, Lt. Col. 34, 38, 39
Cady, Charles L. 842
Cady, David H. 571
Caffyn, Stephen 802
Cafrey, Bernard 842
Cage, William 710
Cagle, Benjamin F. 297
Cagle, Henry 840

Cagnacci, Giovanni 774
Cahill, John 582, 803
Cahill, Thomas 739
Cahow, Miles 833
Cahow, Nichola M. 833
Cain, Charles 557
Cain, John A. 858
Cain, Patrick 619
Cain, Paul 682
Caine, Peter 373
Caine, Thomas T. 836
Cairel, Charles E. 536, 586
Cairns, Robert 619
Calder, Peter 158
Calderon, José de Jesus 315
Calderwood, James E. 245
Calderwood, M.H. 763, 776
Caldwell, Benjamin P. 435
Caldwell, Charles F. 351
Caldwell, Edwin 277
Caldwell, Elbert 394, 687
Caldwell, James 523, 557, 619
Caldwell, Martin V.B. 691
Caldwell, Sam'l L. 179, 277
Caldwell, William 653
Caldwell, William S. 816
Calhoun, Jeremiah 277
Calhoun, John E. 98
Calkins, Hubert 391
Call, David, Jr. 773
Call, Humpsall 619
Callaghan, Daniel 821
Callaghan, Joseph 767
Callahan, Andrew J. 351
Callahan, James 842
Callahan, John 270, 395, 410, 713
Callahan, Michael 138, 653
Callahan, Michael F. 296
Callahan, Patrick 465
Callahan, Peter 500
Calleen, James E. 478
Calletano, Edwardo 318
Calleweart, Augustus 164
Calloway, William P. 47, 372
Calmes, Jerome 253
Calvelage, August 646
Calvert, Joseph R. 163
Camacho, Lorenzo 318
Cambridge, Oliver H. 245
Camedy, John 536, 557

Cameron, Archibald 347, 767
Cameron, Donald M. 632
Cameron, James B. 347
Cameron, John 458
Cameron, Kindall 619
Cameron, Samuel 644
Cameron, Simon 12, 16, 17, 25, 27, 29, 322
Cameron, Vincent 465
Cammel, Robert 639
Camp, Andrew J. 137
Camp, George W. 819
Camp, Harvey E. 695
Campbell, Alexander 465, 493, 777
Campbell, Benoni P. 816
Campbell, Bernard 555
Campbell, Columbus M. 536
Campbell, Edward 212
Campbell, Edward A. 212
Campbell, Edward B. 855
Campbell, Felix 347, 767
Campbell, Francis 793
Campbell, Francis B. 843
Campbell, Frank 347
Campbell, George 138
Campbell, Geo. M. 284
Campbell, George W. 604
Campbell, Henry 164, 500, 664
Campbell, Hugh 733
Campbell, Irving 767
Campbell, James 132, 261, 733, 771
Campbell, John 101, 350, 373, 816
Campbell, John T. 858
Campbell, John W. 110
Campbell, Kendall 471
Campbell, Lemuel 164
Campbell, Nicholas H. 645
Campbell, Raymond 471
Campbell, Rendall 478
Campbell, Robert A. 858
Campbell, Samuel 842
Campbell, Talbut T. 133
Campbell, Thomas B. 424, 440
Campbell, Tolbert T. 270
Campbell, William C. 653
Campbell, William L. 75, 142, 198, 243, 484
Campeon, Peter 355
Campton, Wesley 493
Canary, Martin 270

Canby, Gen. 43, 52, 57, 58, 60, 61, 63-66
Canby, E.R.S. 48
Cane, Michael 739
Canedo, Antonio 308
Canedo, José 318
Canedo, Narciso 308
Canfield, Charles L. 236
Canfield, Francis M. 377
Canfield, Isaac N. 823
Canham, Thomas P. 245
Caniff, James 777
Cannon, Charles 112, 368
Cannon, Ezekiel 405, 410, 713
Cannon, James D. 101, 261
Cannon, John 435
Cannon, Michael 133
Cannon, William 717
Canon, Amos 486
Canovan, Charles 710
Canterbury, Rufus P. 112
Cantillon, James 178, 259
Cantillon, William 179
Cantua, Santiago 315
Canty, John H. 604
Caparoon, Isaac M. 132
Caperton, Capt. 19
Cappleman, John W. 360
Capps, Benjamin P. 92
Capps, William 142
Caravajal, Jesus 806
Caravajales, Sylvester 318
Carbray, Henry 471, 500
Cardin, Robert C. 149
Carey, Calvin 750
Carey, Edmund 611
Carey, James R. 527, 572
Carey, Jeremiah L. 855
Carey, John 691
Carey, John W. 687
Carey, Peter 557, 591
Carey, William 342, 391, 727
Cargle, George M. 523
Carillo, Casimiro 308
Carillo, Juan 315
Cario, Jesus 311
Cario, Juan 311
Carkhuff, Samuel 253
Carl, Christian 449
Carl, William 144
Carle, John 101

Carleton, Charles C. 137
Carleton, George 493, 743
Carleton, Henry 228
Carleton, James H. 16, 21, 22, 29,
32-35, 38, 39, 41, 42, 46-49,
51-54, 56-59, 63, 66, 69-72, 76,
169, 321-23, 325, 335, 506, 510,
668-69
Carleton, Thomas 703
Carley, Charles G. 658
Carley, Charles O. 626
Carlin, Michael 133
Carlin, Peter 204
Carlow, William H. 478
Carlson, Edward 600, 617, 799
Carlson, John 546, 582
Carlton, Henry S. 123
Carlton, John W. 471
Carlton, William 179, 591
Carman, Alexander 577
Carman, James 747
Carmichael, William 158, 527
Carmody, Roger 471
Carn, James W. 159
Carnes, Robert 632
Carnes, Thomas 777
Carothers, Isaac 632
Carpenter, Andrew 619
Carpenter, Belden J. 253
Carpenter, Cary 364
Carpenter, Eben C. 756
Carpenter, George M. 98, 122
Carpenter, Henry 138
Carpenter, John L. 92
Carpenter, Noah T. 278
Carpenter, Orin F. 251
Carpenter, Stephen H. 779
Carpenter, Sylvester 610, 618
Carr, Albert L. 458, 485, 646
Carr, David 739
Carr, Edward C. 226
Carr, Frederick A. 604
Carr, George 864
Carr, George W. 414, 704
Carr, John 220, 278
Carr, Joseph 777
Carr, Patrick 92, 435
Carr, Robert 153
Carr, Sumner 626
Carr, William D. 493

Carraco, Thomas P. 245
Carrahar, Anthony 743
Carrasco, Juan 318
Carrick, William 591
Carrier, Victor 819
Carrigan, William 604, 646
Carrington, Henry 819
Carroll, Edward B. 536, 557
Carroll, George H. 199, 212, 278,
557
Carroll, James 458
Carroll, John 92, 493, 527, 632,
842
Carroll, Joseph 544, 557
Carroll, Patrick 153, 347, 368,
639
Carroll, Patrick J. 639
Carroll, Thomas 581
Carroll, Timothy 368
Carroll, William 435, 567
Carroll, William C. 102, 391
Carson, Charles 211
Carson, Christopher 71, 75, 76,
327
Carson, John 132
Carson, John I. 144
Carson, John J. 245
Carson, Kit 71, 75, 76
Carter, Asa M. 845
Carter, Chas. 137
Carter, Daniel I. 639
Carter, Edward D. 638
Carter, Ethan J. 253, 816
Carter, Henry 465
Carter, John 756
Carter, John L. 337
Carter, Robert 760
Carter, Sylvester 237
Carter, Thomas P. 243
Carter, William H. 143
Carver, David 212
Casano, Edward J. 260, 295
Case, Andrew J. 297
Case, Chester 861
Case, James 125
Case, John A. 657
Case, Samuel 626
Case, Samuel F. 742
Casey, Francis J. 555, 585

Casey, George 753
Casey, Isaac 449
Casey, Joseph 493
Casey, Michael 204
Casey, Patrick 750
Casey, Thomas 691
Casey, William 687, 713
Cashin, William 803
Cashman, John 463
Cashman, William 770
Casiday, John 717
Casnean, E.J. 179
Caso, Charles L. 653
Cason, Calvin 717
Casper, George R. 112, 144, 164
Cass, Hugh 808
Cass, John M. 651
Cassell, Francis M. 431
Casseras, John G. 311
Casserly, Philip 253
Cassidy, John 736
Cassware, Bernard 435
Castaneda, José C. 220
Castello, Jesus 311
Casteyon, Crisarte 311
Castile, John 355
Castillo, Refugio 318
Castle, John 704
Castleton, Henry L. 210
Casto, James 557
Caston, Joseph N. 138
Castro, Jesus 311
Castro, John 311
Castro, José 311
Castro, José L. 308
Caswell, Len 774
Caswell, Thomas 653, 782
Catanach, David N. 144, 149
Cate, Daniel 125
Cate, John P. 617
Cathers, Thomas 800
Cathey, John 833
Cating, Owen 159
Catlin, Brandt T. 354, 799, 823
Cato, Abram 96
Caton, George 813
Catro, John 149
Catterton, David C. 458
Caul, Thomas 639
Causland, John 767
Cavalle, Franchelle 710

Cavanaugh, John 400
Cavanaugh, John K. 695
Cavanaugh, Michael 450
Cayrol, Antonio G. 632
Cearney, George 253
Ceigler, George 137
Chadbourne, Levi 844
Chadd, George W. 833
Chadwick, Peter W. 727
Chadwick, William 691
Chaffee, Daniel K. 864
Chagres, Louis J. 777
Chailley, Eugene 619
Chalmers, John M. 855
Chaloner, George G. 818
Chamberlain, Daniel A. 125
Chamberlain, Edward A. 709
Chamberlain, George W. 287
Chamberlain, Richard S. 864
Chamberlin, William 112
Chambers, Benjamin 251
Chambers, Charles R. 844
Chambers, James 404, 710
Chambers, James M. 604
Chambers, James R. 147
Chambers, James W. 86
Chambers, John B. 799, 807
Chambers, Simon R. 691
Chambers, Walter E. 771
Chambus, James W. 142
Chandler, Asa B. 779
Chandler, Jasper N. 132
Chandler, Osymn 793
Chandler, Robert 638
Chandler, Seth 864
Chandler, Thomas J.A. 342
Chandler, William 557
Chandler, William A. 261
Chandler, William G. 159
Chandler, William S. 855
Chaney, David C. 736
Chapel, Andrew J. 102, 373
Chapin, Alexis B. 816
Chapin, James T. 644
Chapman, Charles 646
Chapman, Henry 814
Chapman, Jeremiah S. 638
Chapman, John 602, 604, 687
Chapman, John P. 833

Chapman, Joseph 278, 287
Chapman, Lewis B. 557, 586
Chapman, Marcellus E. 245
Chapman, Nathaniel 278
Chapman, Reuben D. 435, 557
Chapman, Thomas A. 726
Chapman, Thomas P. 403, 677, 709
Chapman, W. 179
Chappins, Edward 125
Chard, James L. 644
Chares 57
Chartres, Nourrit 611
Chase, A. P. 179
Chase, Charles W. 159
Chase, Daniel J. 639
Chase, Darwin 172, 175, 176, 178-79, 275
Chase, E. C. 178
Chase, Eli 691
Chase, Ezra C. 199, 285
Chase, Fleetwood 747
Chase, George 337, 808
Chase, Hiram A. 527, 586
Chase, Ossian T. 119
Chase, Robert B. 261
Chase, Wellington 774
Chasm, Alexander 486
Chatfield, William 92, 201
Chauncey, Joseph R. 337
Chavane, Charles G. 450, 478
Chaveo, Jesus 318
Cheatham, Richard C. H. 842
Cheek, William A. 824
Cheeney, Ezekiel 691
Cheeney, James 351
Cheeney, William F. 858
Cheeny, Ezekiel 813
Cheffer, Calix 604
Cheney, James H. 201
Cheney, John E. 202
Cherry, James B. 631
Chester, David S. 658
Chestnutt, William 546
Chestnutt, William A. 536
Chettick, Alexander 347
Chew, John W. 585
Chichester, Joseph B. 337, 385
Chicot, Guilliam 310
Childers, Joseph 119
Chipman, John H. 806

Chipman, Warren H. 806
Chipman, William H. 257, 258
Chisholm, Alexander 803
Chism, William L. 373
Chivington, Col. 58-61, 63-64
Cholet, Jacob 696
Chopard, Gustave 639
Chrisman, Henry 604
Christ, Daniel L. 527
Christey, David 727
Christian, Auguste 771
Christian, Carl 478
Christian, Charles 800
Christler, Hiram W. 858
Christophel, Charles 123
Christopher, Charles 98
Chubb, Horace W. 253
Church, Alvah W. 184, 226, 228
Church, Henry C. 182, 245, 284
Churchill, James 807
Churchill, John 144
Churchman, James 800
Cilley, James W. 611
Cillia, August 202
Claffy, Michael 253
Claiborn, Daniel M. 767
Claibourne, Lafayette 245
Clair, Benjamin 803
Clancey, John M. 619
Clapham, Charles T. 774
Clapp, Edwin 604, 777
Clapp, Gotham 788
Clapp, John W. 836
Clapsaddle, Henry E. 784
Clark, Sur. Gen. 72
Clark, Adam 395, 700
Clark, Alexander 803
Clark, Charles 620, 639, 747
Clark, Charles A. 864
Clark, Charles M. 237
Clark, Cyrus D. 172, 258, 275
Clark, Daniel 500
Clark, Daniel P. 819
Clark, De Witt C. 144
Clark, Edmund R. 844
Clark, Eli 131
Clark, Frank G. 211, 212
Clark, George C. 844
Clark, Geo. D. 125
Clark, George S. 261

Clark, Henry H. 785
Clark, Henry M. 620
Clark, Hiram E.W. 867
Clark, Ichabod 638, 695
Clark, Isaac M. 125
Clark, James 536, 691, 803
Clark, James C. 620
Clark, James M. 632, 663–64
Clark, James W. 639
Clark, John 377, 391, 864
Clark, John, Jr. 800
Clark, John C. 442
Clark, John F. 567
Clark, John P. 92, 844
Clark, John W. 760, 808
Clark, Jonathan 832
Clark, Jonathan S. 626
Clark, Laurence 733
Clark, Leonard 261
Clark, Lester G. 286
Clark, Levi K. 864
Clark, Louis 91, 102
Clark, Loyal L. 92
Clark, Marshall 287
Clark, Martin M. 713
Clark, Paul 364
Clark, Peter 311
Clark, Richard 868
Clark, Seth A. 658
Clark, Sheldon H. 261
Clark, Skillman G. 277
Clark, Sylvester K. 164
Clark, Thomas 102, 670
Clark, Thomas A. 245
Clark, Thomas J. 632
Clark, Walter 137
Clark, William 582, 743
Clark, William B. 858
Clarke, Hiram E.W. 858
Clarke, John 144, 220
Clarke, Sheldon H. 220
Clarke, William T. 463
Clarkson, Prince 478
Clarry, Peter 220
Classon, Otto H. 557, 582
Claud, Philip 228
Clauson, Cornelius 658
Clauson, Ferdinand 270
Clauss, Jacques 442
Claussen, William 767

Clavel, Pierre 450
Clawell, Robert 865
Clawson, Cornelius 808
Claxton, William C. 819
Clay, George W. 861
Clear, William L. 245
Cleary, James 739
Cleghorn, William 152, 157
Clemens, Martin 297
Clement, Auguste 311
Clement, Charles 811
Clement, Francis 747
Clement, John 717
Clement, Leonard 102
Clement, William 159
Clements, John 816
Clements, John D. 270
Clements, Robert 821
Clements, Robert H. 110, 717
Clements, Rufus H. 243
Clency, Michael 710
Clendenen, Henry 435
Clendenin, Louis W. 350
Clenford, Charles 450, 493
Clermont, Aime 311
Cleveland, John 99, 119, 260
Cleveland, Lewis C. 253
Cleveland, Reuben S. 749
Clifford, Edward D. 750
Clifford, John 651
Clifton, Thomas 211
Cline, Frank 653
Cline, John P. 287
Cline, William 154
Clink, David 686
Clock, Jacob 459
Clock, James G. 204
Cloet, Charles 824
Clohecy, William P. 604
Clongher, Thomas 228
Clore, John 577
Close, Myron C. 807
Clothier, William B. 630
Clough, Henry 618
Cloves, J. 178
Clow, Edward 611
Clowes, Joseph A. 260, 296
Cloyes, John H. 284
Clukey, Charles 760
Clunie, James 253

Clyde, George W. 779
Clymer, Lewis 793
Coalson, William A. 567
Coates, Benjamin F. 784
Coates, Henry 537, 546
Coates, James 602, 630
Coates, Miles T. 790
Coates, Richard M. 632
Coats, William H. 227
Cobb, Daniel S. 102, 112
Cobb, Joseph L. 767
Cobb, William 459
Cobby, Thomas W. 858
Coberly, Enoch 582
Coblens, David 743
Coburn, John 245
Coburn, Judson C. 700
Cochran, Charles 493
Cochran, Edward 664
Cochran, James A. 342, 390
Cochran, Warren 861
Cochrane, Charles 759
Cockburn, George 471
Coda, Marvil 717
Coddington, Edmund W. 212, 305, 315, 317
Coddington, James 806
Coddington, James R. 459
Codington, Edmund W. 639
Cody, Albemarle 720
Cody, Benjamin F. 821
Cody, Michael 435
Coe, Edward B. 147
Coe, Emery 405, 414, 677, 683, 717
Coffee, George 478, 479
Coffey, William 471
Coffien, Robert 159
Coffin, William H. 603
Coffman, Byron 500
Coffman, Byron C. 440
Coffman, Byron S. 432, 470
Coggeshall, John H. 747
Coggshall, John H. 658
Coggsville, Osman 261
Coghlan, Jeremiah 478
Coghlan, Thomas 337
Cogswell, Henry S. 779
Cogswell, Horatio F. 465
Cogswell, Osmond 295

Cohen, Solomon 544, 586
Cohl, Henry 604
Cohle, John 405, 683
Cohn, John H. 753
Cohn, Oscar 459
Cohn, Samuel B. 747
Cohoun, Hugh 479
Cokely, Dennis 204
Coker, Francis 450
Coker, Noah B. 154
Cokes, William H. 777
Colberson, Ivor 779
Colburn, George 756
Colby, Eldridge G. 448
Colby, William 821
Colclesser, Benjamin 687
Colcord, Wm. D. 833
Cold, Waldemar 102, 112
Cole, Albert 665
Cole, Asa W. 351
Cole, Charles W. 821
Cole, Colie M. 577
Cole, Daniel D. 237
Cole, Elliott G. 492
Cole, George H. 816
Cole, Henry 777
Cole, John 803
Cole, Joseph 771
Cole, Justice H. 435
Cole, Lewis D. 364
Cole, Lyman W.A. 527
Cole, Samuel C. 154, 527
Cole, Thomas 527, 557
Cole, Thomas J. 774
Colegrave, James 537
Coleman, Charles F. 149
Coleman, Harlow 767
Coleman, James 861
Coleman, James H. 87
Coleman, John 846
Coleman, Perry H. 465
Coleman, Thomas 486
Coleman, William 658
Coleman, Wm. T. 28
Coles, Theodore 500
Coles, William M.B. 746
Colform, Edwin L. 816
Colgan, George 609, 663
Colgrove, James H. 486
Colley, Horace F. 245

Collier, Robert 479, 500
Collin, George 537
Collins, Benjamin, Jr. 749
Collins, Charles 486
Collins, Denis 125
Collins, Dennis 713
Collins, Edward 470, 486
Collins, Edward R. 653
Collins, Hiram 395, 678
Collins, James 471, 683, 713, 777
Collins, John 109, 133, 369, 414,
  500, 546, 572, 703
Collins, John B. 524
Collins, John F. 646
Collins, John P. 459
Collins, Michael 221
Collins, Patrick 760
Collins, Thomas 253, 261, 270, 450
Collins, Thomas H. 747
Collins, Timothy 219
Collins, W.M. 179
Collins, William 102, 350, 442,
  846
Collins, William L. 441
Collins, William W. 297, 855
Collinson, Joseph 204
Collis, Albert 620
Collis, Edward 743
Collohan, Francis P. 743
Collough, Charles M. 725
Colly, Horace F. 278
Collyer, Frederick H. 760
Collyer, Paul 771
Colman, Henry 753
Colman, John F. 868
Colocio, Seberino 318
Colohan, William J. 557, 577
Colorado, Mangus 71
Colquette, Henry 663
Colter, Henry 665
Colter, Hugh 546
Colton, D.D. 12
Colton, James 479
Colton, Joseph 639
Colton, Rufus 743
Colville, Charles A. 259
Colwall, William 133
Colwell, Charles 537
Colyer, James 678
Comar, Patrick 546, 572

Combs, Joseph W. 678
Combs, William H. 691
Comerford, John 658
Comfort, Hugh 759
Comfort, Sylvester M. 603
Comins, Ralph E. 86, 88, 130, 152
Commerstadt, Adolph A. 646
Compton, Andrew 696
Compton, Martin 808, 819
Comstock, Asa L. 221
Comstock, George H. 477
Conalin, John 747
Conant, Abram 92
Conchin, George W. 546, 557
Condon, Asaph 638
Condron, John 582
Condy, Richard 523, 557
Condy, William 523
Conery, Peter 218
Coney, John 287
Congdon, Stephen C. 464, 493
Conger, Charles C. 799, 823
Congers, Benjamin D. 527
Congleton, Gordon 457
Conklin, Alexander 144
Conklin, John I.W. 297
Conlan, Andrew 653
Conley, John 132
Conn, John 803
Conn, Robert 638
Conn, William D. 733
Connell, Anthony 470, 493
Connell, Hugh 486
Connell, James 343
Connell, John 450
Connell, Patrick 577
Connell, Peter 844
Connelly, Barney W. 364
Connelly, James 228, 868
Connelly, John 471
Connelly, Patrick 364, 395, 756
Connelly, Thomas 739, 753
Connelly, Timothy 259, 400, 687
Conness, George W. 154
Connington, H. de Lacy 500
Connolly, Barney W. 112
Connolly, Cornelius 750
Connolly, Daniel 465, 750
Connor, Enoch 125
Connor, Hugh 178, 261

Connor, John 395, 410, 717
Connor, Joseph 626
Connor, Patrick Edward 7-12, 14, 15, 17, 19, 38, 39, 172, 174-78, 180, 182, 185, 505-6, 522
Connor, Roger 465
Connor, Samuel 555, 582, 585
Connor, Thomas 459, 577
Connor, William 204, 287
Connors, David 450
Connors, Edward 221
Connors, Michael 692
Conolly, Daniel 665
Conolly, John 369
Conover, Addison V. 355
Conover, Addison V.D. 386
Conover, James L. 585
Conover, William 212
Conrad, George D. 169, 172-73, 182, 184, 186-87, 209, 250, 275, 293
Conrad, George W. 159
Conrad, Jacob 814
Conrad, John 479, 800
Conrady, Conrad D. 92
Conroy, Francis 665
Conroy, Michael 814
Considine, Michael S. 750
Consor, John 364
Contell, James 243, 523, 591
Contrillas, Rafael 386, 395, 410
Converse, Bushrod W. 626
Convery, Thomas 861
Convis, Charles C. 441, 485
Conway, Dennis 465
Conway, James 450, 486
Conway, James C. 221
Conway, John 750
Conway, Michael 450, 486
Conway, Patrick 525, 581
Conway, Richard 557, 582
Conway, Thomas D. 557
Conway, Thomas J. 620
Conway, William 535, 555
Conwell, James 404, 681
Cook, Adam 287
Cook, Benjamin F. 221, 245
Cook, Ceylon A. 125
Cook, Charles 620
Cook, Charles W. 821

Cook, Clark W. 819
Cook, Daniel 287
Cook, Eldridge F. 646
Cook, Eli 723, 749
Cook, Frank 285
Cook, Frederick 861
Cook, George 651
Cook, George F. 779
Cook, Henry 620
Cook, James 790
Cook, John 369, 747
Cook, John P. 785
Cook, John W. 269
Cook, Joseph 471, 646
Cook, Moses 228
Cook, Moses W. 527
Cook, Nelson 626
Cook, Peter 777
Cook, Thomas 527, 546
Cook, William F. 611, 861
Cook, Willoughby 639
Cooke, Henry 842
Cooke, John E. 500
Cooke, John R. 645
Cooledge, Walter S. 763, 773
Cooley, Lemon 626
Coolidge, Henry H. 865
Coombs, Charles H. 261
Coombs, James 546
Coombs, Joseph A. 535
Coombs, Oliver M. 527, 546
Coon, Andrew 212
Coon, George 159
Coonen, Timothy 450
Cooney, Charles 527, 577
Coons, William H. 687
Coons, William W. 226
Cooper, Charles 577
Cooper, David 228
Cooper, David M. 270
Cooper, Fred 259
Cooper, George H. 760
Cooper, George R. 102
Cooper, Henry 221
Cooper, James A. 790
Cooper, James B. 566
Cooper, James C. 653
Cooper, James G. 197
Cooper, Joel B. 212
Cooper, John G. 653, 663

Cooper, John R. 632
Cooper, S. 15
Cooper, Seth H. 868
Cooper, Stephen T. 657
Cooper, Theophilus 703
Coover, George W. 555
Coovey, Jason 395
Copeland, James H. 846
Copeland, John 653
Copeland, John W. 261, 287
Copeland, Josiah S. 626
Copeland, Samuel D. 297
Copeland, Willis 395, 700
Copely, Alexander W. 601, 609, 726
Copp, John 405, 710
Copper, Edwin 259
Coppinger, Charles 665
Coppins, William 620
Copple, Milton W. 270
Coray, Eliakim 591
Corbett, George 125, 713
Corbett, Hugh 739
Corbett, John 747
Corbett, Michael 434
Corbett, Robert 124
Corbett, Samuel J. 855
Corbin, Warren 154
Corcoran, Michael 557, 572, 811
Corcoran, Patrick 777
Corcoran, Thomas D. 733
Cordero, Francisco 315
Cordero, José Antonio 315
Cordero, Juan de Jesus 315
Cordero, Malachi 112
Cordero, Manuel 316
Cordero, Romaldo 316
Cordova, Nicolas 318
Cordova, Santiago 318
Corello, Francisco 319
Corillo, José 315
Corkhuff, Samuel 287
Cornelius, Patrick 465, 493
Cornell, George P. 653
Cornwell, James 537
Corona, José 318
Corona, José Ma 318
Corona, Teodocio 319
Corothers, William E. 819
Corpear, John 405, 683
Corrales, Loreto 316

Corrigan, Thomas 149, 369
Corrilla, Bisento 277
Corrington, Wilson R. 312
Corsen, John 736
Corson, Alonzo V. 355
Corson, George 355
Corson, Sylvester 600
Corwin, Mr. 25-26
Cory, Liness C. 816
Cosgriff, Matthew 618
Cosgrove, Henry 546, 577
Cosgrove, Terrence 405, 710
Cossell, Jackson 861
Cosser, John 760
Cossett, Russell 259
Costa, Jose Ignacio 316
Costello, James 610
Coster, John H. 470, 491, 752, 790
Costerly, John 546
Costigan, Patrick 557
Costigan, Thos. 125
Cota, Miguel 316
Cota, Pedro 315
Cotter, David 477
Cotter, John 756
Cottingham, Robert J. 811
Cottle, Augustus C. 819
Cottle, Leonard J. 228
Cotton, Edward 591
Cotton, James W. 164
Cottrell, Andrew J. 785
Cottrell, Robert J. 858
Couch, Campbell 112
Coulson, Joseph A. 821
Coult, Theodore A. 56, 62, 66, 325, 676
Coulter, Edward C. 624
Counington, Hugh 743
Countryman, Josiah 218
Couran, John 582
Courlayne, Rice H. 204
Courtaine, Rice H. 297
Courter, David 500
Courtney, Frank 499
Courtois, Julius 312
Courtright, Abram J. 278
Courtright, Alson B. 626
Courtright, Geo. S. 76, 77
Couse, William 201

Coutrie, James 842
Couture, Fabien 204
Covacewich, Dionicio 307
Covaney, John 287
Covell, Louis 351
Cover, Levi 245
Covey 700
Cowan, Henry J. 687
Cowan, Isaac 119
Cowan, James 338
Cowan, John 253
Cowan, William 557, 572
Cowden, Frank 639
Cowden, William 144, 338
Cowen, Thomas 639
Cowgill, Latham 261, 295
Cowins, James W. 571
Cowins, Williams 572
Cowles, Frederick H. 557, 753
Cowles, Henry O. 678
Cox, Charles 604
Cox, David M. 727
Cox, George 164, 493
Cox, George C. 178, 297
Cox, Henry C. 278
Cox, J. Clement 305, 317
Cox, John 586, 665
Cox, Nathan 537
Cox, Patrick 471
Cox, Thomas 367
Cox, Valentine H. 676
Cox, Vowell H. 385
Cox, William 736
Coxen, Jacob 814
Coyle, Charles 204, 492
Coyle, John 471
Coyle, Patrick 572, 803
Coyne, Patrick 312
Crabb, Jeremiah 572
Crabbe, Jeremiah 557
Craft, Frederick 131
Craft, John A. 557, 591
Crafts, George H. 808
Craig 36
Craig, Alexander C. 443
Craig, Jackson 806
Craig, John 727
Craig, Joseph 736
Craig, Robert 546
Craig, Robert S. 572

Craig, Thomas H. 799, 802
Craig, William 646
Crain, Norris 253
Crall, Edward L. 704
Crall, George A. 245
Cramer, John 572, 591
Cramer, John W. A. 753
Cramer, William 774
Crampton, Charles A. 631
Crampton, Henry M. 611
Crandall, Robert M. 326, 336, 346, 363
Crane, Charles 582
Crane, James T. 777
Crane, John 102
Crane, Owen 727
Crane, Robert 102, 125
Crane, Tunis V. 611
Cranmer, Walter McD. 824
Crannall, Abraham 546
Crapo, John 261
Cravens, James G. 373
Crawford, Henry 270
Crawford, Henry H. 493
Crawford, James 245
Crawford, James C. 753
Crawford, Josiah H. 858
Crawford, Martin L. 790
Crawford, Philip 771
Crawford, Richard 735
Crawford, Robert 814
Crawford, Samuel 493
Crawford, William 159
Creath, Carroll A. 112
Cree, John L. 182, 278, 287
Creed, Austin G. 253
Creeden, Patrick H. 102
Creedon, Patrick 125
Creevey, Samuel 343, 364, 391
Creighton, George 835
Creighton, John W. 342
Cremoney, John C. 196
Cremony, John C. 62, 65, 67, 169, 209, 304, 307
Creviston, Jacob C. 788
Crews, Lorenzo W. 261
Crilley, Peter 732
Cripe, Joseph B. 800
Crippin, David R. 395, 696
Cripse, Henry 471

Crisby, Joseph T. 227
Crist, George 536, 544, 571
Crittenden, Andrew 261
Crittenden, James G. 699
Croal, John 739
Croasdale, William 665
Crocker, Anson S. 727
Crocker, George B. 261
Crocker, Henry H. 857
Crocker, John R. 798, 823
Crocker, William F. 261
Crockett, Amos 821
Crockett, Charles 138
Crockett, Jason 484
Croden, James 537
Croft, Charles 138
Croft, Charles J. 88, 98
Crohn, Christian 237, 261
Cronen, Patrick 658
Croness, James 771
Cronin, Frank 125
Cronin, Frank J. 212
Cronin, Patrick 465
Crooks, James 658
Crosby, Francis 149
Crosby, Frank W. 527
Crosby, John 653
Crosley, James 750
Cross, Alfred 450
Cross, Leonard 92
Cross, Lorenzo 777
Cross, Robert S. 807
Crossley, Alfred 261, 297
Crosson, John J. 212, 354
Crouch, John S. 354, 359, 367, 390
Croucher, William 840
Crow, Albion T., Jr. 793
Crow, George 92, 109
Crow, Wayman J. 368
Crow, William N. 493
Crowell, Amos E. 760
Crowell, William E. 396, 700
Crowley, Cornelius 360
Crowley, Daniel 212
Crowley, Daniel F. 244
Crowley, Geo. W. 287
Crowley, Patrick 739
Crowley, Thomas 537, 546, 577
Crowley, Timothy 756

Crowley, William 611
Crowninshield, Caspar 848
Crowninshield, John C. 630
Crozier, Henry 557
Crozier, James 270
Cruise, Harvey A. 811
Crum, Almon 278
Crum, Christopher N. D. 572
Crum, Henry 855
Crum, William H. 658
Crump, Chas. T. 119
Crumpton, Wesley R. 855
Crutchfield, Albertus 138
Crutz, Charles 477
Crystal, John H. 253
Cuddahy, James 287
Cuddeback, Henry 833
Culbertson, Jacob C. 527
Cullen, David 739
Cullen, John 179, 297
Cullen, Lewis 237
Cullin, Lewis 270
Cullum, Allen W. 637
Culver, Alexander S. 779
Culver, Lewis G. 784
Culver, Orrin B. 766, 785
Cummings 510
Cummings, Andy 782
Cummings, Geo. W. 270
Cummings, John 287
Cummings, John F. 405, 682
Cummings, Michael 343, 369, 391
Cummings, Samuel 414, 704
Cummins, John 297
Cunan, Hugh 102
Cunard, James H. 790
Cuneus, Julius 471
Cunningham, George 803
Cunningham, James 450, 486, 604, 632
Cunningham, James V. 819
Cunningham, John 112, 149, 355, 369, 479
Cunningham, John A. 347
Cunningham, John W. 311
Cunningham, Joseph A. 253
Cunningham, M. C. 836
Cunningham, Nordacai 683
Cunningham, Orin 537
Cunningham, Peter 683

Cunningham, Robert 739
Cunningham, Stephen M. 788
Cunningham, William 450, 500, 557, 611, 855
Cuppet, David 774
Cups, John 727
Curless, Joseph 626
Curley, John M. 338, 351
Curley, Patrick 414, 704
Curlis, Joseph H. 133
Curn, Henry 459
Curo, Joseph Angel 312
Curoas, Ruperto 319
Curran, John 604
Curran, William H. 204
Currey, Cornelius 142
Currie, John 237
Currier, George 736
Curry, William 400, 410, 692, 756
Curtin, Cornelius 537, 546, 577
Curtis, Andrew Torg 218
Curtis, Charles 861
Curtis, Darius S. 119
Curtis, George 159
Curtis, James F. 18, 305, 431, 595, 599
Curtis, James W. 261
Curtis, John 692
Curtis, John L. 450
Curtis, William 472
Cushing, John T. 486
Cushing, Manly P. 787
Cushman, George H. 459
Cushman, Zenas 558, 572
Cutler, Benajmin Clark 48-51, 54-57, 60-64, 67, 70, 335
Cutler, John M. 558, 572
Cutler, Nathaniel T. 459
Cutting, Charles H. 732, 742, 759
Cutting, Hiram E. 710

D

Daggett, Samuel 610
Dailey, Lewis E. 131
Daily, James 443
Daily, Jeremiah 873
Daily, John 275
Daily, Robert 234, 500
Daker, John 653, 873

Dakin, Charles C. 297
Dakin, Nathan H. 759
Dalbke, Simon H. 479
Dale, Denis B. 658
Daley 179
Daley, James R. 237
Daley, John 178
Daley, John S. 251
Daley, Thomas 739, 873
Daley, William 632, 739
Dally, Theodore 391
Dalton, James R. 112, 119
Dalton, John 261, 297
Dalton, Thomas 732
Dalton, William 338, 386
Daly, Bernard 727
Daly, Dennis 465, 493
Daly, James 212
Daly, John 221, 486, 527, 743
Daly, John C. 567, 577, 586
Daly, John S. 226
Daly, Patrick 727
Daly, Thomas 414, 704
Daly, William 343, 391
Daly, William D.A. 743
Dame, Charles E. 577
Dameron, Daniel 347, 391
Damon, Anson C. 137
Damon, Erastus 777
Dana, John P. 405, 410, 687
Dana, Wm. A. 28
Danbay, John J. 785
Danforth, Charles A. 235
Danforth, David 811, 816
Dange, Gustav 756
Daniels, Charles 102, 112
Daniels, James 138
Daniels, James H. 717
Daniels, James M. 620
Daniels, Joseph 337, 385
Daniels, Seth 620
Danley, Edwin J. 154
Danneleit, August 501
Danneman, Christian 125
Danner, Charles 297
Darby, Franklin 604
Darius, Christopher 228
Darley, Jeremiah 747, 874
Darling, Edwin 790
Darling, Franklin L. 237

Darling, George 338, 386
Darling, William R. 652
Darnell, Walter D. 807
Darragh, John M. 261
Darris, William A. 465
D'Artagnan, Yoes 727
D'Artois, Gaston 732, 742, 796, 802
Daton, George 582
Davenport, Horace 700
Davenport, John A. 753
Davern, John 144
Davidson, Francis 152
Davidson, Frederick A.W. 766, 793
Davidson, George 537, 546, 591
Davidson, Harlan 364
Davidson, Robert P. 524, 572
Davidson, Solomon 125
Davidson, William 144
Davies, Benjamin E. 119
Davies, John 159
Davis, Albert 450, 479
Davis, Alfred 287
Davis, Alonzo E. 657
Davis, Asa M. 858
Davis, Augustus S. 237
Davis, Benjamin B. 787
Davis, Benjamin F. 68, 87
Davis, Benjamin R. 369
Davis, Charles E. 262
Davis, Daniel 612
Davis, David 782, 873
Davis, David A. 164
Davis, David M. 777
Davis, David W. 228
Davis, Edward 287, 609, 617
Davis, Elwin 355
Davis, Erastus H. 558, 577
Davis, Francis A. 93
Davis, Franklin 486, 639
Davis, George 400, 410, 435, 713, 873
Davis, George F. 855
Davis, George L. 245
Davis, George W. 790
Davis, Henry 727, 779
Davis, Henry F. 527
Davis, Jacob R. 435, 558, 572
Davis, James 149, 537, 782, 785, 874
Davis, James B. 816

Davis, James M. 369, 874
Davis, John 149, 154, 213, 346, 472, 612, 800, 816
Davis, John F. 727
Davis, John J. 733
Davis, John S. 714
Davis, John W. 212, 250, 621, 726, 873
Davis, Joseph W. 766
Davis, Joshua 338
Davis, Louis 493
Davis, Lyman 524
Davis, Martin V. 604
Davis, Nelson H. 74
Davis, Nicholas S. 54-55, 336, 376
Davis, Peter 253
Davis, Pryor N. 833
Davis, R.D.W. 28
Davis, Richard 743
Davis, Richard R. 658
Davis, Roach S. 119
Davis, Robert 527, 546, 572
Davis, Rufus T. 278
Davis, S.B. 15
Davis, Samuel N. 753
Davis, Stephen R. 218, 234, 284
Davis, Thomas 658
Davis, Thomas J. 450, 477, 479
Davis, U.H. 671
Davis, W.M. 178
Davis, William 138, 179, 297, 435, 717, 727, 873
Davis, William J. 93
Davis, William P. 742
Davis, William R. 153
Davis, William S. 736
Davis, Wm. T. 270
Davis, William W. 164, 350
Davison, Albert N. 755
Davison, Americus V. 152
Davison, Charles 459
Davison, Daniel C. 816
Davison, George W. 459
Davison, James 617, 624
Davison, Milton C. 785
Davner, Charles 221
Dawe, Joseph 443
Dawley, Daniel 479
Dawley, Thomas H. 87, 125

Dawson, Edwin 535, 544
Dawson, John 663
Dawson, Thomas M. V. 297
Dawson, William 486, 493
Day, Augustus 861
Day, Charles 626
Day, E. U. 828
Day, Elias W. 840
Day, George C. 93
Day, Henry 626
Day, James M. 806
Day, Jedidiah 774
Day, Jules 819
Day, Oliver 612
Day, Smith J. 435
Day, Thomas 799, 806
D'Bois, John 803
Deakins, James 228
Dealand, Henry 287
Dealing, Charles A. 865
Dealling, Charles A. 126
Dean, George P. 246
Dean, James E. 646
Dean, James H. 267
Dean, Samuel 93, 100
Dean, Samuel C. 269
Dean, Thomas 89
Dean, William 364, 873
Deane, Frederick A. 359
Deans, William C. 725
Dearbon, David 840
Dearbourn, Valorus 855
Deardorff, William P. 774
Dearin, Robert 591
Dearing, Jno. T. Del 276
Deband, Leopold 112
De Bois, John 567
De Castro, Charles C. 219, 221
De Cecil, Lafayette 630
Decker, Benjamin F. 486
Decker, Charles 164
Decker, Isaac 582
Decoman, Baptiste 164
Decoster, Samuel 351, 873
De Coux, William N. 732
Decrow, Thomas 351, 391
Deemer, John F. 494
Deemer, William 728
De Forrest, William F. 868
De Freesh, Martin 682

De Freylin, Joseph 312
De Frouville, Frederick 133
Degaldillo, Domingo 308
Degarmo, Seth 246, 253
De Golia, Joseph 394, 686
Degraff, Nathaniel 472
De Groff, Charles E. 760
De Hague, James M. 369
De Hague, Joseph A. 102
De Haven, Francis A. 803
Deirking, William H. 620
De La Haape, Frederick 93
Delahanty, John M. 813
De La Mothe, Gaston 311
De Lamotte, Laurence 714
De Lancie, Richard 91
Deland, George 612
Delaney, James 351
Delaney, James H. 463, 470, 484, 491
Delaney, James W. 572
Delaney, Peter 443, 450
Delaney, Samuel 501
Delaney, William 93
De La Noix, Frederico 312
Delanoix, Frederico 308
Delany, Samuel 472
De La Osa, Feliciano 312
Delarge, John 112
De Lashmutt, Van B. 577
Delay, Timothy 750
Deliardo, Auguste 308
Delisle, Charles 646
Delius, George 138
Dellahan, Peter 204
Delmore, James 147
De Long, Oliver P. 640
De Long, Sidney R. 342, 347, 354, 385, 390, 409
De Long, Thomas 89
Delouche, Desire 537, 546
Deltine, Joseph 307
Demasters, William 164
Dement, George W. 355
De Merritt, David A. 242, 850, 861
Deming, Geo. S. 237
Demoffe, Victor 312
De Monroe, Louis 609
Demontreville, Eugene 308

Dempsey, Cyrus F. 855
Dempsey, James 297, 486, 873
Dempsey, James D. 450
Dempsey, Joseph 808
Deneen, Timothy 138
Denham, Simon 756
Denn, John 790
Denney, Henry 253
Denninger, John 756
Dennis, Hugh 297
Dennis, Joseph 347
Dennis, Policarpo 164
Dennison, William 808
Denny, Pirie B. 275, 284
De Noeville, Arnold 278
Dens, Capt. 76
Dense, Jacob 756
Densmore, Samuel 465
Denver, J.W. 23, 25, 32
Denver, John J. 450
Denvers, William 494
De Party, James 119
Departy, James 102
Depew, John 819
Deporte, Henry 874
De Prate, Ernest 126
Depuy, Anson A. 253
Depuy, Austin 566
Depuy, Joseph 251
Depuy, Samuel 567
Depuye, James B. 479
Derbin, Charles 632
Derby, Horace R. 409, 695
Derome, Edward 472
Derproskey, Wm. F. 270
Derrington, Thomas H. 808
Derry, Michael 790
Derstine, Joseph K. 617, 651, 656
Dervey, Henry G. 126
Descorutis, Edward A. 209
Desere, Chalefour 312
Desjardin, Alfred 486
Desle, Andrew 237
Desmond, Cornelius 558, 591, 604
Desmond, Daniel 501, 586
Des Moulins, Benoit H. 377
Desporte, Henri 612
Desprez, Celestino 459
Dessaint, Louis A. 472
Destint, George 494

Desty, Samuel H. 228
Detenering, Frederick W. 228
Detlow, Thomas G. 753
Devanney, Michael 253
Devanny, Michael 486
Devany, Bartholomew 546, 558, 567, 743
Deveilhe, Auguste 450
Deveney, John 204
Devere, William 434
Devereux, Frank 728
Devertier, Francis M. 262
Devin, Gen. 852
Devin, Charles 874
Devine, Charles 414, 696
Devine, John 687, 739
Devine, Owen 727
Devine, Timothy 873
Devlin, Edward 262
Devois, Simon 237
De Wald, Frederick 861
Dewar, Donald 612, 620
Dewey, Charles S. 855
Dewey, John N. 324
Dewire, John 435
De Witt 28
De Witt, Franklin P. 246
De Witt, Levi 278
Dexter, Andrew J. 219
Dexter, Benjamin F. 806
Dexter, George 824
Dexter, Henry H. 868
Dexter, John 479
Diamond, Daniel 396, 687
Dias, José M. 308
Dibble, Samuel C. 528
Dickens, Enoch S. 710
Dickerson, Andrew J. 640
Dickerson, William H. 377
Dickes, Albert 472
Dickett, Henry C. 728
Dickey, George S. 324, 364, 873
Dickey, Samuel A. 338
Dickinson, Seth J. 821
Dickson, Henry C. 868
Dickson, James 811
Dickson, James C. 246
Dickson, John F. 501
Dickson, Robert 678
Diegle, William 405, 678

Dieken, Thomas II. 347
Dieman, Albert 612
Diemar, Philip 102
Diener, John 558
Dierstein, William 112, 113
Dierstphise, Adolpho 308
Diez, Francisco 312
Dignan, Michael 472
Dill, Columbus 253
Dill, Ottaway 459
Dillahanty, Henry J. 839
Dillane, Jeremiah 138
Dillenbeck, Caleb 543, 554, 576
Dilley, Jonah V. 785
Dilliard, Louis 262
Dillon, James 658
Dillon, John 213, 546, 558
Dillon, Richard 93
Dillon, Thomas 93, 133, 790
Dillon, William 547, 558, 591
Dillon, William P. 450
Dimock, Asa J. 814
Dinan, Patrick 577
Dindried, Manuel 246
Dineen, John 821
Dingman, Lewis C. 372
Dinie, Patrick 138
Dioux, Louis 213
Dirks, Henry 310
Disc, De Witt C. 534, 590
Dittmar, Christian F. 278
Diver, John A. 110, 350
Diverson, Eugene 312
Divine, Andrew P. 472
Divine, Timothy 448
Dixon 28
Dixon, Edward 465
Dixon, George W. 228
Dixon, Henry 485
Dixon, John 558
Dixon, Nathan 777
Dixon, William 360, 873
Dixon, William H. 229
Doan, Wallace 695
Doane, Gustavus C. 855
Dobbins, John J. 499
Dobbins, Marcus D. 676
Dobbs, John 399, 410, 717
Dobbs, Richard 728
Dobbs, Thomas A. 347, 394, 409, 716

Dobbs, William 653
Dobson, James 753
Dobson, William C. 405
Dobson, William E. 710
Dobson, Wm. M. 270
Dock, Michael 312
Dockery, Hugh 450, 479, 486, 873
Dockrey, Patrick G. 632
Dodd, Benjamin 868
Dodd, Edward 612, 620
Doddridge, Benjamin F. 646, 874
Dodds, Charles 808
Dodds, William H. 524, 534, 570
Dodero, Domingo 284
Dodge 28
Dodge, Charles R. 450, 486
Dodge, Edward E. 246
Dodge, John 591
Dodge, Leonard 844
Dodge, Nicholas P. 123
Dodge, Oscar P. 276
Dodgren, B. F. 760
Doe, George W. 535
Doherty, Bernard 814
Doherty, John 297, 567, 604
Doherty, Owen 760
Doherty, Patrick 612
Doherty, William 604
Dohrman, Henry A. 287
Dolan, Edward 435
Dolan, James F. 287, 873
Dolan, Michael 577, 873
Dolan, Thomas 501
Dolan, Timothy 154
Dole, Charles 471, 554
Dolf, Andrew 443
Dolland, John 788
Dolloway, Chas. C. 144
Dolman, Henry 632
Dolton, Robert 632
Domingo, José 319
Dominguez, Dolores 319
Dominguez, José A. 319
Dominguez, José Maria 319
Dominick, John 750
Donaghue, Daniel 591
Donaghue, Daniel G. 472
Donaghue, John 747
Donaghue, Thomas 537
Donahoe, John 808

Donahoe, Philip 126
Donahue, Daniel 179, 547
Donahue, James 213, 253, 459
Donahue, John 343, 391
Donahue, Matthew 450
Donahue, Michael 443, 494
Donahue, Peter 28
Donahue, Thomas 144, 547
Donaldson, Charles W. 253
Donaldson, John 779
Donally, Thomas 658
Donalson, William H. 154
Donatella, Antonio 528, 547, 558
Donato, Ego 811
Donelson, John 824
Donely, Daniel 777
Donevan, John G. 305, 307
Donivan, Michael 131
Donly, Thomas 646
Donnell, Major F. 472
Donnelly, Andrew 262
Donnelly, Bernard 547, 591
Donnelly, Hugh 400
Donnelly, James 528, 577, 612
Donnelly, John 213, 472, 501
Donnelly, Martin P. 369
Donnelly, Patrick 486
Donnelly, Peter 821
Donnelson, John 632
Donnolly, Peter 270
Donohoe 28
Donohue, James 270, 501
Donohue, John 728
Donohue, Thomas 678
Donolan, Thomas 572
Donovan, Bernard 633
Donovan, Jeremiah 728
Donovan, Morris 494
Donovan, Patrick 400, 690, 803, 873
Dontremont, Victor 99
Donylas, James 873
Donzelat, Francis 605
Donzelat, John 640
Doody, Dennis 760
Dooermallen, John 144
Doole, David 336
Dooley, Francis 536, 591
Dooley, Patrick 544, 605
Dooley, Robert 640, 873

Dooling, Michael 479
Doolittle, Uriah H. 612
Doom, Cyrus N. 816
Dopp, David 537
Doran, Andrew J. 696
Doran, Michael 873
Doremus, Harry E.W. 259, 294
Dorland, Robert R. 102, 113, 118, 162
Dorman, John 767
Dorr, William A. 779
Dorsey, Robert 782
Dose, Frederick 278
Dosher, Henry 671
Dosher, Henry J. 714, 873
Dotry, Leonard 873
Dotson, Calvin 677
Doty, John 782
Doty, Leonard 288
Doty, Samuel 633
Doubleday, Charles D. 633
Doubleday, Delos S. 630
Doubleday, Frank 793, 873
Doud, Franklin 343, 391
Dougherbee, Daniel P. 760
Dougherty, Barney 760
Dougherty, Daniel 126, 833
Dougherty, George 665
Dougherty, Hugh 743
Dougherty, James 704
Dougherty, James H. 414, 704
Dougherty, John 501, 739
Dougherty, Joseph 747
Dougherty, Leander 90
Dougherty, Mannus 399, 687
Dougherty, Neal W. 620
Dougherty, Patrick 653, 739
Dougherty, Reuben 102, 873
Dougherty, William 138, 472, 528, 547, 612, 633
Dougherty, William H. 138
Dougherty, William J. 523, 547, 582
Doughty, James C. 225, 250, 267
Douglas, Adam 547, 558
Douglas, Charles D. 420, 427, 470
Douglas, Edward 246
Douglas, George 435
Douglas, James 343, 733, 803
Douglas, Martin V. 528

Douglas, Robert A. 753
Douglass, Alexander 728
Douglass, Charles 450
Douglass, Orman L. 364
Dountremont, Victor 873
Douthill, Charles 347
Doveton, Charles J. G. 626
Dow, Franklin W. 788
Dow, James 577
Dow, Weston W. 678
Dowd, Hugh 704
Dowd, James 814
Dowd, Milo F. 658
Dowd, William J. 122
Dowden, James 808
Dowell, John 868
Dowerty, Henry 756
Dowley, Russell P. 547, 558, 582
Dowling, John K. 237, 873
Dowling, Thomas 133
Downard, Thomas 262
Downer, James S. 839
Downey, Byron A. 760
Downey, Cornelius 262
Downey, John 665
Downey, John G. 5, 12, 13, 28, 322
Downing, Charles 691
Downing, James S. 717
Downing, Lawrence 692
Downing, Samuel A. 808
Downs, Harry 221
Downs, James S. 246
Downs, Sidney B. 665
Downs, William F. 767
Doyle, James 612, 620
Dozier, Alexander T. 591
Dozier, Enoch F. 618
Drace, Sidney A. 443, 450
Drahor, Adam J. 243
Drake, Judge 510-13
Drake, Alpheus F. 144
Drake, Francis 288
Drake, George H. 537
Drake, William 612, 808
Dralle, Louis 435
Drane, George W. 620
Drane, Thomas M. 620
Drant, Nicholas 472
Draper, Charles H. 823

Draper, Thomas D. 653
Dreifos, Adolph 152
Dreman, John 612
Drenan, Benjamin 777
Drennan, John 410, 609, 714
Drescher, Valentine 341
Dresser, Charles H. 605
Dresser, John G. 373
Dresser, Joseph C. 605
Dresser, William O. 605
Drew, Cornelius 405, 683
Drew, Rodackway 771
Drey, Ferdinand 229
Drinan, John 93, 103
Drinkhouse, Henry S. 126
Driscoll, Dennis 811
Driscoll, Eugene 486
Driscoll, Florence 537, 547
Driskell, Elijah H. 295
Drolet, Augustine 308
Drulard, Allen J. 777
Drum, John 802
Drum, R. C. 8, 9, 11, 14, 17-19, 22, 33, 39, 49, 51-53, 57, 64, 66, 172, 174, 305, 419, 430, 505, 669
Drummond, Benjamin 777
Drummond, Geo. W. 767
Drury, Wendell W. 779
Dryer, John 873
Dryer, John H. 756
Dryes, John 646
Drynan, John B. 776, 874
Drynan, Robert 777
Duane, Henry J. 583
Duarte, Francisco 319, 873
Duarte, Reyes 308
Dubois, Samuel 494
Ducette, Louis 547, 572
Dudley, Charles P. 766
Dudley, Gilbert 119
Dudley, John 149
Dudley, John E. 354
Dudley, John G., Jr. 739
Due, William 572
Duensing, Ernest 604
Duer, Beverly C. 726
Duffield, Thomas A. 187, 213
Duffinie, James 262
Duffy, Charles 400, 410, 717

Duffy, Henry W. 771
Duffy, John 472
Duffy, Michael 733
Duffy, Michael M. 262
Dugan, Erastus 297
Dugan, Michael 525, 572
Dugan, Nicholas 377, 873
Dugan, Patrick 159
Dugdail, Thomas 785
Dugid, George 338, 386
Duhain, Henry 288
Duhaine, Henry 204
Duhamelt, Ferdinand 312
Duhem, Constant 704
Duhem, Victor 705
Duhern, Victor 414
Duhig, Timothy 459
Duke, Owen 760
Dulin, Bushrod 451, 499, 528
Dumas, Joseph 737
Dumont, Henry 307
Dumont, Joseph 297
Dunawain, Martin V. 229
Dunbar, Thomas H. 658
Duncan, Lt. 187
Duncan, Archibald 528
Duncan, Benjamin F. 717
Duncan, Chas. H. 237
Duncan, George B. 164
Duncan, James H. 752
Duncan, John 126, 131
Duncan, McCune H. 227
Duncan, Noel 782
Duncan, Reuben 836, 873
Duncan, Robert 229
Duncan, Robert L. 243, 275
Duncan, William 229, 728
Duneman, C.F. Louis 755
Dunham, Hiram 276
Dunham, John 235
Dunkert, Johannah 133
Dunkert, Michael 229
Dunlap, Charles 288
Dunlap, James M. 152
Dunlap, John 547, 572
Dunlap, Samuel C. 774
Dunlap, William H. 747
Dunleary, James 262
Dunleavy, George 360, 873
Dunlop, John S. 93, 103

Dunn, Alexander 558, 572
Dunn, Andrew 144
Dunn, Daniel 577, 873
Dunn, David 823
Dunn, Henry 811
Dunn, James F. 824
Dunn, James W. 803
Dunn, John 472, 808
Dunn, John A. 204
Dunn, Lawrence 346
Dunn, Patrick 844
Dunn, Richard 237
Dunn, Thomas 229, 343, 377, 528, 586
Dunn, William J. 625
Dunnigan, James 793
Dunning, James M. 204
Dunning, Ozro 790
Dunnington, William P. 201
Dunscombe, Henry 435
Dunsing, William 733
Dunton, Ebenezer 459
Dupont, Joseph 126
Dupray, Frank 808
Dupuis, Auguste 646
Durand, Gustave F. 583, 586
Durat, John 861
Durazo, Ramon 316
Duress, Patrick J. 537
Durgin, William P. 657
Durkey, Miles 555
Durkin, James 246, 665
Durkin, John 288
Durnett, William A. 93
Durnin, Patrick 119
Duro, Antonio 75
Durway, Henry 659, 814
Dusenberry, John 620
Dusenberry, Walter S. 771
Duskey, Robert F. 543, 554
Dusky, Andrew V. 828, 840
Dusky, Robert F. 528
Dutton, Evlyn 288
Dutton, George 671, 716, 717
Dutton, George B. 612
Duty, Daniel 774
Duval, Louis 558
Duval, Moses 204
Duval, Samuel C. 759
Duvall 179

Duvall, Levi 364
Duvall, Moses 288
Duvall, Robert W. 288, 873
Duve, Frederick H. 377
Dwyer, James 137
Dwyer, John 103, 760
Dwyer, Michael 653
Dwyer, Samuel 262, 270
Dwyer, Thomas 262
Dwyer, William 343, 391
Dye, James P. 646
Dyer, Andrew B. C. 858
Dyer, Hiram 119
Dyer, James 179, 297
Dyer, Michael 471
Dyer, Richard E. 718
Dyre, Edward 612, 633
Dyre, John R. 448
Dysart, John 405, 683
Dyson, Isaac 537, 547

E

Eady, Joseph 811
Eagan, George L. 355
Eaman, William M. 750
Eames, Jonathan 767
Earl, James R. 288
Earl, Samuel P. 377, 385
Earl, William 486
Earle, William 103, 113
Early 850, 852-53
Earnest, Thompson W. 803
Earnshaw, Enos 470, 486
Earp, William 747
Eastabrook, Alfred 162
Easte, William 494
Easterly, James W. 696
Eastham, Theodore H. 270
Eastman, Francis 547
Eastman, George W. 839
Eastman, Jacob D. 816
Eastman, Lorenzo D. 126
Easton, Henry W. 99, 119
Eaton, Albert 824
Eaton, Charles 679
Eaton, Charles E. 677
Eaton, Chas. H. 234
Eaton, James 246
Eaton, James H. 149

Eaton, John 229
Eaton, John L. 457
Eaton, William 221
Ebeling, John 808
Eberly, Nicholas 811
Ebner, George 219
Eby, James N. 868
Eckert, Philip 152
Eckstin, Samuel 376
Eddy, Caleb M. 794
Eddy, John 227
Eddy, Walter 759
Eddy, Wm. 132
Ede, William 93
Edgar, Lt. 76
Edgar, Harmon 733
Edgerton, George A. 451
Edgerton, George O. 354, 403, 709
Edmiston, Robert 350, 376, 384, 385
Edmonds, Benjamin F. 113
Edmonds, Henry 338
Edmunds, Harvey 386
Edsall, Walter J. 566
Edward, Jesse 154
Edwards, Alexander 209
Edwards, Edmund F. 278
Edwards, Frank 486
Edwards, George F. 394, 409, 712, 874
Edwards, Henry P. 739
Edwards, Isaac 585
Edwards, James 788
Edwards, James C. 268, 270
Edwards, James T. 187
Edwards, John 237, 443, 816
Edwards, John C. 640
Edwards, Joseph 785
Edwards, Joseph C. 164
Edwards, Louis A. 246
Edwards, Napoleon 235
Edwards, Philander 824
Edwards, Richard 739, 780
Edwards, Stephen 435
Edwards, William 586
Effingham, Henry 221
Egan, James 434, 528
Egan, Patrick A. 774
Egbert, Christopher 152

Egbert, Jesse S. 271
Eger, Sidney 486
Egersdorf, George 451, 486
Eggleston, David A. 780
Eggleston, Harrison 774
Eggleston, Lorenzo D. 373
Eglize, Michael 308
Egloff, John P. 158
Ehle, Oscar E. 612
Ehmer, John M. 157
Eichenburger, Jacob 443
Eichhoff, Edward 110
Eichler, George 777
Eidol, Martin 737
Eigenbrodt, Charles S. 850–52, 857
Eighel, Frederick 791
Eisenger, Joseph 665
Eiser, Lewis 378
Eisfeldt, Theodore 600
Eitel, George 612
Eizel, John 213
Ekins, John 501
Elder, Nathaniel 733
Elder, Robert 821
Elder, William 378
Eldred, Nathaniel 262
Eldred, William 577
Eldred, William H. 523
Eldridge, Perez H. 743
Eldridge, William 577
Elias, John 844
Elizalda, Francisco 316
Elizalde, Diego 319
Elizalde, Dolores 319
Elkins, David 347
Elleg, M. 178
Ellend, Lewis 220
Eller, Henry 113
Ellert, John A. 836
Ellery, Henry C. 528, 547
Elles, William H. 640
Ellett, Richard S. 855
Ellicott, Thomas 435
Ellig, Carl 204
Ellingson, Hiram 288
Elliot, Jacob H. 874
Elliot, William 633, 687
Elliott, Charles 119, 620
Elliott, Frank 143
Elliott, Jacob H. 567

Elliott, John 633
Elliott, Lewis M. 646
Elliott, Richard J. 110, 221
Elliott, Stephen F. 599
Elliott, Stephen P. 246
Elliott, William 640
Elliott, William R. 716
Elliott, William W. 242, 262, 275, 278, 865
Ellis 28
Ellis, A. Irving 338
Ellis, Alfred 278
Ellis, Andrew D. 288
Ellis, Charles 113, 278
Ellis, Charles E. 72, 91
Ellis, Charles L. 237
Ellis, Daniel W. 338
Ellis, Edward H. 197
Ellis, Frederick 164, 874
Ellis, Henry F. 733
Ellis, John, Jr. 800
Ellis, Thomas 229, 537, 558, 785
Ellison, John W. 152
Ellison, Riley 679
Ellsworth, Henry A. 815
Ellsworth, William E. 494
Ellsworth, William F. 336, 378
Elmer, Peter 528
Elmore, William H. 537
Eloin, Francis 819
Elsey, Thomas 537, 547, 586
Elster, Henry 747
Eltz, Frederick 586, 874
Elwood, Edward L. 806
Ely, George G. 843
Ely, John 113
Elzcorn, Peter 782
Emerson, Charles 537
Emerson, Charles H. 874
Emerson, Joseph D. 364
Emery, Charles H. 157, 874
Emery, Edward C. 537
Emery, Enoch H. 840
Emery, Herbert L. 612, 620
Emery, Jesse B. 254, 262, 271
Emery, John 338
Emery, Jonas D. 737
Emery, Josiah S. 612, 620
Emery, Leander 126
Emery, William E. 766

Emmerson, Howard 567
Emmett, Edmond 528, 558
Emond, Louis J. 494
Engelbrecht, John H. 133
England, Carsten 605
England, Joseph M. 93
English, George 159, 874
English, Richard 844
English, Walter M. 525, 535
English, William F. 760
Ennessey, John H. 733
Ennis, Richard 262
Enos, Benjamin W. 692
Enos, Erastus 858
Enos, Frank 861, 865
Enright, Lucius 558, 572, 612
Enright, Lucius E. 436
Enriquez, Martin 319
Ensign, Heman B. 472
Ensign, Thomas S. 246
Ensley, Allen 246
Epes, John 610, 618
Epner, Gustav 725
Epner, Joseph 756
Epperson, James E. 179, 558, 591
Erhart, Joseph 774
Erick, Julius H. 276
Erickson, Niel 760
Erixson, Andrew 718
Ernst, Adam 784
Erskine, John 659
Ertle, John 653
Erwin, Alonzo M. 363
Erwin, Arthur C. 646
Erwin, George W. 625
Erwin, Henry 759
Erwin, William W. 537
Esberg, Henry 528
Esburg, Henry 586
Escart, Jesse S. 663
Eschenburg, John R. 494
Eslick, Richard 396, 700
Esmer, Alexis 312
Espelle, Frederick 139
Esperon, Louis 633
Espinosa, Clemente 316
Espinosa, Joaquin 316
Espy, Thomas C. 626
Espy, William 277
Esselstyn, James M. 120

Estabrook, John D. 405, 709
Esteffe, Emanuel 204
Esten, Stephen H. 858
Esterbrook, John D. 677, 692
Estes, Abraham 131
Estes, Albert E. S. 816
Estes, Francis G. 103
Estes, Robert 647
Estill, Thomas 733
Estrada, Francisco 319
Estrada, Manuel 319
Estrado, Demetris 312
Estrado, Francisco 312
Ethen, Anthony 201
Etling, Richard O. 201
Ettien, George W. 743
Euler, Conrad 620
Ewell, Gen. 852
Ewing, James P. 347
Ewing, John 229
Eyre, Edward E. 46, 47, 51, 54, 56-58, 60-62, 64-69, 87
Eyrick, George 254
Evans, Col. 179
Evans, Daniel 794
Evans, Edward 773
Evans, George S. 3, 168, 177, 196, 305, 849
Evans, James 637
Evans, Jeremiah 229
Evans, John 683
Evans, John R. 459
Evans, John S. 435, 780
Evans, Jonathan T. 347
Evans, Mark 547
Evans, Owen 760
Evans, Stephen W. 821
Evans, Thos. 157
Evans, Thomas R. 833, 874
Evans, Warren H. 351
Evans, Wilber 874
Evans, William 144, 728, 753
Evans, Wilson 709
Evans, Youngs 821
Everbeck, Charles 773
Everett, Charles 391
Everhard, Henry 413, 705
Everling, Charles H. 800
Evers, Deitrich 736
Every, Isaac 842

Evoy, Hugh J. 528

F

Faber, George W. 640
Fabian, James W. 159
Fair, William 868
Fairbanks, Austin A. 756
Fairbanks, Ferdinand 139
Fairbanks, James 737
Fairbanks, Oscar 268
Fairbrother, Alfred 679
Fairchild, Alfred S. 771
Fairchild, Chauncey P. 491
Fairchild, Elliott C. 109, 122
Fairchilds, John 705, 874
Fairfax, Claudius 133
Fairfield, Chauncey P. 433, 440, 463
Falcot, Henry 465
Falkenberg, William 311
Falkner, Henry I. 204
Falkner, Joseph F. 479
Faller, Joseph 149
Fallon, John 459, 486, 554, 576
Falls, Richard J. 218
Fanel, Martin 133
Fanger, Edward 288
Fann, Oliver H. P. 229
Fannes, Francis 803
Fannin, John 528, 547, 558
Fanning, George 221
Fanning, John M. 653
Fanning, William D. 262, 874
Fark, Frederick 351
Farley, C. C. 197
Farley, Ebenezer C. 806
Farley, F. 178
Farley, Frank A. 259, 294
Farley, James 814
Farley, Joseph F. 659, 824
Farley, Patrick 612
Farley, William 297
Farlin, Michael 753
Farnell, J. D. 28
Farney, Henry 806
Farnham, Alphonso G. 791
Farnham, Nason T. 813
Farnham, William H. 179, 591, 824
Farnsworth, Gilbert 131

Farnsworth, Oliver H. 782
Farr, Frederick L. 226
Farr, Jedediah 874
Farrar, William 726
Farrar, William H. 100
Farrell, John 665, 737
Farrell, Michael 213, 221, 692, 733
Farrell, Michael F. 229
Farrell, Michael J. 229, 874
Farrell, Newell E. 695
Farrell, Patrick 746
Farrell, Royal J. 243
Farrell, Royall J. 816
Farrell, Sylvester 465
Farrell, William 204, 213
Farren, John 110, 136, 152
Farren, Robert 731
Farrington, Abram B. 739
Fassett, Mortimer S. 626
Faucett, Robert 528
Faucyre, Louis 465
Fauel, Martin 874
Fauntleroy, Arthur E. 378
Faust, Michael 747
Fauth, Jacob 369
Faverau, Louis 443
Favour, John 254
Fay, Dennis 237
Fay, George 705
Fay, Hiram 111
Fay, John P. 237
Fay, Melvin G. 659
Fay, Prescott P. 620, 782
Fay, William 369
Faye, Thomas 811
Fazakerly, James 237
Feagan, Patrick 617
Federle, Gustave 278
Federle, Max 278
Feeks, Julius J. 213, 315
Felch, John H. 865
Feldwick, Henry 99
Feliciano, Verongo 874
Feliz, Francisco 319
Felker, Herman 400, 410, 718
Felker, Nicholas 840
Fellna, George 771
Fellows, Augustus 164
Fellows, Thomas 728

Fellows, W.H.H. 776
Felmer, Joseph 73, 89, 109
Fencel, Henry C.W. 858
Fenn, Silas T. 845
Fennell, James 747
Fennell, Thomas H. 788
Fenner, James K. 558
Fenner, Nicholas 246
Fenton, William 133
Ferber, William 583
Ferguson, Andrew J. 816
Ferguson, Benjamin 620
Ferguson, Charles B. 640
Ferguson, Cornelius S. 364
Ferguson, George 753
Ferguson, Ira G. 749
Ferguson, John 348
Ferguson, Patrick 400
Ferguson, Peter F. 436
Ferguson, Thomas 459, 472, 486
Ferguson, William H. 659
Fergusson, Benjamin F. 672, 696
Fergusson, David 56, 66, 68, 87
Ferlig, George H. 472
Fernon, John 529
Ferrell, Robert 605, 749
Ferrera, Carlos 308
Ferrier, George W. 868
Ferrill, David C. 865
Ferris, Charles 221
Ferris, Dewitt C. 774
Ferris, James H. 774
Ferris, John M. 162
Ferry, George F. 846
Fetridge, Thomas M. 705, 874
Fetter, Henry 494
Ffrench, William 399
Ffrench, William F. 384
Fialon, Rev. 183
Fick, Joseph H. 743
Ficken, Henry 443
Fickett, Isaac S. 665
Ficklin, John 761
Ficklin, John J. 785
Field, George L. 126
Field, George O. 226, 254
Field, James A. 842
Field, Lewis A. 780
Field, Waterman 833
Fielding, William P. 501

Fieldman, Julius 861
Fields, Lorenzo 93
Fields, Richard 213
Fields, Wesley 679
Fike, George W. 612, 647
Filbrook, George 626
Fillebrown, Henry H. 848, 855
Filmore, Charles P. 537
Fimbres, Nicolas 319
Fimple, Parden C. 373, 874
Finch, John W. 833
Finch, Robert J. 612
Finch, Solon 833
Finch, Thomas J. 833
Findley, James H. 791, 794
Finigan, Timothy 819
Fink, Daniel 842
Fink, Joseph 262
Finlayson, James M. 479
Finley, John L. 865
Finley, John W. 351, 391
Finley, Robert 808
Finley, Welton B. 819
Finn, Charles 152
Finn, Edward 470
Finn, Michael 368
Finnegan, Peter 144
Finnegan, Terry 262
Finnegan, Thomas 204
Finnegin, James 351
Finnerty, James 566, 575
Finnerty, John 558, 572
Finnerty, John B. 487
Finney, John 472, 653, 663
Finney, Samuel G. 728
Finnigan, Richard 547
Firn, Daniel 400
Firn, Richard V. 400
Fisch, Frederick D. 601
Fischer, Daniel 612
Fish, Frank W. 465
Fish, Latrop 360
Fisher, August 132
Fisher, Augustus 836
Fisher, Charles A.B. 133
Fisher, Erasmus P. 262, 288
Fisher, Frank 103, 806
Fisher, George 179, 443, 485
Fisher, George W. 547, 581
Fisher, Henry L. 262

Fisher, Jackson 858
Fisher, Jacob 154, 164
Fisher, James 605
Fisher, John 633
Fisher, John L. 221, 229
Fisher, Joseph 120, 874
Fisher, Samuel 343
Fisher, Simeon 338
Fisher, William J. 653
Fisk, Augustus 126
Fitch, Charles H. 120
Fitch, George M. 791
Fitch, J. Ives 609
Fitch, Oscar 791
Fithian, Amos 602
Fithian, William S. 733
Fitz, John F. 472
Fitzclarence, George 640
Fitzgerald, David 262, 298
Fitzgerald, James 365, 391
Fitzgerald, James C. 535, 543, 570
Fitzgerald, John 93
Fitzgerald, Stephen 271
Fitzgerald, Walter 807
Fitzgibbon, John 739
Fitzmorris, Thomas 471, 487, 814
Fitzpatrick, James 159, 600, 617
Fitzpatrick, John 237
Fitzpatrick, William 360
Fitzsimmons, Matthew 484
Flagg, Adam 369
Flagg, Joseph A. 816
Flahave, Michael 819
Flanagan, Edward 159
Flanagan, John 537, 811
Flanders, Samuel K. 136
Flanders, Sullivan B. 525, 547, 555, 576
Flanigan, Thomas 229
Flannagan, Michael 767
Flannery, Dennis 528, 577
Flannigan, James A. 235
Fleece, John C. 761
Fleehart, Irving 625
Fleming, Capt. 763
Fleming, Arthur 522, 591
Fleming, John H. 365
Flemming, John 487
Fletcher, Charles H. 487
Fletcher, Edward E. 659

Fletcher, John 855
Fletcher, John W. 372
Fletcher, Patrick 487
Fleurs, Pierre L. 139
Flin, James 659
Flinn, Samuel 396, 700
Flinn, William J. 640
Flint 28
Flint, Mr. 21, 30
Flint, Maj. 36
Flint, Eugene V. 558, 572
Flint, James W. 558
Flint, John 821
Flint, Richard 537
Flint, Robert 753
Flock, John 431
Flood, Heman N. 213
Flood, Herman N. 612
Flood, James J. 806
Flood, John 451, 528, 547, 811
Flood, Stephen 858
Flora, Joshua C. 278
Flores, Amado 318
Flores, Jesus 800
Flourney, Charles H. 858
Flowers, John 221
Floyd, James 213
Floyd, Samuel 351
Fluke, Eley A. 142
Flynn, Denis 221
Flynn, Edward 466
Flynn, Henry 419-21, 433, 470, 505
Flynn, James 653, 699
Flynn, John M. 750
Flynn, Michael 144
Flynn, Patrick 547
Flynn, Richard L. 558
Flynn, Thomas 343, 351, 369, 391
Fogg, Henry N. 360
Fogg, Nathan H. 865
Foley, Daniel 113
Foley, Daniel B. 312
Foley, David 683
Foley, Edward 229, 653
Foley, Frank 93
Foley, James 278, 298
Foley, John 459, 472, 501
Foley, Mark S. 237
Foley, Michael 645, 811

Foley, Patrick 113
Foley, Peter 132, 133
Foley, William 448
Foljaine, Henry C. 677
Follmer, John 154
Folsom, James W. 492
Folsom, Louis 494
Fonck, Victor 262
Fones, Dioniseo 316
Fongar, Edward 204
Fonner, John C. 833
Fontaine, Henry 443
Foot, Andrew N. 836
Foote, Charles 405
Foote, Charles D. 861
Foote, Charles S. 683, 874
Foote, Grotius D. 803
Foote, John F. 558
Foran, George W. 794
Forbert, Pierce 803
Forbes 28
Forbes, Alexander C. 855
Forbes, Eli B. 93, 111
Forbes, George F. 126
Forbes, James H. 298
Forbes, John J. 271
Forbes, Joseph 298
Forbes, M. 178
Forbes, Martin 202
Forbester, Archibald 537, 567, 591
Forcum, Wesley M. 771
Ford, Benjamin 808
Ford, James 433, 466, 743, 747
Ford, James P. 733
Ford, Michael 811
Ford, Milo G. 868
Ford, Patrick 742, 743
Ford, Silas P. 673, 694
Ford, William 246
Fordham, Nathan C. 865
Fordney, James M. 816
Forehand, Gehile H. 537, 591
Foreman, Ferris 38, 39
Foreman, James 443
Foreman, James E. 819
Foresman, Robert E. 768
Forest, William 246
Forey, William 599
Forhob, John 733
Forkhimer, Bartnett 204

Forman, David H. 131
Forman, Ferris 22, 595, 599, 669
Forman, James 244
Forner, Frederick 487
Forrest, Charles 470
Forrest, John 537
Forrest, William H. 633, 782
Forrester, Francis 414, 705
Forrestier, Auguste 308
Forscutt, Mark H. 537, 567
Forsha, St. Clair 262
Forsman, James S. 431
Forster, Frederick W. 93
Forsythe, George W. 139
Fortner, Charles N. 399
Fortner, Charles W. 686
Foss, Benjamin R. 771
Foster, Andrew 472
Foster, Benjamin F. 152
Foster, Charles 756
Foster, Charles R. 577
Foster, Charles T.F. 737
Foster, Christian 404, 410, 671, 716
Foster, Edward 868
Foster, Frederick 683, 874
Foster, Frederick W. 874
Foster, George 133
Foster, George F. 159
Foster, George H. 791
Foster, George P. 126
Foster, Isaac F. 204
Foster, James 868
Foster, James G. 617, 630
Foster, John 528
Foster, John B. 149
Foster, John W. 246
Foster, Squire 791
Foster, William 204, 237, 391
Fostman, Henry 865
Fouche, Charles 705
Fouches, George 749
Fougherty, Patrick 443
Foulds, John 844
Foundeway, John 647
Fountain, Albert J. 354, 363
Fountaine, Louis 612
Fouquet, Louis A. 647
Fourcade, Joseph R. 653
Fouts, Andrew J. 374

Fowler, Franklin 785
Fowler, Harvey 494
Fowler, Henry G. 840
Fowler, John 459, 737
Fowler, John F. 647
Fowler, John T. 251
Fowler, William H. 816
Fowles, Albert 692
Fox, Benjamin F. 77, 136, 151
Fox, David 451
Fox, Francis 144, 246
Fox, Frank 443
Fox, Hiram W. 784
Fox, James 466, 620
Fox, John 612, 750
Fox, John H. 645
Fox, Martin L. 234
Fox, Thomas 743
Foxwell, George W. 836
France, John 254
Francis, Henry C. 735
Francis, James 647, 844
Francis, John 133, 487, 874
Francis, Samuel 800
Francis, William 794
Francois, John 221
Francois, Richard 312
Francois, Vernot T. 164
Franey, Moses 785, 874
Frank, Charles H. 625
Frank, Frederick 756
Frank, Frederick J. 599, 605, 644
Frank, John 259, 294
Frank, Victor 757
Frank, William 459
Franklin, Antony 788
Franklin, Frederick 692
Franklin, Isaac W. 846
Franklin, Mark A. 547
Franklin, James 237
Franklin, John 262
Franklin, Joseph 343, 369, 390
Franklyn, J. 178
Franks, Alexander 163
Franks, Charles 737
Franks, Edward 113
Franks, Fred J. 609
Franks, John 163, 288
Franks, Robert 164
Frantz, John W. 298

Fraser, James A. 640
Fraser, John 202
Frautfelter, Andrew 351
Frawley, Patrick 178-79, 259, 874
Frawley, Timothy 737, 777
Frazer, Abner 120
Frazer, Ebner 103
Frazer, George 692
Frazer, John 120
Frazer, Magnus 833
Frazier, Abner 400, 410
Frazier, George W. 227
Frazier, John F. 149
Frazier, William W. 830, 843
Fredericks, Jacob 120, 213
Freeborn, Hugh 391
Freeborn, Hugo or Hugh 343
Freeman, Ellis C. 555
Freeman, James 855
Freeman, James B. 835
Freeman, Oscar J. 288
Freeman, William 93, 213, 874
Freese, George D. 768
Freiedeman, John L. 210
Freiler, Marcus 559
Fremont, Anton de 665
Fremont, Louis 137
French, Albert H. 71-74, 79, 89, 117, 161
French, Charles 676
French, George D. 181, 225
French, Henry 621, 803
French, Henry H. 139
French, James A. 800
French, John 494
French, Marquis H. 237
French, William 278
French, William F. 86, 690
Frentress, Frederick N. 144
Freshhom, William 271
Freshour, Joseph T. 800
Freunde, Auguste 312
Frew, John 700, 874
Frey, Fridolin 768
Freylin, Joseph 312
Friedenburg, Wm. 211
Friel, Patrick 351
Fringuelle, Dypolite 612
Frink, Edwin B. 676-77, 686
Frink, Luman 487

Frisbee, Thomas M. 774
Fritch, Augustus 547
Fritsch, Jacob 810
Fritts, Elias 659
Frittze, Henry W. 823
Fritz, Augustus 494
Fritz, Emil 51, 54, 58, 60, 61, 63, 72, 73, 76, 77, 87, 97
Frobitz, Edward 679
Frohlich, David 753
Frolke, Frederick 788
Frost, Joseph S. 103
Fruit, Enoch 842
Fruth, Melchoir 768
Fry, Calvin H. 621
Fry, Joseph J. 268
Fry, William 583
Frye, James F. 605, 618
Fryer, Joseph 548
Fulkerson, Ezra B. 466
Fulkner, Joseph T. 659
Fuller, Benjamin 780
Fuller, Charles H. 811
Fuller, Frank 510
Fuller, Horace 559
Fuller, Horace B. 288
Fuller, Lycurgus D. 365, 369
Fuller, Sir Knight Frank 179
Fuller, Patrick 612
Fuller, W.H. 234
Fullerton, James 365
Fullerton, William 585
Fulmer, John A. 278
Fulton, Robert 844
Fulton, Samuel 739
Furgeson, Robert R. 288
Furguson, Benjamin F. 394
Furman, George R. 788
Furness, William H. 378
Furnier, Jean 312
Furnung, Ferdinand 771

G

Gaberel, August Henry 213
Gabler, John 757
Gadbury, Frank 761
Gadd, William 204
Gaddy, Collins 700
Gadjie, Joseph H. 605

Gaffney, Luke 782
Gaffy, Patrick 747
Gage, Daniel W. 613
Gage, George 753
Gagnon, Francis 451, 466
Gahagan, David 610
Gahagan, Dennis 459
Gahagan, Peter 414, 705
Gaillard, Luis 312
Gainer, John 414, 718
Gainer, Joseph 875
Gainor, Thomas 653
Gaiser, Louis 434
Galbreath, Joseph 774
Gale, William N. 363
Galea, Lucas 308
Galindo, Francisco 308
Gallagher, Andrew 567
Gallagher, Charles 472
Gallagher, Daniel 103, 581
Gallagher, Dominick 312
Gallagher, James 647
Gallagher, John 93, 278
Gallagher, Joseph 229
Gallagher, Patrick 665
Gallagher, Patrick A. 175, 177-78, 180, 182, 522
Gallagher, Peter 710, 791
Gallahan, John A. 785
Gallaher, Samuel E. 836
Gallandette, James 586
Galligan, Thomas 494
Gallop, Hiram J. 279, 288
Galvin, Alexander 577
Galvin, John 537, 559
Galvin, Maurice 237
Galway, James 463
Gamber, William 626
Gamble, Orlando F. 824
Gamel, William J. 90
Gammans, Andrew S. 665
Gandell, Pierre 312
Gandri, Joseph 451
Ganerd, Patrick 472
Ganey, Daniel 494
Gang, David 600
Ganley, Thomas 696
Gannon, Anthony 621
Gannon, Luke 93
Ganoe, Thomas 528

Ganoe, Thomas S. 577
Ganong, Henry W. 743
Gansey, John 479
Gant, Obediah 271
Garber, Anthony 279
Garcelon, Samuel D. 663
Garcia, Antonio 319
Garcia, Dionicia 318
Garcia, Francisco 316, 319
Garcia, Jesus 308
Garcia, José Dolores 316
Garcia, José J. 316
Garcia, José Maria (1st) 316
Garcia, José Maria (2nd) 316
Garcia, Liberato de J. 316
Garcia, Manual 316, 528
Garcia, Prudencia 307
Garcia, Tomas 319
Garcia, Vicente 315
Gard, George E. 788
Gard, John 479
Gardiner, Antonio D. 577
Gardiner, Charles D. 279
Gardiner, George 219
Gardiner, William 683
Gardner, Capt. 60
Gardner, George 298
Gardner, George W. 466
Gardner, Howard 262
Gardner, James 624, 638, 718
Gardner, Leonard M. 156
Gardner, Patrick 748
Gardner, Samuel 605
Gardner, Stephen E. 219
Gardner, Taylor M. 800
Gardner, William 387
Gardner, William A. 271
Garland, Charles W. 448
Garland, Elbridge A. 144
Garman, John A. 338
Garmestone, George 494
Garner, Joseph 154, 875
Garnica, Yginio 319
Garon, Dennis 451, 479
Garrback, Charles 441, 443
Garrett, Henry 651
Garrett, John 633, 782
Garrett, Robert 126
Garrett, William J. 464
Garrison, Joseph G. 229, 254

Garritt, Mount Etna 833
Garritt, Wm. H.H. 355
Garrity, Edward 846
Garrity, John H. 743
Garrity, Thomas 858
Gartley, Alonzo L. 808
Garvey, Frank 103, 113
Garvey, George H. 298
Garvin, Sylvester O. 806
Gascard, Edmons 414, 718
Gasch, Frederick 756
Gascon, Paul Leon 312
Gaskey, Hazard F. 683
Gaskill, Aaron A. 865
Gaskill, Henry W. 862
Gass, George V. 213
Gass, John B. 294
Gastman, Henry 837
Gaston, John W. 477, 479, 846
Gaston, Theron R. 179, 260
Gateley, Thomas B. 534
Gately, Martin 743
Gately, Thomas B. 522
Gatens, Peter 487
Gates, A.K. 494
Gates, Charles 640
Gates, Charles A. 204
Gates, Messenger E. 767
Gates, Roderick R. 293
Gatewood, Ephraim H. 548, 586
Gattiker, John 351
Gaugh, Peter 833
Gaugham, Patrick 806
Gault, John 613, 654
Gauph, John 221
Gautrot, Charles 459
Gavan, Anthony 586
Gaver, David W. 479
Gay, Charles A. 739
Gay, Henry C. 793
Gay, James 794
Gaylor, Lewis 221
Gaylor, Louis 288
Gaylord, George P. 271, 875
Gaylord, Theodore 768
Gaywood, James 785
Geary, Cornelius 355, 404, 679
Geary, Michael 842
Gee, Lewis 131
Geelan, Edward 501

Geer, Knyphausen 832
Gehagan, David 710
Gehiker, Henry 538
Geinado, Leandro 318
Geit, Frederick 821
Gelcich, Vincent 599
Geleich, Vincent 307
Gellick, Herman 262
Gemmil, John M. 780, 875
Genlack, Frederick 113
Genthner, Gustave E. 91
Genthner, Gustavus 147
Genthner, Gustavus E. 122
George, Chief 181
George, Franklin A. 229
Geran, Anthony 603, 633
Gerard, Emilio 308
Gerber, Henry 443
Gerhart, Joseph 378
Gerke, Maximilian A. 605
Gerke, Maximillian 782
Gerlach, Frederick 355
Gerlach, Theodore 559, 587
Germain, Peter 443
German, George 178, 204, 874
German, Joseph 179, 298, 591
German, Manuel 316
German, Peter H. 373
German, Thomas 204, 578
Gerrity, James 254
Gersbacker, William 811
Gesford, Preston G. 202, 204
Getchell, George 229
Getchell, Johnson T. 819
Getens, Peter 868
Getty, Harry 605
Getty, Harry W. 858
Getty, Samuel 436
Getzendenner, Ezra T. 626
Gevern, John 739
Geyer, John 757
Ghering, William 654
Gheslette, Joseph 479
Ghivadelli, Geambattista 774
Gibbings, William R. 279, 298
Gibbins, John D. 165
Gibbons, Gerrard R. 501
Gibbons, John 369, 733
Gibbons, Thomas 777
Gibbs, Byron D. 855

Gibbs, Charles F. 459, 529
Gibbs, David A. 750
Gibbs, Eugene B. 426, 463
Gibbs, James O. 269
Gibbs, Marshal 179
Gibbs, Thomas H.H. 269
Gibney, John 494
Gibson, Alexander 770
Gibson, Charles 254
Gibson, Charles H. 726
Gibson, George 466
Gibson, Henry 369, 391
Gibson, James W. 288
Gibson, John 538, 810
Gibson, Joseph 753
Gibson, Joshua L. 494
Gibson, Merritt P. 165
Gibson, Pleasant M. 404, 682
Gibson, Samuel 605
Gibson, William G. 209
Gibson, William K. 817
Gibson, William W. 817
Giddings, Orestes 774
Giequel, Charles A. 221
Gierl, John 663
Gifford, William H. 139
Gignac, Augustus A. 740
Gignel, Jean Pierre 312
Gilber, Luis 316
Gilber, Miguel 316
Gilbert, Alonzo 578
Gilbert, Edward P. 640
Gilbert, Erastus 803
Gilbert, Henry W. 378
Gilbert, James D. 113
Gilbert, John M. 559, 578
Gilbert, John W. 819
Gilbert, Robert C. 647
Gilbirth, William 246
Gilbuth, Henry 791
Gilday, Patrick 487, 875
Gildersleeve, John W. 583, 590
Gildersleeve, Robert 638
Gile, Gideon 794
Giles, George W. 718
Giles, Isaac B. 285
Gill, Charles W. 833
Gill, Thomas J. 93
Gill, William 360
Gillespie, Christopher 205, 874

Gillespie, Eugene 126
Gillespie, James 761
Gillett, Henry G. 133
Gillett, Randolph G. 131
Gillette, George M. 294
Gillick, Owen 626
Gilligan, Patrick 621
Gilligan, Peter 811
Gilliland, John M. 785
Gillin, Pvt. 75
Gillin, Owen 360
Gillingham, Edward N. 624
Gillis, James 484
Gillis, John 451, 472
Gillis, Robert 89
Gillman, Charles R. 559
Gillman, Jacob 348
Gillman, John 626
Gillman, Manly B. 126
Gillman, Moses 640
Gillmore, George A. 396
Gillon, Thomas 154
Gillpatrick, George 262
Gilman, Caleb 575, 581, 589-90
Gilman, John 436
Gilman, Joseph A. 732, 752
Gilman, Manly B. 103
Gilmore, Archibald 501
Gilmore, George A. 700
Gilmore, James 753
Gilmore, John H. 746
Gilmore, Rufus H. 103, 120
Gilmore, Silas 633, 640
Gilmour, George A. 875
Gilroy, Charles 800
Gilson, William 246
Gimie, Francois 312
Gingras, Louis 470
Ginn, Thomas 369
Ginner, Joseph 149
Gist, Henry 259
Given, Charles 771
Givens, Jabe D. 89
Gladding, George H. 605
Glaize, Amadie 757
Glancey, Thomas 90, 342
Glandon, John 583
Glann, Peter 120
Glasby, Melton L. 676
Glasby, Milton L. 412, 690, 692

Glasman, Henry 401
Glass, John 559, 587
Glass, Joseph A. 743
Glass, Joseph H. 529
Glass, Norman 348
Glaus, Henry 211
Gleason, Cyrus S. 254
Gleason, Cyrus W. 605
Gleason, John 559
Gleason, Simon 396, 687
Glen, John 757
Glenn, Henry J. 288
Glenn, Michael 501, 587
Glennon, Thomas 154
Glidden, Frank A. 436
Glover, Asa 718
Glover, Jacob O. 451, 477
Glover, Jesse C. 487
Glynn, Frederick W. 823
Glynn, John 298
Goard, Archey B. 229
Goble, John 246
Godart, Henry 548, 572, 578
Godbold, C.H. 179
Godbold, Charles 590
Godding, August 271
Godell, William W. 813
Godfrey, Charles H. 613
Godfrey, Eli A. 736
Godfrey, Frederick 441, 451, 479, 529
Goetz, William 559, 757
Goetze, William 200, 298
Goff, George 110
Goff, Peter 451
Goggin, Edward 123
Goggs, John 139
Gohrman, Henry 768
Going, James H. 757
Golden, Patrick 738
Golding, Daniel 205
Golding, Isaac D. 757
Goldsberry, Nathaniel B. 381, 414
Goldsbury, Nathaniel B. 700
Goldsmith, Adam 811
Goldsmith, Charles 791
Goldsmith, Gustavus S. 279, 288
Goldsmith, Wilson 757
Goldspring, William 139
Goldthait, John W. 578

Golia, Joseph de 686
Golighty, John 229, 443
Golphe, Oscar 311
Gomez, Antonio 316
Gomez, Francisco 318, 875
Gomez, José 309
Gonnison, John H. 463
Gonzales, José 312
Gonzales, José M. 309
Gonzales, Silvestore 309
Gonzalez, Jesus 319
Good, Henry 780
Good, Henry A. 621
Good, James H. 613
Goodaker, Samuel C. 294
Goodale, Frederick W. 654
Goodell, Myron E. 218
Goodell, William W. 179, 263
Goodfellow, John W. 858
Goodman, James 154, 875
Goodman, John F. 839
Goodman, Julius V. 93
Goodman, Marcus H. 688
Goodman, Philip W. 605
Goodman, Theodore H. 197, 200, 250
Goodman, Thomas F. 263, 875
Goodnow, Theodore L. 466
Goodrich, Henry 548, 587
Goodrich, Henry M. 868
Goodrich, John M. 585
Goodrich, Marco B. 626
Goodrich, Thomas 824
Goodrich, William V. 659
Goodwin, Aaron L. 139
Goodwin, Charles 806
Goodwin, Cyrus 205
Goodwin, George 529
Goodwin, George B. 633
Goodwin, George R. 665
Goodwin, James 487
Goodwin, James R. 821
Goodwin, Patrick 748
Gordon, Asa H. 165
Gordon, Ben. 559
Gordon, Charles G. 213
Gordon, Charles W. 651
Gordon, Elijah W. 294
Gordon, James 254, 354
Gordon, James H. 271

Gordon, James W. 459
Gordon, John G. 753
Gordon, John M. 159
Gordon, William H. 205
Gorham, Peter J. 466
Gorham, Samuel A. 77, 136, 151, 152
Gorin, Joseph 201
Gorley, Hugh A. 350
Gorman, James 78, 87, 156
Gorman, John 369, 602, 776
Gorman, John C. 374
Gorrie, Robert 338, 387
Gors, Henry 355, 387
Goshen, Hector J. 369
Goshorn, Thomas H. 343
Gosler, August 451, 479
Gosser, John 633
Gossett, Leon 626
Gothie, William 774
Gott, John W. 501
Goudy, Henry 794
Goudy, Isaac 405, 683
Goudy, Washington 794
Gould, Charles 120
Gould, Daniel 842
Gould, Frank 387
Gould, Frank J. 356
Gould, James 120
Gould, John F. 88, 126
Gould, William 144
Gould, William H. 559
Goulding, Daniel 288
Goulding, George W. 855
Gourley, Eliakim T. 487
Gourley, James 352
Gower, Joshua 688
Goyen, Charles 613
Gozzen, Herman 868
Grace, Frederick 436
Grace, James T. 148
Grace, Oliver P. 782
Grady, John 777
Graeff, Jacob E. 691
Graffell, Charles 267
Grafton, Harker M. 126, 221
Gragg, Edward 811
Gragg, William 837
Graham, Alexander 645
Graham, Ambrose S. 714

Graham, Andrew S. 751
Graham, Arthur 529, 578
Graham, David 229
Graham, James J. 263, 566
Graham, Jerome B. 268
Graham, John 591
Graham, John W. 808
Graham, Joseph 436
Graham, Martin K. 263
Graham, Michael 279
Graham, Richard 844
Graham, Robert 743
Graham, Samuel A. 244
Graham, Thomas W. 788
Graham, Wesley A. 538, 683
Graham, William 529, 538
Graighan, Frederick 743
Gram, David H. 683
Gram, Denis 221
Gramer, Frederick 205
Granger, Elmer 645
Grant 28
Grant, Alfred S. 644
Grant, Charles M. 494
Grant, James 436, 743
Grant, James A. 491
Grant, James W. 777
Grant, John 692, 743
Grant, John F. 479
Grant, Joseph 271
Grant, Lewis T. 524, 570, 813
Grant, Lorenzo 93
Grant, Louis T. 470, 797
Grant, Thos. B. 159
Grant, William 405, 683, 726
Grant, William T. 559
Granville, John B. 757
Granville, Richard 733
Grass, Frederick 443
Graver, John 659
Graves 28
Graves, Alexander F. 692
Graves, Charles H. 480
Graves, Stephen H. 581, 587
Graves, William H. 246
Gravier, Edward 665
Gravins, Peter 791
Gray, Albert G. 205, 288
Gray, Edithel 149
Gray, Francis M. 472

Gray, George 790
Gray, George W. 814
Gray, Harvey P. 819
Gray, James 205, 587, 801
Gray, John 406
Gray, John M. 771
Gray, Joseph H. 285
Gray, Nathaniel A. 548
Gray, Patrick 473
Gray, Peleg C. 862
Gray, Reuben P. 529
Gray, Robert 633
Gray, Stephen 746
Gray, Timothy W. 794
Gray, William 100
Gray, William H. 118
Graybill, Madison 396, 700
Grayson, George H. 842
Grayson, Ralph 137
Greaves, William 433
Greaves, William S. 451
Grebner, August 221
Greely, Edwin 743
Green, Capt. 324
Green, Alfred 728
Green, Caswell C. 289
Green, Charles D. 487
Green, Charles N. 865
Green, Cornelius 578
Green, Deming 254
Green, Deming J. 271
Green, Duane M. 742
Green, Edwin R. 103
Green, Ferdinand 144, 621
Green, Francis C. 226
Green, Frank 837
Green, George 559
Green, George L. 788
Green, Howard 705
Green, James 436, 485, 487
Green, James W. 90, 98
Green, Jerry K. 705
Green, John 529, 757
Green, John A. 801
Green, John W. 714
Green, Joseph 312, 801
Green, Lawrence W. 654
Green, Levi J. 118
Green, Philander W. 93
Green, Thomas 43, 229, 459

Green, William 154, 538
Green, William F. 120
Green, William H. 760
Green, Wright W. 244
Greene, Henry A. 363
Greenleaf, Curtis 477
Greenleaf, James L. 821
Greenlee, Robert A. 768
Greenwood, John 801
Greer, Alexander 791
Greer, Hugh B. 279
Gregg, Chauncey S. 627
Gregg, John 298
Gregg, William D. 451, 591
Gregory, Charles M. 139
Gregory, Gilbert 269
Gregory, James 621
Gregory, Wm. C. 133
Greir, Samuel 862
Grentert, Jacques 221
Grey, Daniel F. 748
Grey, John 688, 718
Grey, Stephen 736
Gribben, Joseph P. 374
Grieve, John 803
Griffey, Ezekiel 791, 794
Griffin, Daniel 179, 298, 875
Griffin, Francis M. 524, 543, 590
Griffin, John 279, 494
Griffin, Joseph H. 768
Griffin, O.H. 28
Griffin, Robert 436
Griffin, Thomas 436, 782
Griffin, William 840
Griffing, Charles C. 858
Griffith, Charles 289
Griffith, David E. 631
Griffith, James 501, 587
Griffith, James W. 162
Griffith, Marshall 743
Griffith, Rockwell A. 621
Griffith, Thomas 499
Griffiths, Charles 205
Griffiths, Daniel 613
Griggs, Joseph 756
Grigsby, Alfred T. 374
Grigsby, John 647
Grigsley, Alfred T. 113
Grijalva, Jesus 718
Grillo, John 538, 548

Grimes, Isaac 365
Grimes, Joseph M. 821
Grimes, Michael 718, 875
Grimm, John 728
Grimshaw, Pvt. 187
Grimshaw, George 227
Grimshaw, Thomas 567, 875
Grimsley, Martin V.B. 627
Grist, George O. 785
Griswold, Charles W. 463
Griswold, John M. 246
Grob, Frederick 463
Groce, John F. 335
Groh, George 714
Gron, Mathias 480
Gropengiesser, Albert 824
Grosse, Julius 473
Grote, Simon C. 369, 414
Grout, Charles M. 247
Grout, William 451, 559, 578
Grove, David 785
Grove, William H. 202
Grover, Byron H. 858
Grover, Edwin H. 142
Grover, Lucien D. 352
Grover, Morgan 807
Grover, Morgan S. 797
Grow, Ambrose 312
Grubb, Caswell W. 627
Gruin, Jacob 647
Gruman, Francis 748
Gudith, John C. 865
Guelleman, Antonio 309
Guerin, Adolphus 309
Guerin, Cleophas 529, 559
Guerin, Frederick L. 640
Guerra, Antonio M. de la 305
Guerra, Antonio Maria de la 315
Guerra, Juan J. de la 315
Guerra, Santiago de la 305, 315
Guerre, Francisco 310
Guertler, Robert 743
Guess, James W. 740
Guilderoy, John 360, 365
Guillaume, Philip 640, 654
Guilman, Antonio 305
Guirado, Francisco 317
Guirado, Juan Francis 98
Guiraido, Francisco F. 305
Guirard, Charles 659

Guivey, William 645
Gullegher, Charles 605
Gulliver, George W. 801
Gum, Henry 298
Gumm, Eli L. 133, 700
Gundlach, Henry 487, 492
Gunn, Chester 238
Gunnison, Harvey 733
Gunsenhouser, August 113
Gunther, John J. 451, 477
Gunzenhauser, August 714
Gurkey, John 254
Gustamante, José 319
Gustavus, Alexander 837
Gustin, Amos 633
Gutaran, Pierre 451
Guthrie, Flavel 728
Gutierres, Sebastian 309
Gutierrez, Catarino 319
Gutierrez, Catarino E. 315
Gutierrez, Diego 316
Guy, John 748
Guyot, Alphonse 451
Guzman, Andres 801
Gwinn, James K. 93
Gwyther, George 378

H

Haack, Albert 463
Haas, Jacob 742
Haas, James C. 785
Haber, Jacob 221
Haberfeldt, George 279, 298
Haberkorn, Charles 120
Habick, Henry 559
Hacke, Henry 201
Hacker, John M. 736
Hacker, Jonathan 833
Hacket, Patrick J. 868
Hackett, Charles W. 785
Hackett, Hannibal B. 732
Hackett, Jacob P. 725, 731, 749
Hackett, James 378, 691
Hackett, Thomas 126
Hackleman, John 298
Hackney, John 219
Haddlesten, Daniel 659
Haden, Porter 58, 69-70, 109, 142
Hadley, George W. 378, 391, 401

Hadley, John 633
Hagan, John 145, 538
Hagan, Michael B. 774
Hagarty, William 452
Hagedon, Eber A. 808
Hagen, George 811
Hager 36
Hagerton, Thomas 221
Haggart, Gilbert 338
Haggerty, Patrick 555, 571, 810
Haggett, Charles G. 679
Hahn, Albert 432, 443, 477, 755
Hahn, Charles F.R. 524
Hahn, George 238
Haigh, George B. 753
Haight, John E. 640
Haikmain, Charles 263
Hailer, Henry 647
Hailman, Martin 587, 876
Haine, Arthur 484
Haines, Henry 728
Haines, John 538, 559
Haines, John W. 782
Hairbush, William 205
Hakes, James 93
Hale, Charles S. 378
Hale, David H. 260
Hale, Edward 835
Hale, Edward O. 213, 356
Hale, Enoch K. 229
Hale, Frank 480
Hale, Henry P. 613
Hale, James A. 441, 637
Hale, John W. 406, 679
Hale, Simon 742
Halegan, Anthony 740
Haley, Cornelius J. 803
Haley, Daniel 495, 751
Haley, David 665
Haley, James 822
Haley, John 753
Haley, Thomas 263, 538
Halfman, Thomas 413, 705
Hall, Alesci Ira 591
Hall, Alexander 399
Hall, Americus 396, 696
Hall, Augustus H. 662
Hall, Calvin 221
Hall, Charles E. 740
Hall, Daniel C. 602

Hall, Edmund 203
Hall, Enos A. 759
Hall, Fred G. 271
Hall, Frederick 855
Hall, George 692
Hall, George W. 659
Hall, Henry 495, 559, 572, 578
Hall, Henry J. 271
Hall, Hiram S. 213
Hall, James 72, 103, 113, 221, 743, 875
Hall, James A. 728
Hall, John 103, 271
Hall, Joseph H. P. 613
Hall, Julius C. 378
Hall, Lemon G. 495
Hall, Osmer 374
Hall, Peter 761
Hall, Robt. H. 123
Hall, Samuel 238
Hall, Thomas 142
Hall, Thomas W. 875
Hall, William 184
Hall, William E. 696
Hall, William Ex. 394
Halleck, Henry W. 517
Halleck, J. Y. 28
Haller, Frederick 145
Haller, John 365
Halleran, James 436
Hallers, Sebastian 374
Hallett, James 229
Halley, William 343, 352
Halligan, John T. 862
Halliman, James S. 875
Hallman, John A. 409, 713
Halloran, James 487, 495
Hallowell, C. 178
Hallowell, Charles L. 875
Hallsa, Paul 605
Hallsted, Jacob W. 868
Halman, James S. 229
Halpin, Henry 814
Halpin, John 374
Halsey, David C. 495
Halsey, Wm. H. 865
Halstead, Frank 788
Ham, George F. 814
Ham, George P. 258
Ham, James A. 279, 289

Ham, John B. 801
Ham, Joseph 840
Ham, William H. 263
Hamann, August 343, 352, 391
Hamann, Peter T. 844
Hamar, John P. 627
Hambright, James 149
Hamel, James H. 814
Hames, Benjamin 801
Hamil, Patrick M. 133
Hamilton, Andrew 495
Hamilton, Charles 567, 591, 753
Hamilton, Charles H. 451
Hamilton, David 740
Hamilton, Franklin 90
Hamilton, George 638, 717
Hamilton, George H. 205
Hamilton, James 578
Hamilton, Jasper A. 858
Hamilton, John 495
Hamilton, John P. 585
Hamilton, Merritt 348
Hamilton, Robert 124
Hamilton, Thomas 93
Hamilton, Ziba C. 157
Hamlin, Adrian R. 93, 157
Hamlin, Mortimer J. 451
Hamlin, Orrin E. 338
Hamm, Albert L. 805
Hamm, Charles T. 787
Hammer, Edward D. 149, 654
Hammer, Frederick A. 279
Hammer, Marcus 665
Hammer, Marcus C. 213
Hammer, Melancthon O. 247
Hammerburg, William 855
Hammon, William 613
Hammond, Ansel 700
Hammond, Charles 567
Hammond, Charles H. 263
Hammond, James B. 817
Hammond, John W. 681
Hammond, Lafayette 67, 335, 367
Hammond, Nathaniel L. 238
Hammond, Ulysses H. 159
Hammond, William 202, 591, 627
Hammond, William H. 372, 788, 876
Hampton, William 716
Hanayott, Frederick 136

Hanback, William H. 761
Hance, Foster 374
Hance, John T. 672, 709
Hancock, Francis O. 525, 572
Hancock, George S. 338, 875
Hancock, Henry 599
Hancock, William A. 794
Hand, B.C. 28
Hand, Charles B. 221
Hand, George O. 363
Handley, John 806
Handlin, Thomas 501
Handy, Albert F. 761
Handy, John C. 197
Handy, William W. 365, 875
Hanes, Charles A. 103
Haney, Charles W. 529, 548
Haney, John R. 378
Haney, Thomas 548, 578
Hanford, William T. 725, 735, 746, 755
Hanger, James 613
Hankerman, Albion A. 289
Hanks, Calvin W. 247
Hanks, Cornelius 808
Hanks, Francis 413, 705
Hanks, Julius D. 356, 387
Hanley, Michael W. 271
Hanlin, Cornelius 205
Hanlon, Bernard 538, 559
Hanlon, John 451
Hanlon, Mathew 451
Hanly, Thomas 743
Hanna, Aquila W. 832
Hanna, Hamilton 451, 559, 567
Hanna, James 753
Hanna, John, Jr. 431, 456, 484
Hanna, William P. 832
Hannah, William 473
Hannah, William C. 578
Hannan, John 436, 529, 754
Hannon, James 728
Hannon, Patrick 683
Hannum, John B. 627
Hanscon, Samuel 855
Hansen, Charles 757
Hansen, Hans C. 605
Hansen, Nelson 154
Hansen, William 740
Hanson, Andrew 103

Hanson, Charles W. 259
Hanson, Henry 529
Hanson, Lusander E. 346
Hanson, Neels 809
Hanson, Ole C. 279, 295
Hanson, Paul 205
Hanson, Peter 583, 862
Hanson, Theodore 633
Hanson, William M. 865
Hants, Philip 145
Hanz, Joseph 757
Hapgood, George E. 235
Happ, Conrad 451
Happ, John J. 640
Happ, Simon J. 640
Harbaugh, William 148
Harbeck, Henry R. 868
Harden, Addison P. 137
Harden, Albert 785, 876
Harden, Asa 605
Harden, Henry 495
Hardenberg, James R. 234
Hardenburg, Charles A. 374
Harder, Frank 356
Hardesty, Samuel V. 263
Hardie, Oswald 412, 703
Hardin, George W. 459
Hardin, Robert 459
Hardin, Robert D. 460
Harding, Gov. 510-13
Harding, James 862
Harding, Julius C. 774
Hardman, William H. 865
Hardt, Henry 443
Hardwick, William 149
Hardy, Benjamin W. 794
Hardy, Louis W. 665
Hardy, Samuel 378
Hare, Daniel 538, 743
Hare, James K. 817
Hargedan, Michael 811
Hargedan, Thomas 811
Hargrave, Abram 394, 699
Hargrave, Joseph P. 346, 359
Hargrave, Robert 178, 277
Haring, Henry C. 346
Harkin, Charles 862
Harkness, Allan M. 785
Harkness, Edson 785
Harkness, Thomas 559, 578

Harlan, John W. 640
Harland, John 785
Harlow, Hial 501
Harman, Alva 780
Harmon, John 640, 791
Harmonn, Louis 640
Harms, Henry 785
Harms, Peters H.W. 748
Harn, Anthony 633
Harnett, John J. 728
Harney, Peter 485
Harp, John C. 205
Harper, Charles L. 487
Harper, Conrad H. 443, 466, 875
Harper, Elliott 279
Harper, Horace 487
Harper, Jerome W. 777
Harper, Jesse 659
Harrighansen, Christian 743
Harring, John V. 665
Harrington, Andrew J. 352
Harrington, Cornelius 213
Harrington, Frederick 432, 448
Harrington, Frederick J. 780
Harrington, George 865
Harrington, George L. 126
Harrington, Gregory 250
Harrington, John 466, 875
Harrington, Levi H. 737
Harrington, Michael 279
Harrington, Morey 460
Harrington, Thomas 221
Harrington, William 740
Harrington, William H. 343, 391
Harriot, Christian 234
Harriott, Christian 197, 234, 298
Harris, Albion 436
Harris, Arthur H. 736
Harris, Barney 279
Harris, Benjamin 258, 263
Harris, Charles 809
Harris, Charles W. 473
Harris, Daniel C. 205
Harris, David 163
Harris, Edgar V. 378
Harris, Edward 771
Harris, George 501
Harris, George M. 238, 263
Harris, George W. 491, 647
Harris, Henry P. 794

Harris, James 718
Harris, Jesse 124
Harris, John 202
Harris, John W. 495
Harris, Lorenzo B. 501
Harris, Otis S. 401, 692
Harris, Richard B. 843
Harris, Richard H. 199, 263, 269, 279
Harris, Samuel 222, 696
Harris, Smith 286
Harris, Stephen M. 837
Harris, Thomas 739
Harris, Thomas A. 197
Harris, Thomas S. 173, 197, 200, 247
Harris, William 700
Harris, William C. 640
Harrison, Arthur S. C. 466
Harrison, Benjamin 359
Harrison, James 748
Harrison, John 148, 728
Harrison, Milton 137
Harrison, Richard 348
Harrison, Watson R. 709
Harrlick, Absalom 275
Harrover, Benjamin T. 670, 694, 703
Harsha, Samuel 768
Harshaw, David T. 376
Harshberger, Henry M. 359
Harslett, Michael 587
Hart, Christopher 578
Hart, Edward C. 737
Hart, Edward R. 451, 487
Hart, Hugh 529, 578
Hart, James 754
Hart, James S. 378
Hart, Jesse C. 578
Hart, John 103, 113, 487
Hart, John L. 640
Hart, Martin 263
Hart, Mortimer H. 811
Hart, Oliver 159
Hart, Robert 235
Hart, Robert B. 338
Hart, Thomas 238
Hart, Wm. A. 235
Hart, William R. 396, 688
Harthan, Lucius 113

Hartley, Francis 356
Hartman, Benjamin F. 279
Hartman, Charles 559
Hartman, John J. 585
Hartman, Prince Albert 279
Hartnett, William H. 289
Hartney, Michael 683
Harts, Thomas 436
Hartshorn, William 159, 613
Hartso, Augustus 631
Harvey, Benjamin F. 89
Harvey, George 811
Harvey, Henry G. 794
Harvey, John 120, 263, 436
Harvey, Robert 113
Harvey, Thomas 495
Harvey, William 103, 113
Harwood, Franklin 67
Harwood, Thomas 733
Hase, Nelson B. 627
Hashe, Herman 780
Haskel Daniel B. 346
Haskell, Alonzo C. 601, 609
Haskell, Daniel B. 367, 390, 876
Haskell, Henry 737
Haskell, Randolph K. 100
Haskell, Seth H. 254
Haskell, Washington L. 609
Haskin, David H. 211
Haskins, George 289
Haskins, Henry C. 213, 279
Haskins, Henry E. 559
Haskins, Joseph E. 406, 710
Hassard, Thomas R. 740
Hassig, Frederick 396, 696
Hassler, Henry 480
Hassold, John C. 460
Hasson, Arthur J. 213
Hastin, William 100
Hastings, Frank 605
Hastings, Henry W. 352
Hastings, John 343, 392
Hastings, Lemuel G. 149
Hastings, William 714
Hastings, Wm. D. 234
Hastler, Jacob 548, 559
Hastler, William 538, 548, 591
Hatch, George E. 279
Hatch, Isaac 800
Hatch, Oliver S. 625

Hatch, Richard A. 865
Hatch, Stephen 352
Hatch, William O. 760
Hathaway, Henry I. 147, 157
Hathaway, William 839
Hatheway, Daniel L. 259
Hatheway, Dan. S. 113
Hatton, Samuel P. 254, 534
Hauck, Martin 600
Haullere, Sebastian 768
Haulser, Charles A. 113
Haun, John J. 862
Haupt, Charles 443
Hauskins, George Z. 154
Haven, Franklin 196, 723
Haw, Francis M. 833
Hawes, Albert B. 289
Hawes, Charles A. 88, 113
Hawes, Thaddeus 394, 686
Hawkins, Andrew 238
Hawkins, Clayton T. 229
Hawkins, George W. 460
Hawkins, James 529
Hawkins, James H. 747
Hawkins, James M. 865
Hawkins, Jeremiah 374
Hawkins, John 814
Hawkins, Patrick 356
Hawley, Ashley D. 443
Hawley, David O. 344, 392
Hawley, Everton W. 640
Hawley, Rollin C. 529, 578
Hawley, Samuel 683
Hawn, John B. 605, 633
Hawn, Richard 640, 750
Haws, Alfred 659
Haws, Alfred H. 289
Haws, Sylvanus S. 659
Hay, David C. 806
Hay, George 621
Hay, Thomas F. 788
Hay, Valentine 728
Haybeck, George 473
Haycock, George 644
Hayden, Charles 587, 875
Hayden, Martin 263
Hayden, Peter 263
Hayden, Robert D. 700
Hayes, Andrew 99
Hayes, Andrew A. 771, 876

Hayes, Andrew J. 123
Hayes, Edward E. 555, 566
Hayes, George 754
Hayes, George W. 802
Hayes, Henry A. 683
Hayes, John 613
Hayes, John W. 433
Hayes, Lewis W. 676
Hayes, William E. 605
Hayes, William W. 725
Hayford, James B. 868
Haynes 28
Haynes, John 495
Haynes, Sallush 473
Haynigan, John 451, 480
Hays, Col. 19
Hays, Charles 737
Hays, Francis 289
Hays, Henry S. 346
Hays, Horace H. 238
Hays, John 785
Hays, Joseph 374
Hays, Robert 93
Hayse, Robert H. 139
Hayt, Edward H. 618, 783
Hayt, Louis M. 495
Haywood, George 145
Haywood, J. 179
Haywood, John 591
Hazelett, William 817
Hazelton, John H. 771
Hazen, Eli W. 356
Hazen, George W. 254
Head, David M. 247
Heafron, John 238
Heald, William H. 794
Healey, Daniel 633, 875
Healey, John 876
Healy, George P. 126
Healy, James 473
Healy, John 761, 768
Healy, Thomas 743
Healy, William 692
Heaney, Hiram 495
Hearn, Patrick 737
Hearn, William 559, 803
Hearon, Michael 451, 457, 480
Hearrin, John 295
Heath, Alonzo or Alfonso 159
Heath, Charles W. 179, 559, 592

Heath, David N. 751
Heath, Ebenezer G. 696
Heath, Higer H. 659
Heath, John 336
Heath, Leon D. 768
Heath, Sullivan 76, 151, 152, 162, 243
Heaton, John 740
Heator, Humphrey B. 247
Heber, John 238, 263
Hebert, P.O. 15
Heck, John H. 205
Heck, Mathias 153
Heck, Victor 755
Heckel, John J. 342
Heckman, John F. 828, 840
Hecox, James M. 289, 875
Hedeman, Charles 218
Hedges, Frederick T. 458
Hedman, William 742
Hedrick, Daniel W. 162, 876
Heenan, John 460
Heer, Christian 788
Heffernan, Arthur P. 499
Heffernan, Charles 420, 498
Heffernan, Francis R. 499
Heffner 178
Heffrin, Patrick 470
Hefton, John 443, 451, 640
Heguerra, Francisco 307
Heidlinger, John 199
Hein, George 665
Heineman, Henry 822
Heinings, Joseph B. 780
Heinrich, Lawrence 803
Heins, Christopher 742
Heintmiller, Henry 757
Heintz, Charles 705
Heisley, John W. 238
Heitler, Lawrence 449
Heitman, Charles H. 858
Heitz, Arthur 524, 538, 548, 567
Hekas, Thomas 837
Helder, Herman 230
Helford, Smith 659
Heller, Paul 743
Hellstern, Clemens 448, 742, 755
Helon, William 236
Helstern, Clemens 432
Heltman, Frederick 448

Hely, George V. 529
Hemming, John 247
Hempfield, Isaac W. 829, 835
Hemphill, Ion 238
Hemphill, Joseph 761
Hempter, Eusebius 214
Henderson, Chas. H. 157
Henderson, David 559, 714, 875
Henderson, George H. 149, 473
Henderson, Henry 538
Henderson, Hiram G. 538, 559
Henderson, James 480, 654
Henderson, James W. 548, 567
Henderson, Nat. W. 768
Henderson, Orrington L. 818
Henderson, Peter 374
Henderson, Theodore L. 748
Henderson, William 460, 846
Henderson, William J. 728
Hendley, Shattuck 28
Hendren, John R. 840
Hendricks, William C. 367
Hendrickson, Charles E. 289
Hendry, James 605
Heninger, Thomas J. 765, 784
Henkil, Gabriel 701
Henkin, John 495, 875
Henkle, Gabriel B. 396
Henley, John P. 587
Henley, William 392
Henman, Frederick 238
Henn, Anton 559, 572
Henn, John B. 356
Hann, Wendle 806
Henrahan, Michael 436
Henrich, John W. 222
Henrichs, Christian 374
Henrici, Francis R. 443
Henry, Charles 633
Henry, John 578, 640, 737, 780
Henry, John M. 447
Henry, Peter 268, 876
Henry, Patrick 286
Henry, Thomas 487, 875
Henry, William 163, 213, 238, 263, 647, 676, 710
Henshaw, William 824
Hensley, John 178, 548, 559, 592
Hensley, Richard M. 352
Hentz, William 621
Hepburn, James W. 858

Herbert, P.O. 15
Herford, Augustus D. 185, 876
Herford, Augustus S. 271
Hergate, F. Baptiste 819
Herges, William 728
Herkleman, Chas. 480
Herlow, Palle F. 433
Herlowe, Palle F. 218
Herman, Carl 750
Herman, George 113
Herman, Louis 548
Herman, Louis L. 344
Hermance, Peter 640, 811
Hermann, Louis 352
Hermann, Louis F. 392
Hern, Madison 133
Herold, John 819
Heron, Cornelius J. 451
Herrick, Isaiah B. 837
Herrick, Rufus F. 829, 841
Herring, Henry 751
Herring, Marcus F. 413, 703
Herring, Simeon H. 120
Herring, Thomas 640
Herring, Wm. M. 833
Herron, Andrew M. 403, 709
Herron, Cornelius J. 179, 592
Herron, John 567, 587
Hersey, Albert 436
Hersey, Charles N. 219
Hershberger, John 254
Hershman, Jacob 103
Hertle, John G. 279
Hertle, J.J. 179
Hertz, Peter 222
Herve, Emile 538
Hervey, James 487
Hervey, William S. 566, 875
Heslop, Alfred 103
Hess, Louis 222
Hess, Solomon H. 230
Hess, William 559
Hessen, Arthur 495
Hester, Charles 271
Hetherington, Hugh 437
Hette, Henry 444
Heuft, Jesse M. 451
Heulit, George 436
Heulle, Charles 444

Heuser, Mathias 247
Hewett, A. P. 179
Hewett, Henry 133
Hewitt, Alfred P. 295
Hewitt, Andrew G. 771
Hewitt, James C. 621
Hewston 28
Heyburn, James W. 201
Heydemann, Henry G. 444, 451
Heydinger, Michael 814
Hibbard, Hiram 466
Hibbert, Rufus 247
Hibbetts, John 126
Hickey, John 696
Hickey, Michael 499
Hickey, William 230
Hickman, Sylvester 222
Hickok, William 803
Hicks, Alvah O. 406, 683
Hicks, Charles W. 222
Hicks, Henry 222
Hicks, Hewlet 583
Hicks, Jacob 779
Hicks, Lucius C. 269
Hicks, William P. 559, 592
Hieman, Charles 862
Hierra, Ramon 319
Higby, Lewis 529
Higdon, William H. 403, 677
Higgins 324
Higgins, Benjamin S. 602
Higgins, Elias T. 605
Higgins, Francis H. 406, 683
Higgins, Henry B. 279
Higgins, James 748
Higgins, John 213, 222, 714, 814
Higgins, John C. 448, 466
Higgins, Nelson 548, 560
Higgins, Patrick 344, 390
Higgins, Richard 791, 794
Higgins, Robert 378
Higgins, Theodore M. 369
Higgins, Thomas 213
Higgins, Thomas P. 610
Higgins, William 159, 578
Higgins, William F. 289
High, Charles B. 783
High, Deston 783
High, William 617, 621
Highket, George 271, 875

Hight, John 460
Hightower, Benjamin F. 535, 544
Hightower, William 365
Higson, Alexander 460
Higuera, Francisco 876
Higuera, José J. 309
Hildebrand, Conrad 783
Hildebrand, George W. 451
Hildebrand, Jacob 688
Hildebrandt, George 444, 460
Hilderbrant, Conrad 647
Hildreth, William A. 118
Hill, Allen T. 728
Hill, Alonzo H. 640
Hill, Charles J. 259, 263
Hill, Charles W. 855
Hill, Christopher 396, 696
Hill, Daniel F. 750
Hill, David L. 788
Hill, Edgar S. 647
Hill, Edward 501
Hill, Edwin M. 238, 263
Hill, Eleazer G. 370
Hill, Emerson F. 538
Hill, Francis 279
Hill, Frank 809
Hill, Granville 844
Hill, Harry 754
Hill, Herbert G. 809
Hill, James 862
Hill, James M. 777
Hill, John 645, 761
Hill, John A. 152, 855
Hill, John E. 433, 476
Hill, John J. 683
Hill, John T. 738
Hill, John W. 868
Hill, Joseph 179, 279
Hill, Reuben A. 373
Hill, Richard S. 726
Hill, Robert 263
Hill, Tavitimo 312
Hill, Thomas 451, 567, 571, 578
Hill, Thomas W. 360
Hill, William J. 773
Hillberry, Aaron 833
Hiller, Frederick 356
Hilliard, William H. I. 855
Hilliker, Gillman 437
Hills, Franklin M. 757

Hillyer, Edgar W. 599, 601, 630
Hillyer, James 480
Hilpert, George 757
Hiltis, William C. 835
Hilton, Francis M. 279
Himmermann, Henry 640
Himnan, Jason N. 560
Hinchliff, Zaccheus 822
Hinckley, Edwin C. 222
Hinckley, John P. 495
Hinckley, Samuel 814
Hinckley, William H. 751
Hinds, Hugh L. 674, 703
Hineman, Heinrich 714
Hines, Daniel L. 791
Hines, Gustavus A. 415, 705
Hines, James 701
Hines, Wesley 814
Hines, William 437, 780
Hinkle, George A. 633
Hinkle, William W. 757
Hinkley, Ezra T. 480
Hinkley, John 679, 875
Hinkley, Luther E. 578
Hinman, Alfred C. 238
Hinman, Ashbell G. 805
Hinman, Jason N. 199, 279, 298
Hinman, John S. 819
Hinman, Robert 279, 876
Hinsdale, William P. 267
Hinterlong, Augustus 630
Hipps, David C. 605
Hipsehley, Joseph 444, 452
Hirbschman, Charles 621
Hirth, Frank 613
Hison, Henry 271
Hitchcock, Aaron C. 162
Hitchcock, C. E. 28
Hitchcock, Irving W. 165
Hitchings, Peter 573
Hite, William 718
Hiteshen, John T. 338
Hitman, Moses 732
Hixenbaugh, William F. 692, 875
Hjelm, John 538, 567
Hoadley, Lawrence S. 247
Hoag, Hiram G. 448, 452
Hoag, Philander M. 280
Hoag, Stephen A. 788
Hoagg, Augustus 338, 387

Hoagland, Daniel 339
Hoalton, Michael 473
Hoars, John S. 137
Hoban, Anthony 824
Hoban, Thomas 529, 578, 709
Hobbs, Alfred 247
Hobbs, Walter 139
Hockhausen, John P. 501
Hodgdon, Simon 817
Hodge, William M. 165
Hodges, Frank 356
Hoel, Samuel 139
Hoell, John G. 842
Hoey, George 103
Hoey, Michael 466
Hofedank, William 335, 367
Hoffer, John G. 243
Hoffler, John 149
Hoffman, Col. 21, 42
Hoffman, Charles, alias Charles
  Hirbschman 621
Hoffman, Charles H. 238
Hoffman, Daniel I. 499
Hoffman, David B. 599
Hoffman, Frank 587
Hoffman, Frederick 238
Hoffman, George 842
Hoffman, George W. 728
Hoffman, Gilbert W. 621, 781
Hoffman, Henry 523, 538, 605,
  633
Hoffman, Henry A. 495
Hoffman, Jacob 529
Hoffman, John 560
Hoffmann, Jacob 441
Hoffner, Anton 344
Hoffner, Frederick 613
Hoffner, Samuel 613
Hofsummer, John 757
Hogan, Edward 640
Hogan, John 126, 263, 641
Hogan, John W. 748
Hogan, Peter 401, 688
Hogan, Thomas 538, 757, 803
Hogarth, Emile 654
Hoglang, Saxie 840
Hogue, Geo. W. 243
Hohenstein, William 487
Hohn, John H. 344, 810
Hoil, John 230

Hoin, Peter P. 356
Hoke, Benjamin 148
Hoke, James H. 280
Holbrook, C. E. 197
Holbrook, Charles B. 819
Holbrook, Thomas J. 263, 295
Holcomb, Geo. B. 492
Holcomb, Henry 374
Holcomb, Randolph S. 230
Holcombe, Henry 113
Holden, James 633, 665
Holder, William 460
Holdridge, Jeremiah 211
Holland, Daniel 538, 560
Holland, Henry 814, 858
Holland, Jacob 205
Holland, John 259, 284
Holland, John B. 352, 392
Holland, William B. 247
Hollenbeck, Peter 143
Holliday, Ephraim J. 529
Hollingshead, Wesley 356
Hollis, Benjamin F. 794
Hollister, Dudley L. 656
Hollister, William N. 659
Hollman, John 488
Holloway, George W. 633
Holloway, Leonidas H. 638
Hollowell, Charles L. 263
Hollowell, Henry B. 776
Holman, Wilson 113, 361
Holmes, Alexander 791, 794
Holmes, Amasa A. 733
Holmes, Bartlett R. 822
Holmes, Edward 688, 875
Holmes, George 733
Holmes, James 210
Holmes, James H. 114
Holmes, John J. 613, 621
Holmes, Joseph 437
Holmes, Ralph 761
Holmes, Stephen 803
Holmes, Thomas 647, 875
Holmes, William 560
Holmes, William B. 714
Holski, Edward 538
Holt, Daniel H. 752
Holt, David H. 813
Holt, George I. 855
Holt, John 744

Holt, Levi B. 749
Holthousen, Peter 114
Holton, Charles H. 263
Holygrafer, Pvt. 75
Holzgrafen, Henry C. 139
Homer, George R. 538
Homer, Horatio G. 258
Homer, James 495, 749, 752
Homer, James L. 699
Honey, James P. 776
Honey, William R. 197, 726, 752
Honeyman, Francis 534, 575, 585
Honn, Emanuel D. 271
Honorio, Dubois 312
Honsinger, John 441
Hood, Aaron T. 294
Hood, Edward P. 473
Hood, John 858
Hood, Menzo W. 230
Hood, Smith F. 816
Hood, William H. 178, 298
Hook, George 473
Hook, George A. 460
Hooker, Gen. 849
Hooker, Ambrose E. 196, 725
Hooker, Benjamin 437
Hooker, Henry B. 460, 613, 647
Hooley, John 627
Hooper, Thomas 114
Hooper, William 621, 714
Hooper, William B. 242
Hooton, Goodloe 401, 410, 714
Hoover, Charles, alias Lewis, Charles 621
Hoover, David 254
Hoover, Dewey 259
Hoover, Isaiah C. 573
Hoover, James 93
Hoover, William H. 663
Hope, Augustus 159
Hope, John 641, 876
Hopkins, Benjamin M. 460
Hopkins, Hopkin 605, 634
Hopkins, Samuel 641
Hopkins, William 205, 289
Hopkins, William H. 710, 777
Hopper, John O. 538, 548, 587
Hopper, Joseph W. 392
Hoppock, James L. 613, 634
Hoppy, Hugh 205

Horan, John 473
Horay, William 692
Horlacher, Frederick 814
Horn, George H. 197, 335, 431
Horn, Joseph 432, 441, 448
Horn, William 470
Horne, Franklin N. 771
Horner, Christopher 111
Horner, Samuel 846
Horobin, George 103
Horrlin, Michael 205
Horsfeldt, Gustavus 247
Horsley, J. 75
Horsley, Joseph 154
Horton, Alonzo 587
Horton, George F. 538
Horton, George W. 298
Horton, Samuel 263
Horton, William 488, 757
Hosea, Daniel 627
Hoskins, Henry C. 199
Hoskins, John D. 844, 875
Hosley, Franklin 728
Hosmer, Frank 114, 370
Hosmer, Josiah 565, 568
Hossock, David 794
Hostetter, William S. 230, 875
Hotanick, Joseph 312
Hotchkiss, Stiles 747
Hoten, George W. 178, 875
Houche, James P. 378
Houck, Ernest 744
Hough, Thomas 529
Houghton, Lafayette E. 785
House, Lucien M. 609
Houseley, John 501
Houser, Conrad W. 809
Houston, Albert A. 587
Houston, Charles W. 785
Houston, George 587
Houston, John 757
Houston, John K. 390, 412, 686, 709
Houston, Michael 148
Houston, William I. 213
Hout, Francis 659, 809
Hovey, George D. 437, 466
Hovey, Henry 800
Hovey, John H. 641
Hovey, William P. 822

Howard, Amos H. 865
Howard, Asa F. 178, 296, 875
Howard, Charles 525, 728, 788
Howard, Daniel A. 448, 477
Howard, Francis 728
Howard, Francis E. 488, 495
Howard, Frank 114, 718, 727
Howard, George 679, 875
Howard, George E. 865
Howard, George H. 751, 875-76
Howard, George W. 252
Howard, Henry A. 794
Howard, James 811
Howard, John 370, 627, 744, 803
Howard, John A. 788
Howard, Lewis P. 783
Howard, Patrick 495
Howard, Robert 578
Howard, Samuel A. 211
Howard, Samuel P. 768
Howard, Spencer 219, 875
Howard, William 247
Howard, William A. 289
Howard, William H. 254
Howard, William W. 120
Howe, Col. 63, 64, 65
Howe, Charles B. 179, 275
Howe, George 573
Howe, James 713
Howe, John W. 865
Howe, John W. M. 230
Howe, Wesley C. 868
Howe, William 641
Howell, Ab. 817
Howell, Charles 104
Howell, George 751
Howell, Samuel 627
Howell, Thomas 560, 592
Howell, William 222, 621
Hower, George 679
Howes, Geo. 28
Howey, John B. 737
Howland, Capt. 61, 63
Howland, Joseph A. 298
Howles, Samuel 263
Howlett, Charles E. 154, 165
Howley, John P. 560
Howson, William O. 165
Hoxey, Chester 139
Hoxsie, Benjamin F. 865

Hoxzy, Chester 238
Hoye, Robert 728
Hoyle, Washington 149
Hoyt, E. C. 178
Hoyt, Ebenezer C. 592
Hoyt, Ephraim 336
Hoyt, Ephraim N. 350
Hoyt, John B. 100, 114
Hoyt, Moses 641
Hoyt, Samuel N. 175, 176
Hoyt, Samuel W. 589
Hoyt, Thomas S. 773
Hubbard, Albert 91
Hubbard, Ansil 605, 875-76
Hubbard, Charles G. 499, 797, 816
Hubbard, Charles M. 209
Hubbard, Eli 352
Hubbard, Eli B. 605, 641
Hubbard, Julian A. 696
Hubbard, Samuel S. 621
Hubbard, Timothy 374
Hubbard, William F. 247
Huber, Clinton 466, 768
Huber, John 733
Hubinger, John A. 235
Hucker, Charles 444, 501
Hudleston, Thomas 280
Hudson, Charles 865
Hudson, Frank 269, 876
Hudson, John 701
Hudson, Leonard 529
Hudson, Richard 385, 399, 403, 703, 712
Hudson, Samuel 783
Hues, David 710
Huff, Andrew J. 817
Huff, George W. 809
Huff, William S. 783
Huffner, Antone 452
Hufnagle, Peter 444
Huftale, Peter H. 824
Hug, Lewis 791
Huggins, Ephraim F. 785
Huggins, George 238
Hughes, Alfred J. 705
Hughes, Arza B. 485
Hughes, Charles H. 833
Hughes, David 165
Hughes, Edward 814
Hughes, Edwin C. 548, 560

Hughes, Frederick G. 361, 392
Hughes, Henry L. 415, 705
Hughes, Henry R. 846
Hughes, Hugh 761
Hughes, James 757
Hughes, James E. 447
Hughes, John 230, 289, 748, 845-46, 868
Hughes, John S. 835
Hughes, John W. 837
Hughes, Leander W. 178, 294
Hughes, Levi D. 178, 299
Hughes, Peter 740
Hughes, Stephen 230, 480, 501
Hughes, Stuart 592
Hughes, Thomas 165
Hughes, William 841
Hughes, Willis 740
Hughie, Michael 705
Hughs, William M. 348
Huil, Eugene 312
Hull, Chauncey 865
Hull, Daniel 370
Hull, Edwin M. 158
Hull, Gustavus A. 786
Hull, John A. 499
Hull, Josiah S. 406, 709
Hull, Robert K. 127
Hull, Thomas W. 352
Hull, William E. 422, 425-26, 456
Hull, Zachariah T. 149
Hulme, Richard 641
Hulsinger, Ellis 299
Humbert, P. 178
Humbert, Philip 295
Humble, Christian 534, 802
Hume, Alfred 568
Hume, Charles 378
Hummelkee, Charles 154
Humphrey, Benjamin F. 824
Humphrey, Henry 692
Humphrey, Thomas J. 344, 352
Humphrey, William 842
Humphrey, William H. 93
Humphrys, Thomas 392
Hundermark, John F. 361
Hungerford, Alfred 809
Hunnadey, Charles 444
Hunsaker, Benjamin F. 218
Hunsinger, William 714

Hunssinger, William J. 396
Hunsucker, John 627
Hunt, Charles H. 732
Hunt, Francis A. 835
Hunt, George 733
Hunt, James 252, 299
Hunt, James A. 855
Hunt, James R. 179, 276
Hunt, John W. 701
Hunt, Thomas 583
Hunt, William 679, 733
Hunt, William R. 91
Hunter, Capt. 46, 47, 51, 54, 69
Hunter, Bear 172, 173, 175
Hunter, Edward S. 846
Hunter, Francis D. 263
Hunter, Henry 145, 729
Hunter, James P. 865
Hunter, John L. 855
Hunter, John S. 354
Hunter, Louis S. 415, 705, 876
Hunter, Sullivan 771
Hunter, Thomas 833
Hunter, William 401, 495, 691
Huntington, George C. 251
Huntington, Walter E. 127
Huntington, Ward 250
Huntley, Jeremiah 841
Huntley, John H. 239
Huntsman, David 165
Hupfner, Adolph 295
Hupp, James 539
Hurd, Justus 158
Hurlburt, Isaiah 742
Hurlburt, Isaiah, Jr. 732, 746
Hurlburt, Samuel O. 247
Hurley, Cornelius 163
Hurley, James F. 473
Hurley, Joseph 142
Hurley, Michael 104, 365
Hurst, Henry 790
Hurst, John 361
Hurst, William 835
Husband, James A. 466
Huse, Nelson S. 213
Husman, George 771
Hussey, Harrison 627
Hussey, Stephen 761
Hussey, William 679, 875
Hussey, William H.H. 855

Hustis, Theodore F. 842
Huston, Eli 824
Hutchings, Ezra N. 634
Hutchings, Jackson 529
Hutchings, James M. 480
Hutchings, Moses 876
Hutchings, William M. 548, 568, 587
Hutchingson, B.C. 178
Hutchins, John W. 774
Hutchins, Moses 641
Hutchinson, Armstrong 753
Hutchinson, Bartel C. 263
Hutchinson, David 659, 665
Hutchinson, Geo. R. 247
Hutchinson, James 805
Hutchinson, John F. 88, 89
Hutchinson, Robert 452, 460
Hutchinson, William 127
Hutchison, Thomas A. 752
Hutson, William 592
Hutson, William K. 560
Hutton, Hampton 732, 746, 749
Hutton, John 737
Hutton, William 744
Hyams, Frederick N. 822
Hyde, Charles H. 104, 134, 365,
Hyde, Washington W. 396, 410, 718
Hyde, William A. 771
Hyde, William H. 354
Hydulphe, Michael 452
Hyer, Mathew 875
Hyer, Matthew 285
Hyer, Philip 263
Hykus, Jacob 718
Hyler, Charles 613
Hyney, John S. 840
Hyson, Henry 199, 205, 299, 560

I

Icanberry, Jacob M. 641
Ide, Ezra B. 163
Ide, James A. 295
Ide, John E. 299
Ihrie, George P. 522
Ilbright, Frederick 606
Illig, Carl 205

Illig, Morris 280
Imms, Edwin 823
Ince, John F. 842
Ingersoll, Charles Y. 239
Ingersoll, Daniel B. 289
Ingersoll, Jonas H. 525
Ingham, Edward 522, 534, 585
Ingraham, Frank A. 733
Ingraham, William 271
Ingram, Alfonso B. 460
Ingram, Uriah J. 460
Inks, James 247
Inman, Dolphin S. 587
Inman, Henry 466
Innes, John C. 432, 433, 456, 476, 491-92
Innis, John 348
Innis, William L. 779
Inwood, Allen 149
Ipsom, George 839
Ireland, Corydon G. 239
Irons, Louis D. 263, 568
Irvin, Daniel T. 271
Irvin, Henry 280
Irvine, Alexander 114
Irving, Daniel 280
Irving, Evered 862
Irving, Harry P. 858
Irving, Henry P. 849
Irving, Herbert A. 247
Irwin, Alexander 299
Irwin, John P. 352
Irwin, William W. 813
Isenman, Frank 791, 876
Israel, Abraham 280, 299
Isreal, Newton 630
Ivans, John 733

J

Jack, Alexander C. 529, 583
Jack, James G. 819
Jackins, Charles E. 535, 585
Jackman, Albert 729
Jackman, Frederick T. 259
Jackman, John A. 701
Jacks, Samuel 466
Jacks, Samuel E. 613
Jackson, Charles R. 771
Jackson, Edwin 740

Jackson, George 806
Jackson, George E. 463
Jackson, Isaac H. 289
Jackson, James E. 437
Jackson, John 560, 573, 610, 696
Jackson, Joseph 73, 120
Jackson, Josiah C. 233
Jackson, Robert 466, 495
Jackson, Thomas 659
Jackson, Thos. A.N. 705
Jackson, William 199, 227
Jacob, Julius C. 610
Jacobs, Albert G.D. 139
Jacobs, Albert G.T. 134
Jacobs, Meshack H. 833
Jacobs, Rodney 686
Jacobs, Samuel B. 352, 810
Jacoby, Thomas 93
Jacquel, Julien 202
Jacquell, Julien 285
Jacques, Dennis 634
Jaeger, Francis J. 802
Jahn, August 127
Jahn, Ferdinand 783
Jahnel, Constantine 817
James, Brooks 621
James, Cyrus H. 757
James, George H.C. 448, 499, 548
James, Harrison M. 87
James, Henry 740
James, Horace P. 28
James, Jacob M. 254
James, James M. 437
James, Jesse 777
James, John 729
James, John A. 137
James, Nickerson S. 213
James, Oscar 495
James, Prior L. 473, 488
James, Richard W. 767
James, Robert 205
James, Robert R. 774
James, William 288, 744, 774
James, William H. 280
James, William S. 757
Jameson, J. 75
Jameson, James 259
Jameson, Samuel C. 729
Jamieson, Thomas 94
Jamison, Albert 127

Personal Name Index

Jamison, John, alias Davis, John W. 621
Jamison, Thomas 104
Jamison, William 846
Janes, Jasper N. 832, 835
Janes, John W. 835
Janney, Phineas 154
Jansen, Joseph 134
Janson 28
Janson, Henry 501
Jaquan, Clestine 627
Jaques, Isaac S. 733
Jara, Domingo 319
Jarrell, Henry C. 654
Jarrett, William R. 806
Jarvis, William 205, 289
Jauregny, Pierre 641
Jay, Leroy 361
Jay, William 178, 202
Jefferis, William B. 657
Jeffers, John 254
Jefferson, Henry G. 729
Jefferson, John 751
Jefferson, Lincoln 876
Jeffres, Benjamin 444
Jeffreys, David F. 659
Jefts, Eldridge G. 647
Jehu, William 539, 548
Jehu, William H. 573
Jellings, James 356, 876
Jenkens, Edward S. 793
Jenkins, Benjamin A. B. 840
Jenkins, Charles H. 748
Jenkins, Charles M. 859
Jenkins, George 437
Jenkins, Henry 211
Jenkins, Ignatius 257
Jenkins, Ignatius S. 197
Jenkins, Jas. E. 127
Jenkins, James M. 603
Jenkins, John C. 477
Jenkins, Joseph 222
Jenkins, Joseph P. 808
Jenkins, William 230
Jenkins, William H. 452, 480
Jenks, Andrew 780
Jenks, David W. 819
Jenks, Elon 159
Jennings 28
Jennings, Charles T. 87, 142, 162

Jennings, Fletcher R. 823
Jennings, Francis M. 696
Jennings, Lawrence B. 444
Jennings, William H. 868
Jenny, Alphonso 634
Jenny, David 606
Jenny, Theodore 701
Jeppesen, William 748
Jeremiah, James A. 132
Jersey, Richard M. 276
Jessup, Joseph G. 432, 477
Jessup, Levi T. 794
Jessup, Richard M. 28
Jesus, Jose 134
Jett, Benjamin F. 786
Jewell, David C. 201
Jewell, Lafayette 239, 271
Jewell, Mason 444, 495
Jewett, Charles W. 654
Jim, Joaquin 181
Jim, Smoke Creek 186
Jimenez, Marcelino E. 305, 307
Jimeno, Porfino 305, 310, 315
Joaquin, Jim 181
Jocelyn, Stephen E. 524, 553, 566, 568
Johansen, Peter 601
John, Henry D. 452
Johns, George 814, 846
Johns, Henry D. 488
Johns, William M. 522, 524, 553
Johnson, Adolph 844
Johnson, Alden S. 801
Johnson, Alexander B. 130
Johnson, Alexander W. 165
Johnson, Allen 806
Johnson, Allen D. 627
Johnson, Andrew 222, 652, 833
Johnson, Charles 162, 254, 529, 621, 809, 837
Johnson, Charles A. 819
Johnson, Charles L. 817
Johnson, Charles S. 688
Johnson, Charles W. 610, 613, 652
Johnson, David H. 432, 485
Johnson, Edward K. 247
Johnson, Edwin N. 709
Johnson, Elener 729
Johnson, Eli 139
Johnson, Francis L. 817

Johnson, Frederick 219
Johnson, George 69, 94, 145, 179, 280, 299, 733, 844, 876
Johnson, George M. 855
Johnson, George W. 361
Johnson, Hanlon E. 222
Johnson, Henry 230, 733, 737, 814
Johnson, Henry B. 373
Johnson, Henry C. 356
Johnson, Hugh 525, 544
Johnson, Humphries 263
Johnson, James 213, 312, 348, 396, 525, 548, 560, 576, 606, 634, 641, 654, 701, 811, 819
Johnson, James A. 294
Johnson, James H. 718
Johnson, John 123, 134, 606, 714, 876
Johnson, John (1st) 744
Johnson, John (2nd) 744
Johnson, John B. 810
Johnson, John J. 771
Johnson, Jordan 339
Johnson, Joseph 271, 568, 809, 862, 876
Johnson, Joseph C. 530
Johnson, Joseph H. 718
Johnson, Lawrence 768
Johnson, Lewis 634
Johnson, Louis A. 647
Johnson, Lyman 788
Johnson, Orlando 337
Johnson, Oscar A. 219
Johnson, Owen 392, 401
Johnson, Parish B. 456, 470
Johnson, Peter 254, 285, 535, 665
Johnson, Peter F. 466
Johnson, Richard M. 346, 390
Johnson, Robert S. 151, 324, 365, 876
Johnson, Samuel 205, 280, 295
Johnson, Samuel S. 520
Johnson, Stacy D. 578, 876
Johnson, Stephen H. 747
Johnson, Thomas 214, 654
Johnson, Thomas B. 365
Johnson, Thomas E. 544, 555, 578
Johnson, Thomas J. 372
Johnson, William 254, 342, 370, 627, 705, 714, 733

Johnson, Wm. B. 28
Johnson, Wm. F. 833
Johnson, William H. 840
Johnson, William M. 104
Johnson, William S. F. 104, 134
Johnston, Albert Sidney 6, 7, 852
Johnston, Alexander B. 87, 243
Johnston, Isaac W. 239
Johnston, Jas. Lumpkin 817
Johnston, James R. 254
Johnston, John L. 592
Johnston, Samuel W. 775
Jolly, Francisco 309
Jolly, William 145
Jonas, Louis 473, 761
Jones 28, 58, 61
Jones, Allen 737
Jones, Andrew 525
Jones, Benjamin 714
Jones, Benjamin H. 663
Jones, Charles 794
Jones, Charles J. 269
Jones, Charles T. 219, 225, 876
Jones, Cyrus B. 865
Jones, David A. 729
Jones, David K. 202
Jones, Edward C. 809
Jones, Edwin R. 824
Jones, Eugene B. 579
Jones, Evan P. 641
Jones, Francis M. 230
Jones, Frank R. 247
Jones, Frederick 205, 579, 876
Jones, George J. 134
Jones, George R. 352
Jones, George W. 145
Jones, Hezekiah 473
Jones, Ira C. 581
Jones, John 57, 537, 560, 780, 786, 868
Jones, John C. 759
Jones, John G. 754
Jones, John L. 159, 876
Jones, John P. 777
Jones, John T. 858
Jones, Joseph 835
Jones, Leroy M. 775
Jones, Luther 444, 452
Jones, M.T. 665
Jones, Nelson V. 247

Jones, Ora C. 530
Jones, Ozias Edwin 280
Jones, Peter 280, 686
Jones, Peter C. 222
Jones, Randell 28
Jones, Richard 495
Jones, Salathiel 452, 480
Jones, Samuel 233
Jones, Sylvanus A. 145
Jones, Sylvester 365
Jones, Terah 573
Jones, Theodore H. 651, 686
Jones, Thomas 480, 495, 534, 539,
548, 560, 568, 876
Jones, Thomas C. 770
Jones, Thomas H. 120
Jones, Thomas J. 452, 654
Jones, Thomas W. 94, 157
Jones, William 127, 196, 214, 267,
280, 378, 406, 480, 579, 641,
651, 665, 692, 783, 876
Jones, William B. 545, 549, 592
Jones, William C. 571, 606, 876
Jones, William F. 666
Jones, William H. 222, 299
Jones, William T. 768
Jones, William W. 839
Jones, Zephiniah W. 280
Jordan, Frederick 136, 147, 726
Jordan, George M. 677, 679, 714
Jordan, James 149
Jordan, John 627
Jordan, Joshua 235
Jordan, Reazin 641
Jordan, Richard T. 627
Jordan, William H. 799
José, William 539, 549
Joselyn, Joseph H. 448
Joseph, Albert 149
Joseph, Victorine 452
Joslyn, Frank M. 254
Jourdan, James 247
Joy, John 205
Joy, John L. 344
Joy, Maurice 859
Joyce, David K. 255, 876
Joyce, James 139
Juarez, President 76
Juarez, Leandro 316
Juarez, Pedro 309

Judah, Henry M. 595, 599
Judd, Arthur V. 786, 876
Judd, Harrison E. 165
Judd, Norton E. 251
Judson, Timothy 824
Judson, William 255
Julian, Nathan T. 271
Jungblut, Henry W. 444
Junior, Elijah S. 681

K

Kaar, Philip 239
Kagee, Andrew 437, 560, 587
Kagee, John 530, 587
Kagil, Louis 814
Kahner, Lawrence 495
Kailler, Joseph 165
Kaiser, Ferdinand 627
Kaiser, Frank 602
Kaiser, Jacob 530, 549
Kaiting, James 666
Kale, Wilson 751
Kalean, John 729
Kaley, George 356, 613
Kalmback, Frederick 480
Kamball, Carlos 378
Kammerling, Emil 452
Kamp, Albert 157
Kane, Alexander 401, 410, 714
Kane, Joseph 452
Kane, Michael 761
Kappler, Andrew 794
Karcher, Gottleib 780
Karr, John H. 452
Karros, Max 757
Karshaw, Daniel 877
Karteskind, George 748
Kasler, John 255
Kasson, Elijah 592
Kastner, Francis I. 444
Kathan, Daniel H. 280
Kathan, Jesse H. 280
Katz, Charles A. 374
Kaufman, Alexander 460
Kaup, Simon 437
Kausler, Charles 592
Kavanaugh, William 127
Kay, Daniel B. 501
Kay, James 803

Keahl, John 768
Kean, William H. 263
Kear, Sextus 205
Kearnes, Thomas 104
Kearney, Francis H. 222
Kearney, Frederick 458
Kearney, James 458, 488, 638
Kearney, John 299
Kearney, Matthew 201
Kearns, Thomas 809
Kearns, Thomas V. 114
Kearny, Gen. 24
Kearny, John 205
Kearny, Patrick 822
Kearsing, Henry 560
Kearsing, Henry W. 239, 263, 299
Keating, John D. 94
Keating, John K. 801
Keating, John R. 692
Keating, Patrick 606, 634
Keatinge, Patrick 583
Keatley, William 339, 377, 387
Keaton, Joseph Z. 865
Keber, Louis 251
Kee, Charles T. 706
Keefe, John 222, 539
Keefe, Thomas 473
Keefer, Godfrey 466
Keegan, Andrew 154
Keegan, William 791
Keeler, Erastus N. 205
Keeler, George S. 806
Keeley, Francis M. 783
Keen, Lemuel 239
Keen, Samuel 264
Keenan, Edward 137
Keenan, Frederick 573
Keenan, Peter 788
Keenan, Terrence 205, 877
Keene, George 437, 495, 549,
560, 592
Keep, Robert W. 809
Kehl, Charles M. 840
Keho, Patrick M. 339
Kehoe, James 868
Kehoe, Samuel 710
Keifer, John L. 255
Keiffer, Jacob 833
Keihn, Frederick 791
Keil, William 127, 761

Keim, Oliver F. 214
Keith, James F. 62, 104, 876
Keith, John W. 618
Kelland, John A. 444, 452, 480
Kelland, Richard 452, 480
Kellen, Charles W. 560, 587
Kellen, George E. 361
Keller, Daniel W. 555, 810
Keller, Felix 621
Keller, Jacob 654
Keller, Jefferson D. 530, 549,
587, 592
Kelletta, Julius 466
Kelley, Daniel 768
Kelley, George 356
Kelley, George F. 396
Kelley, James 356
Kelley, John L. 775
Kelley, Wm. H. 877
Kelliher, Andrew 751
Kellner, Emile 243
Kellogg 28
Kellogg, Austin 846
Kellogg, Cornelius V. 356
Kellogg, Henry B. 280
Kellogg, John 668, 676
Kellogg, John W. 352, 748
Kellogg, William L. 295
Kelly 178
Kelly, Andrew J. 817
Kelly, Barney 560, 877
Kelly, Caius P. 859
Kelly, Charles 370, 621, 688
Kelly, Daniel 132, 299
Kelly, Edward 530
Kelly, Egbert 378
Kelly, Frank M. 267, 744
Kelly, George F. 688
Kelly, Henry 757
Kelly, Henry W. 499
Kelly, Ira C. 165
Kelly, James 139, 374, 378, 718,
740, 744, 748, 771, 814
Kelly, James M. 846
Kelly, James S. 726
Kelly, John 114, 202, 230, 239,
264, 370, 381, 399, 410, 501,
666, 692, 714, 877
Kelly, John H. 840
Kelly, John T. 299

Kelly, John W. 370
Kelly, Joseph 214, 255, 276
Kelly, Joseph M. 271
Kelly, Louis R. 165
Kelly, Michael 94, 299, 803
Kelly, Michael P. 157
Kelly, Nelson 803
Kelly, Patrick H. 276
Kelly, Peter 714
Kelly, Peter W. 230
Kelly, Philip 444
Kelly, Robert 480
Kelly, Stephen 145
Kelly, Thomas 227, 280, 613, 659, 819, 833
Kelly, Thomas H. 147
Kelly, Timothy 647
Kelly, William 127, 347, 437, 757
Kelly, William D. 779
Kelly, William H. 432
Kelly, William L. 473
Kelton, Emberson 666
Kelty, Timothy 786, 877
Kemm, Robert S. 621
Kemp, John H. 348
Kemp, Joseph 460
Kemp, William 601
Kempner, Joseph 734
Kendall, Edwin A. 127
Kendall, George D. 765, 790
Kendall, Nathan B. 637
Kendall, Robert 744
Kendall, Uriah J. 819
Kendall, William 740
Kendall, William W. 734
Kene, John 401, 688
Keniston, Francis 579
Kenna, Joseph M. 814
Kennady, James 289
Kennedy, Dennis 473, 488
Kennedy, Hiram 641
Kennedy, James 230, 247, 374, 613, 634, 729
Kennedy, James H. 239
Kennedy, John 205, 587
Kennedy, John D. 94
Kennedy, John J. 94
Kennedy, Joseph G. 255
Kennedy, Richard 127
Kennedy, Robert D. 822

Kennedy, William B. 147
Kennedy, William W. 821
Kenney, James 480, 560, 568
Kenney, Robert D. 696
Kenney, Thomas B. 530
Kenny, James 549
Kenny, John 599, 609
Kenny, Joseph 356, 387
Kenny, Robert 539
Kenoyer, David 840
Kent, Newton 737
Kent, Wharton 460
Kent, William 683
Kent, William H. 243
Kentler, Frederick 501
Kentner, Madison L. 452
Kenyon, George M. 679
Kenyon, Henry P. 289
Kenyon, William H. 568
Keogel, Frederick 370
Keon, Michael 573, 842
Keon, Patrick 344, 392
Keornich, Otto 370
Keough, Patrick 480
Kepfter, Louis 247
Kerby, Andrew 452
Kercheval, Benjamin B. 862
Kerker, Ferdinand 600
Kerlin, Samuel 840
Kern, John 734
Kern, Peter 530, 560
Kerr, David S. 606
Kerr, Frank 475
Kerr, John 370, 437
Kerr, Robert 94, 877
Kerr, William 761
Kerren, John W. 654
Kerrington, William 634, 647
Kershaw, Daniel 444
Kerstine, Charles 654
Kertz, August 205, 473
Kesselhot, William 299
Ketcham, Thomas E. 419-20, 505-6, 524
Ketchum, Marion 666
Keton, Charles 794
Kettelle, Charles 214
Key, John 280
Keyes, Benjamin 312
Keyes, Seth 466, 495

Keyser, Henry 634
Kibbe, Edward 579, 877
Kidd, William 788
Kidder, Henry H. 299
Kidder, John G. 800
Kidder, Munroe C. 801
Kidder, William S. 791
Kief, James 682
Kiernan, Daniel 714
Kiernan, Edward L. 247
Kiernan, James 714
Kiernan, Michael 437
Kierstead, James H. 807
Kilborn, Augustine D. 734
Kilfoyle, Frank 260
Kilgore, Andrew M. C. 259
Kilgore, John W. 179, 258
Kilpatrick, Wm. J. 271
Kimball, Charles M. 877
Kimball, Charles W. 683
Kimball, Heber 511
Kimball, Orville H. 793
Kimball, Parker J. 618
Kimball, Solon D. 865
Kimberly, Jared T. 379
Kimberly, Nathaniel C. 111, 877
Kimbrough, Asa J. 361
Kimbrough, James M. 775
Kimmons, Henry K. 549, 583
Kincaid, David 339
Kincannon, William R. 613
King, Albert 247
King, Andrew 583
King, Bradley W. 214
King, Chas. W. 145
King, David C. 94, 104
King, Fielding A. 845
King, Frank 437, 466
King, Frederick 154, 165
King, George 444, 460, 535
King, George P. 679
King, George S. 768
King, George W. 590
King, Henry 222
King, Henry A. 280, 289
King, Henry D. 753
King, Henry S. 602
King, Jacob 822
King, James 211, 587
King, John 104, 230, 236, 342,
 392, 437

King, John B. 312
King, John R. 625
King, José 319
King, Luther 627
King, Patrick 613, 621, 806
King, Peter S. 688
King, Robert 587, 817
King, Thomas 131
King, Thomas F. 601, 645
King, William 434, 473, 488, 803
King, Wm. W. 370
King, Wilson 444, 464
Kingsbury, Joseph C. 770
Kingsley, Edward H. 865
Kingsley, Spencer J. 609
Kingston, George 740
Kinkaid, John 696
Kinman, Jason N. 227
Kinman, Robert 876
Kinnear, John A. 201
Kinney, Justice 179
Kinney, J. F. 175
Kinney, J. T. 510, 515-17
Kinney, John 127
Kinney, Patrick F. 473
Kinnie, Charles M. 855
Kinsaul, Benjamin F. 839
Kinseld, Peter 613
Kinsey, Ezra 222
Kinsinger, Joseph 379
Kinsinger, Peter W. 379
Kinsley, Alfred 530, 579
Kinsley, N. 178
Kinsley, Nathaniel 275
Kinslow, George 415, 706
Kipp, Jacob 757
Kipp, William J. 801
Kirby, Asa H. 348
Kirby, G. W. 109
Kirby, George 94
Kirby, Henry R. 634
Kirby, Seth 800
Kirby, Silas W. 801
Kirk, Francis M. 602
Kirk, John C. 573
Kirkhuff, Samuel 286
Kirkland, Betty S. 819
Kirkpatrick, Charles A. 522, 799
Kirkpatrick, John 780
Kiser, Jacob 740

Kitchen, William A. 817
Kittle 28
Kittredge, Willard 553, 585
Kittridge, Asst. Surgeon 59
Kittridge, Ruell W. 289
Kizer, Bergin August 748
Klans, Moses 444
Klausman, Francis 748
Klauss, Moses 811
Kleeberger, Edward 777
Klegg, Thomas 104
Klein, Charles 149
Klein, Francis 742
Kleinhoff, Peter 634, 877
Klima, Michael 768
Kline, George L. 280
Kline, George W. 688
Kline, William 361
Kline, William M. 114
Klinger, Andrew 737
Klinker, Frederick 583, 585, 780
Knabner, Henry B. 496
Knapen, Edgar A. 114
Knapp, David 869
Knapp, James 492
Knapp, James W. 275
Knapp, John 729
Knapp, John N. 809
Knapp, Nathaniel O. 441
Knee, Richard 729
Knee, Solomon 729
Kneettle, Frederick R. 788
Knepper, Hugh 205, 230
Knepper, Jesse 222, 230
Kness, Adam 312
Knickerbocker, Geo. M. 457, 484
Knight, John 734
Knight, Michael 549
Knight, Nathaniel 751
Knight, Samuel P. 784
Knight, William G. 165
Knight, William L. 169, 225, 242, 267
Knight, Winfield S. 160
Knighton, William H. 843
Knob, Andrew 134
Knobloch, John 641
Knoblock, John 255, 272
Knoke, Albert 120, 876
Knoll, Frank 444

Knott, Edwin 406, 711
Knott, William E. 379
Knower, Joseph S. 752
Knowles, Amos P. 800
Knowles, Frank 855
Knowles, John P. 606
Knowlton, Joseph, Jr. 800
Knowlton, William 803
Knox, Harrison 109
Knox, James 496
Knox, Moses M. 759
Knuchal, Arnold 654
Knudzen, Charles 822
Kobelt, Louis 613
Kobro, Frederick 748
Koch, Adam 248, 444
Koehli, Jacob 480
Koerber, John 289
Koernick, Otto 392
Kohlman, Charles 361, 387
Koons, Michael 701
Korble, Louis 210, 214
Korthus, Erwin G. 539
Kowell, John 654
Kowlett, William 877
Kraemer, Augustus 444
Kraft, Henry 444
Kraher, Anthony 149
Kramar, Peter 776
Kramer, John 488
Kraus, Andrew 701
Kreps, George A. 230
Kress, John 466
Krim, George 344
Kristian, Peter 289
Kroffs, George W. 780
Kroger, Herm 530
Krona, Frederick W. 219
Krone, George 535
Krouse, Andrew 276
Krug, Jacob A. 579
Kruger, Henry 444
Krumm, Jacob 768
Krumpegel, Edward 114
Kruse, Harry 415, 706
Kruss, Frederick W. 777
Kuhl, Charles 127, 214
Kuhlman, John G. 734
Kuhls, Henry 865
Kuhn, Frederick 218, 219

Kuhn, Peter 264
Kuhns, John Francis 573, 694
Kull, Rudolph F. 248
Kunkler, John E. 87
Kurtz, Jacob 634
Kurtz, John 339, 392
.Kurtz, Louis 444
Kustel, Cassimer B. 809
Kuster, Barney 339
Kuster, Louis 444
Kybury, Samuel E. 227
Kyle, Christopher 97
Kyle, John E. 239
Kyle, Samuel C. 560, 587, 813

L

Labadie 183
La Bean, Alexander W. 356
Labee, George 104
La Bertew, Gabriel H. 560, 587
La Bieau, Alexander W. 387
Labish, Theodore 480
La Boeuf, Francis 118
Laborde, Louis 312
La Campo, Manuel 473
Lace, Thomas K.H. 786
Lackey, William S. 153
Lacy, Frederick D. 150
Lacy, Henry 433
Lacy, Laurence 729
Ladd, Freeman S. 794
Ladd, John P. 684
Ladd, William 289
Lafferty, Albert G. 833
Lafferty, John 305
Lafferty, Zabina 310
Laflash, Franklin 706, 877
Lafrens, John 734
Laget, Paul E. 539
Lagoon, Juba 837
Lagoon, Peter 837
Laguna, Santos 319
La Haape, Frederick, de 93
Laharge, Baptiste 820
Lahay, William 729
Lahey, Patrick 814
Lahey, Thomas 272
Lahey, William 692
Laighton, Alfred L. 856

Lajounie, Lewis J. 810
Lajoye, Charles 539
Lake, David P. 142
Lake, Elisha 846
Lake, William H. 178, 205, 877
Lalazar, Alfego 313
Lally, John F. 272
Lamare, Charles 452
Lamb, Abram 452
Lamb, Alexander 729
Lamb, George J. 299
Lamb, Luther C. 606
Lamb, Peter 568
Lamb, Robert G. 814
Lamb, Thomas 634, 641
Lamb, William 264
Lamb, William H. 677
Lamb, William N. 714
Lambert, Francis H. 370
Lambert, Henry W. 444
Lambert, James H. 431
Lambert, John 222, 671, 694, 699, 709
Lambert, Peter 147
Lambert, William H. 233
Lambly, Patrick M. 501
Lamercier, Alfred 627
Lameroux, Isidore 806
Lamley, Jonas 150
Lamlin, Peter 460
Lamm, George J. 560
Lamon, George W. 530, 539
Lamont, William 352, 415, 706
Lamoreaux, Norbert 444
La Mothe, Gaston, de 311
La Mott, John 280, 290
Lamott, Joshua 230
Lamphear, Edson 573
Lamson, Franklin 136
Lanabee, Seneca 280
Lanagan, Edward 549, 560
Lanahan, James 560, 573
Lanahan, Peter 803
Lancaster, Jeremiah F. 361
Lance, William H. 255
Lancri, Peter Lucie 820
Land, Charles 466
Land, Joseph 481
Landerer, Charles 165
Landergen, James W. 484

Landers, John 467, 502
Landers, Theodore 235
Landes, Benjamin 178
Landgraf, Augustus 264
Landis, Benjamin 276
Landis, Stephen F. 862
Landon, John 641
Landsbury, John 647
Lane, Alexander 460
Lane, Asa F. 272
Lane, Edward P. 865
Lane, George 437
Lane, John R. 684
Lane, John W. 352
Lane, Orshun L. 660
Lane, Percy 275
Lane, Robert L. 290
Lane, Samuel 264
Lane, William 786
Lanfe, Henry 313
Lang, Ferdinand 127
Lang, Jacob 806
Lang, Richard 714
Langan, Thomas 638
Langdon, David 154
Langdon, Joseph H. 356, 387
Lange, August F.C. 877
Lange, Augustus F.C. 127
Langelier, Louis 634
Langford, Henry 761
Langham, Emil 560
Langhans, Emil 264
Langley, Charles 276
Langley, Henry C. 777
Langley, Howell T. 862
Langley, J.S. 178
Langley, John 277, 877
Langley, Joseph 452, 878
Langraf, A. 179
Langton, Timothy 437, 488
Languedoc, William C.E. 806
La Niece, James 747
Lanigan, James B. 226
Lanigan, John 230
Lanigan, Thomas 145
Lannahan, Peter 370
Lannigan, John 214
Lannigan, Rody 214
La Noix, Frederico, de 312
Lansdale, Lewis 777

Lansdall, Lewis 878
Lansdon, Sgt. 186
Lansdon, Alexander 214
Lansey, Michael 437
Lansing, Alfred D.C. 248
Lansing, James 264
Lantz, Milton P. 570
Lantzenhiser, John B. 606
La Osa, Feliciano 312
Lapoint, Lawrence 677, 679, 718
Lara, Matias 316
Larabee, Seneca 877
Larcom, Thos. H. 239
Large, Thomas 729
Largy, John 255
Larichiler, Henry 788
Larkin, John 768
Larkin, Michael 744
Larkin, Patrick 613, 622
Larkin, Townsend T. 255
Larney, Philip 634
La Rose, Wm. L. 344, 365, 392
Larrieu, Lorenzo D. 865
Larsen, Carl C.M. 748
Larsson, John 734
Lash, Thomas J. 350
Laster, Jonathan 729
Latham, George 844
Lathrop, Albert J. 812
Lathrop, Francis M. 751
Latimer, Lt. 183
Latimer, Charles A. 740
Latimer, Elisha E. 98
Latimer, William H. 158
Laton, Washington C. 775
Latour, Edmond 473
La Tour, Jeremiah 452, 488
Latour, Peter 467
Lattie, Alexander 803
Lattimer, Lt. 71
Lattin, Josiah 549
Lattin, William H. 805
Laubersheimer, Anton 346
Laurence, William H. 825
Laurenson, William 437
Laus, Refugio 718
Lautz, Milton P. 526
Laux, Henry 817
Lavalle, Edward 530, 549
Lavery, John 579

Lavish, Otto 801
Lavish, Thomas 801
Lavray, John 488
Lawhern, William 688
Lawless, James 248
Lawless, Thomas 502
Lawless, William 539, 549, 592
Lawlor, Patrick 202
Lawlor, William 470
Lawrence, Austin S. 299, 877
Lawrence, Benjamin F. 555
Lawrence, Charles 729
Lawrence, Frank 840
Lawrence, John 549
Lawrence, Owen 206
Lawrence, Peter F. 467
Lawrence, Simpson 361
Lawrence, Thomas 379
Lawrence, William 473
Lawrence, William H. 869
Lawrier, Alexander 309
Lawry, Edward 660
Laws, Leonard B. 647
Lawson, George 761
Lawson, Geo. W. 460
Lawson, Gustavus 104
Lawson, Henry C. 89
Lawton 28
Lawton, A.T. 28
Lawton, Andrew J. 734
Lawton, David W. 767
Lawton, George 568, 877
Lawton, William 757
Lay, William J. 869
Laycock, Jacob 344
Laycraft, Samuel H. 780
Layet, Paul E. 814
Layett, Paul E. 523
Layton, David 539, 560, 583
Layton, Levi E. 692
Lazanaga, Santos 313
Leach, Chauncey B. 752
Leach, Merritt C. 634
Leach, Oscar F. 230, 878
Leach, Thomas 862
Leadbetter, Robert 264
Leahy, Joseph 768
Lean, Guillermo 316
Leary, Dennis 473
Leary, James 647

Leary, Timothy E. 467
Leaton, Col. 76
Leaton, Robert 114
Leavel, Ambrose 437
Leavick, Simon 370
Leavitt, Holland 549
Leaycraft, Samuel H. 437
Lebendelfer, Daniel S. 602
Le Blonde, Henry 309
Lebrand, George 313
Lecerf, Victor 313
Leckie, Adolph 740
Le Court, Stephen 622
Lectner, William 846
Ledyard, Ebenezer C. 79, 89
Lee, Albert 255
Lee, Alfred 856
Lee, Andrew 583
Lee, Charles H. 701
Lee, Charles J., Jr. 794
Lee, Charles W. 801
Lee, Daniel 877
Lee, David 877
Lee, Edward 437
Lee, Frank 641
Lee, George L., Jr. 865
Lee, George W. 869
Lee, Harvey 599
Lee, Henry 566, 573
Lee, James R. 783
Lee, John 104, 178, 370
Lee, John H. 110
Lee, John S. 280
Lee, Leander 794
Lee, Orlando H. 599, 602, 609, 624
Lee, Peter 264
Lee, Scheuval D. 579
Lee, Silas 740
Lee, Stephen 791, 878
Lee, Thomas 809
Lee, William 502, 783
Lee, William G. 448
Lee, William W. 460
Leeds, Chas. W. 239
Leedy, Samuel R. 352
Leese, Louis V. 305, 307
Leese, Nathaniel 467
Leesenring, James P. 592
Lefebre, Edward 313

Lefever, Andre 613
Leffau, Henry 561
Leflock, Felix 313
Legare, Burnett H. 452
Legget, Joshua 299
Leggett, Joshua 877
Leggitt, J. 178
Leggitt, James 844
Legler, Charles 856
Legrand, Peter 734
Legross, Ernest H. 310
Lehe, Eugene 447
Lehegarat, Charles 437
Lehman, Jacob 638
Lehman, Paul 460
Lehmer, James 561
Lehmer, James C. 198, 206
L'Hommedieu, Ed. W. 484
L'hommedue, Samuel 285
Lehr, Daniel 401, 406, 411, 684
Leibold, Felix 324, 344
Leiding, Fritz 255
Leighton, Daniel 211, 761
Leighton, Stephen 878
Leighton, Stephen H. 290
Leighton, William 91
Leins, John F. 754
Leitch, Joseph 729
Lellemand, Frank E. 290
Lemaire, Auguste 313
Lemaitre, Eugene 313
Lembeck, William F. 434
Lembert, Francis H. 810
Le Mier, John J. B. 634
Lemmon, Alexander 372
Lemmon, John 789
Lemoin, Hugh 877
Lemoine, Hugh 803
Lemon, Frederick W. 780
Lemon, George W. 348
Lemon, John 61
Lemon, Samuel 815
Lemon, William 777
Lemon, William M. 779
Lemons, George W. 415
Lennam, Martin 467
Leo, Daniel 473
Leo, Michael 230, 239
Leon, Abrial 842
Leon, Juan 305, 309

Leonard, David C. 592
Leonard, James B. 794
Leonard, Nelson 839
Leonard, Patrick 452
Leonard, Patrick H. 865
Leonard, Philip 834
Leonard, Richard 313
Leonard, William 202, 296
Leonard, William S. 120
Leonhardt, Carl 641
Le Roy, Charles W. 127
Le Roy, Philip R. 122
Leroy, William S. 573
Lesan, Albert A. 264
Leslie, John 583
Lessenring, James P. 535
Letterman, James 824
Leture, Alexander 647, 877
Leuthold, Casper 464
Level, Ambrose 568
Levengood, Jacob 394
Lever, Frank 452
Levere, Charles F. 227
Levi, Richard 94, 877
Levison, Sigmund 744
Lewin, James D. 139
Lewis, Abram W. 771
Lewis, Antonio B. 502
Lewis, Charles 621
Lewis, Charles W. 763, 766
Lewis, Frederick 549, 561, 573
Lewis, George 280, 299
Lewis, Henry 114
Lewis, Isaac D. 789
Lewis, James 94
Lewis, Jeremiah 452, 877
Lewis, John 473, 502, 754, 822
Lewis, John H. 754
Lewis, Joseph 744
Lewis, Joseph C. 606
Lewis, Major A. 778, 878
Lewis, Micajoh G. 509, 585
Lewis, Morgan C. 660
Lewis, Philip 255
Lewis, Richard O. 561
Lewis, Robert 772
Lewis, Stephen 859
Lewis, Sylvester T. 255
Lewis, Thomas 782
Lewis, William 139, 264, 627

Lewis, William V. 734
Ley, Thomas A. 842
Leya, Frantz 299
Leybourne, Stephen C. 844
Leyden, Francis 206, 214
Leyden, James 248
Leyra, José R. 307
Lhommedue, Samuel 206
Libby, Alvin H. 579
Libby, Frank O. 856
Libby, John 696, 877
Libby, Stephen H. 701
Libby, William H. 701
Liberski, Robert 822
Liddle, William 434
Lienan, Henry 740
Liening, John H. 120, 122, 136
Light, Edward 88, 104
Light, Harvey W. 780
Light, James 339, 817
Light, James M. 835
Lilley, John 692
Limereux, John 313
Lincoln, Abraham 7, 322, 515
Lincoln, Augustine 290
Lincoln, Benjamin 280
Lincoln, Horatio D. 790
Lincoln, J. 179
Lincoln, Jefferson 280, 294
Lincoln, John 281
Lind, Charles J. 290
Lind, Edward 814
Linde, Albert 485
Lindell, Robert 452
Lindeman, John 783
Lindenmath, Peter H. 145
Linder, Charles 811
Linderman, John 631
Lindley, George 502
Lindley, Miles 804
Lindley, William 460
Lindsay, Alexander 481
Lindsay, Fulton 160
Lindsey, Dugald 587
Line, John 837
Lineback, Alfred S. 549
Liner, Joseph 729
Liner, Peter 264, 281
Linn, De Witt C. 264
Linoberg, Jacob 206

Lion, Henry 654
Lipp, Charles H. 488, 530
Lippe, Augustus 786
Lippincott, Benjamin 19
Lippincott, Henry 725
Lippitt, F. P. 38, 39
Lippitt, Francis J. 418-19, 421, 431, 506-7
Lisberger, Augustus 740
List, George W. 290
Lister, Peter V. W. 692
Lithgon, William H. 104
Little, Chester C. 137
Little, Francis 139
Little, George 154
Little, Hazen D. 866
Little, Horace L. 264
Little, John C. 214
Little, Mountain 76
Little, Robert 467
Littlefield, Alonzo 793
Littlefield, Nathan I. 775
Littlefield, Rufus J. 434
Littlefield, Theodore A. 452, 499
Littleton, James E. 268
Livingston, Alexander 539, 549
Livingston, Frederick 522, 539, 583, 592
Livingston, Henry 761
Livingston, Robert P. 415, 706, 878
Livingston, William 392
Livergood, Daniel W. 267, 268, 877
Livergood, Jacob 699
Lloyd, Andrew 437
Lloyd, George A. 374
Lloyd, Thomas C. 365
Loane, Abraham 856
Lobbering, Antonio 109
Lober, Joseph 214
Lobough, Ephraim 143
Locke 28
Locke, Benjamin 856
Locke, George C. 657
Locke, John M. 869
Lockey, George 94
Lockhard, A. G. 179
Lockhart, Andrew J. 264, 299
Lockhart, William 365

Lockwood, Arthur J. 347
Lockwood, Charles E. 344, 368, 392
Lockwood, Truman D. 634
Loder, Richard B. 231
Lodge, Michael 801
Loft, Thomas 822
Loftus, Anthony 754
Loftus, Charles 299
Logan, Elza 94
Logan, Frank 145
Logan, James V. B. 695
Logan, John 222
Logan, Lorenzo L. 365
Logan, Robert C. 137
Logan, Sampson A. 786
Logan, Samuel 695
Logan, Thomas 645
Logan, William 127
Logsdon, James 862
Logsdon, William H. 235
Logue, James 178, 264, 272
Logue, John 206, 268
Lohman, John 793
Lohmeyer, August 757
Lohse, Louis S. 379, 447, 805
Lomax, John H. 783
Lombard, Frank 94
Lombarts, Joseph 761
London, John 248
London, Thomas E. 751
Lonergan, Nicholas 696
Loney, Phillip 613
Long, Charles W. 827, 832
Long, Daniel 539
Long, David C. 583
Long, Edward 866
Long, Erick 846
Long, George 734, 842
Long, John 165, 244, 452, 481,
    499, 877
Long, Michael 613, 666
Long, Robert 134
Long, Silas C. 791, 878
Long, Thomas 437
Longenback, Frederick 622
Longhurst, William 754
Longley, Abraham S. 602, 617
Longley, Napoleon B. 437
Longley, Sylvanus S. 275
Longshore, Archer B. 688

Longworth, Cyrus 363, 810
Lontzenhiser, John B. 877
Loomis, John N. 214
Loomis, Mills S. 684
Loomis, Salmon H. 638, 810
Loomis, Willis S. 406
Loose, Justus 729
Lopez, Bernardino 316
Lopez, Ermenejildo 316
Lopez, Jesus 319
Lopez, Joaquin 309
Lopez, José Antonio 319
Lorain, John 474
Loran, Robran 488, 530
Lorber, Joseph 227
Lord, Ivory D. 820
Lord, Joatham 300
Lord, John McHenry 779
Lord, Richard 840
Lord, Thomas H. 859
Loredo, Miguel 309
Loring, Edward B. 200, 209, 210
Loring, Elijah 222
Loring, Levi A. 614
Loring, Samuel B. 94
Lorr, Anthony 357, 387
Lorton, Samuel 666
Loser, Peter W. 214
Loss, Frank 757
Lossee, William 606, 634
Lottillier, Adolph M. 313
Loud, Eugene 866
Louderback, Daniel 210, 214
Louget, William 127
Loughead, James 86, 99, 109
Loughnan, Jeremiah 379, 387
Loughrige, Charles 114
Lounds, John 666
Louning, Albert 768
Loutzenhizer, John C. 625
Love, George C. 609, 637, 662
Love, Jerome W. 114, 718
Love, John 679
Love, John A. 281, 300, 365
Love, William 549, 561
Lovejoy, Dana B. 862
Lovejoy, Jabez F. 877
Lovejoy, Jabez T. 255
Lovejoy, Paul 751
Loveland, Darwin C. 467

Loveland, John F. 561
Lovell, Maj. 36
Lovell, Francis M. 206
Lovering, William 614
Lovern, William 622
Lovewell, Alfred 530, 877
Lovewell, Thomas 530
Loving, Frederick 549
Lovitt, Abel H. 220
Lovitt, Charles 248
Low, Aaron 474
Low, C. Adolphe 28
Low, F.F. 5, 305
Low, Frank 794
Low, Perley 94
Low, Warrington M. 460
Lowarey, David 281
Lowe, Augustus H. 625
Lowe, Kindle B.P. 744
Lowee, John 627
Lowell, Charles 165
Lowell, Wilson 290
Lowen, John 453
Lower, Oliver 601, 666
Lowery, Zachariah 768
Lowman, Samuel 352
Lowring, Edward B. 877
Lowry, Felton 823
Lowther, Robert J. 379
Loy, Martin M. 791
Loyd, John W. 235
Loyd, Thomas 474
Loyde, James 134
Lubeck, Henry E. 481, 877
Lubeck, John 231
Lubeck, Julius 641
Lucas, Charles H. 281
Lucas, Hamilton S. 822
Lucas, Michael 815
Lucas, Thomas 127
Luce, Charles A. 91
Luce, Simon 834
Luce, William 840
Luckey, Andy 352
Luckey, Charles 840
Lucky, Charles 877
Ludewig, Otto 549
Ludlow, Chauncey 214
Ludlow, John H. 357
Ludwig, Alvin B. 348

Lugo, Francisco 316
Lugo, José 316
Luis, Pedro 313
Luisano, Pedro P. 309
Luke, Charles A. 300
Luke, John 768
Lull, Abner C. 77, 143
Lumley, Edward 114
Lumm, John 281
Lund, George P. 614
Lund, Peter 530
Lundbeck, Lemuel S. 706
Luning, Andrew 488, 747
Luning, Charles 361
Lunn, William 150
Lunn, William F. 877
Lunsford, John 768
Lunsford, William 767
Lunt, John M. 255
Lunt, William P. 859
Luse, Luther S. 581
Luskey, George 401, 692
Lusser, Louis 539
Luther, Chauncey 641
Luther, George A. 837
Luttrall, James 561, 573
Luttrell, George W. 775
Luttrell, John 775
Luttrell, Marion F. 775
Lux, Nicholas 757
Lux, William 840
Lycan, William M. 865
Lydon, Peter 814
Lyman, Edward 264, 300
Lynam, Daniel 641
Lynch, Alexander 813
Lynch, James 606, 654, 761
Lynch, John 206, 751
Lynch, John F. 600
Lynch, Martin 272
Lynch, Michael 231, 740
Lynch, Patrick A. 481
Lynch, Patrick E. 761
Lynch, Sandy 401, 411, 696
Lynch, Thomas 231
Lynch, Timothy 437, 877
Lynch, William 445
Lynd, James A. 206
Lynde, Isaac 43
Lynham, Thomas 104

Lynn, Robert 648
Lyon, Albert E. 583
Lyon, Henry A. 676, 699
Lyon, James H. 94, 104, 139
Lyon, John 127
Lyon, Wendell P. 344
Lyon, William A. 679
Lyons, Charles 134, 877
Lyons, George 272
Lyons, John 641, 711
Lyons, Michael 822
Lyons, William 467
Lysle, Francis 139
Lythe, Nicholas N. 706
Lytle, George 775
Lytle, George W. 824
Lytle, Nicholas N. 638

M

M' see Mac and Mc
Maber, W.M. 179
Maber, William 264, 300
Mabray, Oliver S. 648
Mac see also Mc
Macauley, James 609
Mace, Joseph W. 453
Mack, Frederick 437
Mack, George W. 737
Mack, James 627
Mackintosh, James 561, 583
Mackney, John B. 783
Macnamara, Maurice 693
Macondray 28
Macowitzki, Charles 153
Macy, George 357
Madden, Francis 748
Madden, John 445
Maddocks, Enos F. 290
Maddox, Samuel B. 862
Maddux, David 344
Maddy, Andrew J. 231
Maden, Christopher 549
Madigan, Simon 370
Madigan, Thomas 453, 812
Madison, John 663
Madison, William F. 206
Madruena, Jesus 316
Madson, Antonio 846
Maduaga, Aniceto 309

Magan, John 842
Magary, Alfred 856
Magary, Charles 583
Magary, George P. 134
Magee, Joseph T. 579
Magill, Hugh R. 706
Magill, James 114
Magill, William 361
Magry, Paschal 693
Magstaff, Jeremiah 879
Maguire, Daniel 264
Maguire, George 614
Maguire, John 142, 255, 437
Maguire, John D. 453
Maguire, Thomas 654
Maguire, Thomas F. 866
Maguire, Thomas J. 457
Maguire, William D. 751
Magy, Alexander 441
Mahar, Barney 231
Mahar, Thomas 359
Maher, James 693
Maher, John 693, 727
Maher, Joseph 94
Maher, Michael 814
Mahin, Thomas H. 231
Mahler, Edward 727
Mahler, Joseph 729
Mahon, Daniel 453
Mahoney, Andrew 622
Mahoney, John 461, 488, 622
Mahoney, Patrick 837
Maier, Gottlieb 789
Mailley, Thomas 264
Mails, Abraham 775
Mains, Joseph 120, 729
Maison, John 344
Maitheson, Thomas 879
Maize, Montgomery 433
Major, George J. 206
Major, John 666
Majory, Levi H. 157
Malcolm, Henry 488
Malcolm, Hugh 370, 392
Malcolm, Lorton 654
Malcolm, Walter 339
Malcolm, William H. 754
Malcom, Hugh 344
Malcom, Walter 387
Malcomb, Lewis 272

Malichi, Francis 396, 701
Mallard, Barnard H. 561
Mallet, James 693
Mallet, William 214
Malley, William 817
Mallock, Silas R. 561
Mallon, Michael 748
Mallon, Philip 502, 666
Mallory, Abner T. 859
Mallory, Avrell 114
Mallory, William E. 260
Malone, John 145, 474, 688
Malone, John (1st) 401
Malone, John (2nd) 401
Malone, Michael 231
Malone, Thomas 693
Maloney, Daniel 530, 583
Maloney, Jeremiah 579
Maloney, John 104
Maloney, John M. 463, 491
Maloney, Peter 62, 878
Maloni, John 392
Malot, Francols 311
Maloy, Edward 761
Malson, William 648
Manchester, Luman A. 859
Manes, Noble C. 791
Mangus, Colorado 71
Manion, John 768
Manjanes, Carlos 311
Manker, William A. 859
Mankinney, Peter 248
Mankins, John 837
Manley, Aaron R. 335, 363
Manley, Charles 392
Manley, Edgar 401, 688
Manley, James 581
Manley, Thomas 339, 386
Manly, Martin 634
Mann, Alonzo P. 801
Mann, Henry 793
Mann, Jacob 396, 688, 706
Mann, Lewis W. 118
Mann, Louis 670
Mann, Silas B. 641
Mann, Stephen B. 794
Mann, Thomas H. 206
Mann, William J. 555
Manners, Edward 790
Manners, Frederick 726, 742, 752

Manning, George A. 243, 850, 867
Manning, James 744
Manning, John 179, 539, 549, 592
Manning, John M. 688
Manning, Michael 757
Manning, Patrick 401, 411, 415, 684
Manning, William C. 243, 850-51, 864
Manon, Gabriel 319
Manon, José de R. 319
Mansel, George 481
Mansfield, Carmel H. 800
Mansfield, Ellis F. 699
Mansfield, James A. 239
Mansfield, Lawrence 370, 392
Mansfield, Lawrence J. 344
Mansfield, Walter 539, 579
Mansfield, William 561
Manso, Charles 272
Manter, Charles 822
Manter, Fordyce R. 142
Mantis, Frodyce B. 879
Manuel, José 817
Manville, Henry 684
Mapes, Pvt. 75
Mapes, John W. 105
Mapes, William B. 105
Maples, William M. 300
Marble, Archibald P. 499
Marble, Charles M. 433
Marble, Francis B. 206
Marble, Lewis L. 579
Marble, Oliver J. 822
Marces, Alva W. 823
Marchand, Prospero 309
Marchello, Dominic 737
Marcher, James J. 122
Marckey, John F. 248
Marcon, Leon 309
Marcovitch, John 94
Marcus, Charles 834
Marcy, James M. 878
Marenzo, Francois 313
Marie, Goanvie C. 844
Marie, Julius 239
Marin, Francis 453
Marin, James 481

Marino, Antonio 481
Marion, Timothy J. 248
Markel, David D. 648
Markel, David L. 445
Marken, David W. 648
Marker, John D. 179, 206, 290
Marker, Peter 549, 561
Markey, Francis 846
Markham, John 660
Markham, William B. 134
Markle, John 618
Markley, Henry H. 432, 492
Marks, John 214
Marks, Samuel A. 744
Maroney, Matthew 684
Marple, Samuel W. 198, 272
Marsh, Franklin 840
Marsh, George D. 202, 206, 290
Marsh, James 561, 566, 592
Marsh, Joseph 748
Marsh, Pembroke S. 822
Marsh, Richard 786
Marsh, William P. 211
Marsh, William T. 862
Marshall, Mr. 61
Marshall, Anton 812
Marshall, Benjamin 744
Marshall, David L. 834
Marshall, Edward B. 701
Marshall, George W. 467, 772
Marshall, Henry 438, 561, 573
Marshall, Henry W. 352
Marshall, Herman 445, 496
Marshall, James H. 737
Marshall, John A. 789
Marshall, Richard T. 94
Marshall, Samuel 105
Marshall, Seneca 300
Marshall, Seneca S. 255
Marshall, Thomas 353, 654
Marshall, William 549
Marsland, Matthew H. 218
Marstadt, Francis 199
Marstall, George E. 160
Marston, Frank 842
Marston, Frederick 461
Marston, Ivory R. 239
Marstrand, Charles 313
Martell, Theodore 523, 561
Martin, Abraham 348, 878

Martin, Andrew J. 801
Martin, Barney 641, 654
Martin, Caspar 844
Martin, Charles Q. 231
Martin, Christopher C. 837
Martin, Ebenezer 94
Martin, Fritz 365
Martin, George 530
Martin, George A. 94
Martin, George H. 406, 684
Martin, George I. 227
Martin, George M. 688, 878
Martin, George T. 210
Martin, George W. 114
Martin, Henry 461, 573
Martin, Henry J. 105, 127
Martin, Hiram F. 496
Martin, James 94, 264, 457, 570, 744, 751
Martin, John 231, 350, 474, 496
Martin, John A. 754
Martin, John H. 252, 281
Martin, John R. 844
Martin, Joseph 530
Martin, Lawrence H. 744
Martin, Ledyard H. 800
Martin, Lemuel W. 235
Martin, Patrick 606
Martin, Pedro 812
Martin, Peter 222, 729
Martin, Philip 94, 105
Martin, Philip J. 778
Martin, Thomas 134, 453
Martin, Tyler 461
Martin, Wiley 114
Martin, William 290, 502
Martin, William C. 830, 841
Martin, William H. 136
Martinete, Emile 817
Martinez, Francisco 319
Martinez, José 844
Martinez, José M. 309
Martinez, Rafael 319
Marts, Elias 373, 392, 400
Martz, James 231
Marvin, Henry G. 448, 749
Marvin, John A. 406, 684
Mase, Nathaniel H. 587
Mason, Alva 154
Mason, Charles 99, 150

Mason, James 778
Mason, James E. 218, 433, 445
Mason, John 406, 502, 655, 711
Mason, John I. 231
Mason, Joseph 820
Mason, Joseph M. 778
Mason, Lyman 160
Mason, Matthew 530, 561
Mason, Richard B. 381, 401, 693
Mason, Robert 734
Mason, Thaddeus W. 281
Massa, José 737
Massen, Auguste 539
Massey, Albert W. 239
Massey, Charles C. 445
Masson, August 878
Masson, Horatio J. 592
Masten, Peter 837
Masters, Leonard 787
Masters, William, Jr. 357
Matheson, Thomas 535, 555
Mathews, Benjamin F. 789
Mathews, Henry 453, 561, 579
Mathews, Henry R. 492, 739
Mathews, John 259
Mathews, John H. 706
Mathews, Nicholas 453, 461
Mathews, William 281
Matlock, William 844
Matthew, Nicholas 648
Matthews, Elisha F. 772
Matthews, Henry 614
Matthews, John H. 381, 415
Matthewson, Dugal 666
Matthewson, Henry B. 845
Matthey, Henry U. 693
Matthis, Upton L. 290
Mattice, Edwin W. 523
Mattis, Edwin W. 573
Mattison, Oscar 406, 684
Mattox, Henry A. 869
Maubert, Ferdinand 272
Mauliner, John 614
Maurice, John F. 648
Maury, Pierre 768, 878
Mawson, Richard 701
Max, Martin 561, 878
Maxcey, James M. 682
Maxey, George 844
Maxfield, Francis M. 461

Maxim, Henry 453, 878
Maximillian, Emperor 76
Maxon, John 94
Maxsen, Bonnevie 467
Maxwell, Arthur 614, 879
Maxwell, John 91, 105, 137
Maxwell, Luther 222
Maxwell, Thomas 780
May, Charles 361
May, Henry M. 539, 561
May, John 300
May, John H. 543
May, Joseph 846
May, Peter 453, 496
May, William H. 467, 791
Mayberry, Charles W. 693
Mayer, Louis 748
Mayers, Daniel 281, 300
Mayfield, Emory 759
Mayfield, James 627
Mayher, John H. 467
Maykins, William H. 801
Maynard, Chas. E. 123, 222
Maynard, Eli F. 225, 234, 243
Maynard, Jesse T. 210
Mayo, Carter H. 622
Mayor, Oscar 284
Mays, William 809
Mazeaux, Francis T. 255
Mazon, Abel 318
Mazy, Henry 856
Mc see also Mac
McAfee, Anselem A. 770
McAllister, Alfred 214, 269
McAllister, J. 38, 39
McAndrew, John 415, 606, 706
McArthur, Alvin 822
McArver, John 701
McAtee, Hezekiah 300
McAuliff, Daniel S. 778
McAuliffe, Thos. F. 290
McAuslan, Francis 772
McBean, John A. 264, 579, 592
McBee, Robert H. 588
McBride, Isaac 201
McCabe, Charles M. 215, 272
McCabe, Edward 272
McCabe, Henry 365
McCabe, Terrence 438
McCabe, William 492

McCadden, William 139
McCaffrey, Charles 272
McCaffrey, Cornelius 239
McCaffrey, James E. 359
McCaffrey, John 474
McCain, William H. 651
McCall, Bernard 128
McCall, Henderson 754
McCallan, James 772, 801
McCallum, John C. 866
McCamant, Lewis 248
McCammen, J. S. W. 869
McCann, Bernard 231
McCann, Francis 729, 744
McCann, Henry 617
McCann, James 165, 453
McCann, John 622, 789, 869
McCann, Michael 374
McCann, Samuel 365
McCann, Thomas 300, 641
McCanne, Barney 778
McCardle, Philip 688
McCarlton, Michael 438
McCarrak, Joseph 859
McCarten, John 740
McCarthy, Charles 539, 744
McCarthy, Cornelius 438
McCarthy, Dennis 339, 370
McCarthy, Edward 809
McCarthy, Jeremiah 434
McCarthy, John 628
McCarthy, John D. 856
McCarthy, Timothy 453
McCarty, Charles 470, 481, 817
McCarty, John 95, 666, 856
McCarty, John D. 502
McCarty, Justin 474
McCarty, Lemuel 862
McCarty, Owen 539, 550, 561
McCaughtry, Alexander 114, 348
McCauley, Daniel 622
McCauley, James H. 812
McCauley, John 272
McCauley, Peter 379
McCauliff, John 215
McCauly, Thomas 231
McCawley, Charles 748
McCawley, Daniel 614
McClaim, Francis 805
McClain, John 697

McClanahan, Allen 791, 794
McClanahan, Enoch 791, 794
McClane, John 748
McClanin, James 128
McClannin, Isaac K. 252
McClarrin, George 361
McClatchy, William 525
McCleave, William 46, 57, 60,
  61, 68, 71, 76, 79, 87, 89, 324
McClellan, George B. 20, 33, 34,
  35, 40, 43, 46
McClellan, William 786
McClelland, Andrew P. 821
McClelland, Hamilton 804
McClelland, John 339
McClelland, Thomas 671
McClelland, William 397, 679
McClenahan, John 477
McClimans, James D. 95
McClintock, William 822
McCloud, Donald 290
McCloud, John 481, 812
McCloud, Slathiel 817
McClure, George 150
McClure, Henry 145
McClure, Samuel 561, 573
McClure, William 579
McCluskey, John 579
McCoach, William 474
McCollum, George E. 817
McCanaughy, William 361
McConigal, Robert 879
McConihe, George 614, 648
McConkev, Milton 878
McConkey, Harvey 670
McConkey, Harvey M. 121
McConkey, Hugh B. 786
McConkey, Milton 714
McConnell, James 215, 277
McConnell, John 531
McConville, John 163
McCool, Richard H. 757
McCord, Isaac 583
McCord, William H. 227
McCorea, James 631
McCormack, Edward 110
McCormack, John 576, 740, 783
McCormack, Michael 573
McCormack, William 775
McCormic, Charles 524, 576

McCormic, Thomas 568
McCormick, Charles 588, 804
McCormick, James 348, 354, 387, 539
McCormick, John 374, 878
McCormick, Joseph 813
McCormick, Thomas 264
McCormick, William 239
McCormick, William B. 346
McCorney, Peter 281
McCouliff, John 120
McCourt, Michael 744
McCoy, Alexander 178, 780, 879
McCoy, Alonzo A. P. V. 281, 295
McCoy, Daney 666
McCoy, Daniel 634
McCoy, Francis 641
McCoy, Harrison 634
McCoy, Henry C. 206, 550, 561
McCoy, Hiram C. 602, 776
McCoy, Hugh 641, 666
McCoy, James H. 845
McCoy, John G. 786
McCoy, Michael 634
McCoy, Nelson A. 778
McCoy, Robert 568
McCoy, Robert F. 573, 579
McCoy, William 165, 227
McCracken, S. 828
McCracken, Samuel H. 837
McCrea, James 606
McCready, Henry C. 502
McCreary, Alexander 711
McCreary, Marion 252
McCreery, Alexander 404
McCrellis, Albert B. 761
McCrimmon, John W. 734
McCrindle, James 821
McCue, James 179, 206
McCue, James P. 202
McCue, Martin 780
McCue, Patrick 657
McCue, Patrick W. 231
McCuistion, Robert M. 348, 370, 390
McCuistion, Thomas J. 348
McCulloch, John 697
McCulloch, William F. 206
McCullock, John 394
McCullock, Thornton B. 438

McCullough, Charles 744
McCullough, John 566
McCullough, John H. 878
McCully, Emery H. 618
McCumber, William 231
McCumming, Robert 791
McCune, Bernard 140
McCune, John 239
McCurdy, Albert M. 652
McCurran, Patrick 290
McDade, Martin 140
McDaniel, James 461
McDaniel, James R. 834
McDaniel, Wm. H. 837
McDaniels, Benjamin F. 677
McDermit, Charles 196, 293
McDermitt, Peter 140
McDermott, Charles C. 625
McDermott, George 327, 379
McDermott, Michael 589, 592
McDermott, Michael J. 757
McDermott, Peter 137, 154
McDermott, Peter W. 348
McDermott, William 281
McDermott, William P. 336, 812
McDonald, Bryan 785
McDonald, Calvin 748
McDonald, Duncan T. 746
McDonald, Edward 154, 160, 406, 684
McDonald, Felix 222
McDonald, George 441, 531, 862
McDonald, George R. 200, 257, 267
McDonald, Harry A. 179, 264, 290, 561
McDonald, Henry A. 198
McDonald, James 588, 862
McDonald, John 99, 123, 128, 438, 474, 502, 522, 531, 539, 579, 768, 780
McDonald, John B. 794
McDonald, Joseph 488, 539, 573
McDonald, Julian S. 693
McDonald, Reynold 701
McDonald, Thomas 740
McDonald, Walter 740
McDonald, William 344, 754
McDonald, William H. 816
McDonnell, Francis 502

McDonnell, James 804
McDonnell, John F. 231
McDonnell, John W. 820
McDonough, Michael 740
McDonough, Philip 227
McDonough, William 206
McDougal, Capt. 16
McDougal, Daniel 866
McDougall, Donald 739
McDougall, Frederick 433
McDougall, Jackson A. 95
McDougall, James 502, 812
McDowell, Maj. Gen. 430
McDowell, Andrew J. 660
McDowell, Isaac W. 614
McDowell, John 628
McDowell, Thomas C. 794
McEachem, Hugh 588
McElhanon, Hugh B. 128
McElhose, Thomas 397, 697
McElroy, John 652, 714
McElroy, Stephen C. 339, 386
McElroy, Wm. L. 239
McElroy, Wilson 801
McElwee, John 457, 744
McEnany, Thomas 730
McEneany, Patrick 121
McEnerney, Edward 666
McEnneny, Patrick 105
McEnturff, Columbus 660
McEwen, Dougal 239
McEwen, Warren L. 859
McFadden, Abner W. 614
McFadden, Alexander 453
McFadden, John 531
McFadden, Moses H. 488
McFadin, Benjamin 740
McFall, William 769
McFarland, Alexander 453
McFarland, Andrew J. 150
McFarland, George A. 706
McFarland, George P. 879
McFarland, George W. 481
McFarland, John B. 737
McFarland, Robert 461
McFarland, Thomas 866
McFarlin, Andrew B. 794
McFarlin, James F. 206
McGann, James 128
McGannon, Darby A. 706

McGar, James 588
McGarey, Ambrose 666
McGarey, Thomas 655
McGarry, Edward 18-19, 168,
    172-73, 175-77, 180-81, 196,
    508-9
McGarvey, John 481
McGarvey, Thomas 461, 754
McGeary, George P. 878
McGee, Arthur 737
McGee, James 397, 688, 862
McGee, John 370
McGee, William 348
McGehn, Marion 272
McGiff, James 614
McGill, Neal B. 531, 581
McGill, William 387
McGilveray, John M. 198, 226
McGilvery, John 298
McGinley, Theodore B. 160
McGinnis, Bernard 438
McGinnis, Cornelius 434
McGinnis, Frank 121, 215
McGinnis, John C. 387
McGinnis, Michael 140, 150
McGinnis, Patrick 140
McGinniss, John C. 677, 693
McGivney, Alexander 152
McGloin, James 734
McGoldrick, Thomas 95
McGonagal 179
McGonagle, Joseph B. 387
McGonigal, Joseph B. 339
McGonigal, Robert 780
McGonigal, William 140
McGonigle, Eli 248
McGonigle, John 300, 573, 706
McGorran, William 206
McGoven, Thomas 474
McGovern, James 550, 561
McGowan, Abraham 573
McGowan, Alexander B. 367, 726,
    738
McGowan, Daniel 401, 411, 684
McGowan, George 453, 485, 489,
    648
McGowan, Henry 801
McGowan, James 663
McGowan, William 878
McGrade, Albert 264

McGrath, Daniel 342
McGrath, James 481, 635, 691, 748, 878
McGrath, Patrick 152, 772
McGrath, William 812
McGraw, Hugh 740
McGreer, John 248
McGreevy, Edward 666
McGreevy, Patrick 754
McGregor, Archibald 361, 387
McGregor, Hugh 734
McGregor, William H. 769
McGrew, Finley A. 215
McGrindley, John 834
McGuffy, James 281
McGuire, Arthur 859
McGuire, Edward 300
McGuire, Francis D. 105
McGuire, George 846
McGuire, Horatio N. 583
McGuire, James 399, 687, 757
McGuire, John 592, 641
McGuire, Joseph 688
McGuire, Patrick 748
McGuire, Thomas 761
McGuire, William H. 115
McGuirk, John 778
McGurvey, Thomas 878
McHale, Luke 453
McHale, Ulrick S. 285, 525
McHenry, James P. 339, 387
McHenry, M. 660
McHirron, Henry 525
McHoey, Peter 726
McHugh, Andrew 716
McHugh, James 555, 571, 734, 745
McIlray, Capt. 82
McIlroy, Robert H. 122
McIlvain, Alden 688
McIlvain, Alden S. 401, 677, 715
McIlvanan, Andrew N. 110
McIlveran, Andrew N. 718
McInarney, Patrick 688
McIng, James 353
McInteer, Edward F. 801
McIntire, Donald 579
McIntire, Francis 502
McIntire, John 375
McIntire, John A. 807
McIntire, Peter 759

McIntosh, Isaac R. 856
McIntosh, James 150
McIntyre, Archibald 406, 711
McIntyre, James 474, 622
McIntyre, John 461
McIntyre, John A. 799
McIntyre, Robert G. 260
McJones, Eli 375
McKane, William 290
McKay, Duncan 751
McKay, James 820
McKay, John L. 448
McKay, Joseph 433
McKay, Rudolph 481
McKay, William 806
McKean, Robert 761
McKean, William S. 786
McKeber, James 879
McKee, Albert 145, 879
McKee, David B. 645
McKee, Emory C. 145
McKee, Henry N. 145
McKee, Michael 445, 489
McKee, Samuel 846
McKee, Wm. H. 676
McKee, William H.H. 258
McKeeber, James 606, 641
McKeefry, David 772
McKeen, Benjamin F. 281
McKeever, Craig 666
McKeever, Edward 769
McKeever, Michael 474
McKelvey, John W. 806
McKeman, James 614
McKendry, Archibald 854
McKenley, Daniel 215
McKenley, Peter 124
McKenley, Richard W. 561
McKenna, Francis 218, 250
McKenna, James C. 222
McKenna, Michael 251
McKenna, Thomas 655
McKenna, William 239
McKennan, Daniel 264
McKenny, James 809
McKenny, John W. 866
McKenzie, Alexander 165, 561
McKenzie, Francis M. 561
McKenzie, John 445
McKenzie, Joseph 751

McKenzie, Thomas C. 166
McKeon, Barney 666
McKeon, Bernhard 474
McKey, Robert 239
McKillipps, Alonzo 684
McKim, John 397
McKinley, Joseph W. 606, 635
McKinley, Thomas C. 841
McKinley, William H. 693
McKinn, John 697
McKinney, Ivory 701
McKinney, William D. 606
McKinney, William R. 248
McKinnon, John 843
McKinnon, Malcolm A. 136
McKinstry, Levi A. 234
McKnight, John 622
McKnow, J. 179
McKown, Isaac D. 372
McKown, James 276
McLain, David 689
McLane, Bernard 879
McLane, John 285
McLane, Louis 35
McLane, Neil 817
McLean, Alfred A. 866
McLean, Allen 730
McLean, Daniel 172, 175-76, 177, 178, 257
McLeary, Samuel 730
McLellan, Josiah T. 160, 166
McLelland, Albert 255
McLeod, Alexander 438
McLeod, Samuel 778
McLaughlin, Sgt. 181
McLaughlin, Charles 371, 824
McLaughlin, Daniel 231
McLaughlin, Henry M. 837
McLaughlin, John 406, 496, 550, 679
McLaughlin, John B. 610, 618
McLaughlin, Moses A. 181-82, 225
McLaughlin, William 467
McLoud, Malcolm 745
McLoughlin, M. J. 666
McMahon, Barnard 290
McMahon, Bernard J. 367
McMahon, Hugh 761
McMahon, James 757
McMahon, Jhew 840

McMahon, John 137, 438, 481
McMahon, Lawrence 834
McMahon, Martin 531, 579
McMahon, Michael 614, 761
McMahon, Patrick 657, 748
McMahon, Thomas 115, 411, 715
McMahon, William B. 592
McMalcolm, James 837
McMann, John 531
McMann, William 843
McManns, John 90, 215
McManus, Michael 795
McMartin, John 780
McMichael, John 614, 648
McMillan, James 693
McMillan, Mauly 878
McMillan, Nelson 215
McMillan, William J. 95
McMillen, John 822
McMillen, Robert 264
McMiller, Alfred 878
McMillin, Alfred 679
McMinds, Ira 780
McMinn, William H. 543, 570
McMullen, Alexander 573
McMullen, William 51, 66, 335, 346
McMullin, Rankin 644
McMunn, George S. 679
McMurray, David 128
McMurray, John R. 660
McMurry, Francis A. 775
McMurtry, Innins 635
McMurtry, James T. 227
McMurtry, Julius T. 641
McNabb, William 748
McNally, James 467, 737
McNamara, James T. 115, 354
McNamara, John 100, 115
McNamara, Michael 568, 878
McNanny, Owen 648
McNarry, Owen 878
McNaughton, James 95
McNeal, Gain 235
McNeal, Montreville 502
McNeal, Webster 223
McNeil, Alonzo 339
McNeil, John T. 222
McNeil, Lachlin 614
McNeil, William H. 856

McNeile, William   754
McNeill, John T.   300
McNeill, William   790
McNeish, Thomas   453, 499
McNelly, David   525, 554
McNelly, John W.   660
McNichol, Daniel   778
McNichols, Daniel   474
McNiel, Daniel   140
McNulty, James M.   67, 335
McNulty, R. M.   179
McNulty, Roger   201
McNulty, William C.   718
McNutt, James F.   769
McNutt, Robert J.   711
McPartland, Andrew   339, 388
McPheeters, David   223
McPherson, George   496
McPherson, Jackson   628
McPherson, James   150, 568
McPhilimy, Thomas   239
McPhilipps, Thomas   140
McQuade, James   467
McQuade, John   210, 879
McQuade, Patrick   795
McQuade, Paul   635
McQuade, Thomas   814
McQuaid, John   878
McQueen, William A.   590, 878
McQuillan, John A.   815
McQuillin, William   666
McQuynn, John   239
McRea, George W.   776
McReynolds, Daniel   281, 878
McShaffer, John   701, 712
McSorley, Hugh   579
McTarnahan, Samuel   268
McTernan, John   843
McThomas, Robert   780
McWayne, Chandler   776
McWilliams, Barton   689
McWilliams, Borden   754
McWilliams, Isaiah   223
McWilliams, James   628
McWilliams, Manly   817
McWorther, John M.   206
Meacham, William   453
Mead, Charles O.   628
Mead, Gaylord K.   284
Mead, John V.   679

Mead, William   730
Mead, William C.   82, 122
Meader, Charles B.   851-52, 869
Meador, Reuben N.   684
Meagher, John   496, 502
Mealey, Martin   215
Meanor, Robert   693, 879
Means, Bernard   311
Means, Timothy   313
Mears, Otto   371
Medina, Lorenzo   550, 588
Medina, Theodore   550, 588
Medley, John C.   736
Meehan, Patrick   758
Meek, Abram L.   244
Meek, Arthur J.   375
Meek, Samuel C.   365, 392
Meeks, John   648
Meeney, Thomas   145
Megerle, Louis H.   244
Megerley, Frederick   550, 573
Megerly, Ernest P.   448
Megginis, Johnston   502
Mehan, James   606
Mehl, Peter   550
Mehrand, Louis   313
Meirer, José   732
Meier, William   734
Meigham, Henry   397, 689, 879
Meincke, Adolph W.   734
Meinking, Frederick   786
Meis, Joseph   453
Meister, John   105
Meister, Robert   496, 655
Meizle, William   453, 481
Mejia, Braulio   401, 715
Mejia, Brulio   411
Melaney, Edward   641
Melcalf, Jabez S.   783
Melhouse, Theophilus   357
Mellen, Henry B.   218
Mellert, Lewis   791
Mellish, Walter   718
Mellon, Maj.   187
Mellon, Edward   453
Mellville, James   239
Meloy, John H.   348
Melro, Walter F.   625
Melrose, Alfred   635
Melton, Chapel   406, 684

Melville, Frank 140
Melville, George 730
Melville, William 231
Melvin, Adveno L. 375
Melvine, Edward R. 115, 712
Mendell, Henry B. 660
Mendes, Besenta 313
Mendibles, Angel 319
Mendibles, Trinidad 319
Menine, Jean Baptiste 693
Menio, Charles 453
Mensinger, Henry 474
Menter, Almon 300
Menter, Martin V. B. 300
Menter, William D. 300
Mentro, Susafe 313
Mentz, Herman 842
Meranda, Pedro 311
Merce, Charles 248
Mercer, Francis 339, 388
Mercer, John 160
Merchant, Lt. Col. 33
Merchant, Abraham 255, 878
Merchant, William 255
Merickle, Bernard 461
Meriwin, Daniel E. 660
Merling, John 342
Merrem, August 223
Merriam, Adney D. 234
Merriam, John L. 156, 239, 244
Merriam, Jonathan 856
Merrick, Gideon 655
Merrick, Murphy 264
Merrill, Augustus M. 879
Merrill, Benjamin F. 239
Merrill, Daniel E. 859
Merrill, George E. 693
Merrill, George O. 791
Merrill, Giles 787
Merrill, Griffin S. 211, 215
Merrill, Irwin S. 248
Merrill, Isaac N. 534, 555
Merrill, Joseph C. 522
Merrill, Leander 210
Merrill, Theodore 815
Merritt, Edward S. 140
Merritt, Gilbert R. 869
Merritt, Sam. 28
Merry, Thomas H. 866
Merts, Gustave E. 496

Mesa, Antonio 309
Mesenheimer, Manson A. 211
Messenger, Hiram A. 764, 779
Metcalf, Henry S. 345
Metcalf, Jabez S. 666
Metcalf, John J. 105, 353
Metcalf, Sheron 655
Metcalf, Warren T. 642
Mettkoff, Barnard 550, 561
Metzger, Elias B. 115
Metzger, Martin 806
Metzger, Theophilus 365, 392
Metzradt, Ferdinand 198, 812
Mewhinney, Hugh 201, 225
Mewhinney, John 226
Meyer, Anton F. 539
Meyer, August 758
Meyer, Conrad 474
Meyer, William 438
Meyerhoff, Frederick 496
Meyers, Amos P. 648
Meyers, Amos T. 105
Meyers, Arthur H. 606
Meyers, Geo. L. 223
Meyers, John 846
Meyers, John H. 644
Meyers, Louis A. 550
Meyers, Peter 748
Meyers, William 539, 786
Meyers, William H. 846
Michael, Dettlief F. 264
Michael, William 806
Michaelis, Frederick 411
Michallis, Fritz 401
Michan, John 791, 795
Michealis, Frederick 718
Michell, John 474
Michels, Theodore 812
Michely, Bertoni 474
Michner, Jesse 272
Middaugh, Nelson 878
Middaugh, Nelson D. 272
Middlesworth, Peter Van 228
Middleton, John J. 568
Middleton, John M. 148
Middleton, Thomas 829, 832, 839
Mieure, George F. 816
Miggitt, William B. 730
Mihay, William 859

Milaney, Edward 128
Miles, Charles S. 354
Miles, George S. 415, 704
Miles, Henry P. 869
Milford, Edmund N. 561
Milhahan, Frederick 264
Millan, Thomas R. 711
Millard, William H. 539
Miller, Abraham 614, 829, 839
Miller, Alpha P. 206
Miller, Amoa 264
Miller, Andrew 376
Miller, Anton 755
Miller, Archibald 339
Miller, Augustus B. 783
Miller, Caleb B. 115
Miller, Charles 105, 115, 231, 401,
   411, 457, 496, 630, 679, 693,
   781, 879
Miller, Charles A. 353, 878
Miller, Charles G. 843
Miller, Chauncey 540
Miller, Christian 568
Miller, Clemens 745
Miller, Curtis C. 272
Miller, David 628
Miller, Edward 206
Miller, Elijah 540, 695
Miller, Francis 464, 531
Miller, Fred 502
Miller, George 812
Miller, George F. 231
Miller, Henry 123, 453, 481, 622,
   666, 680, 812, 834
Miller, Henry A. 155, 684
Miller, Henry B. 196
Miller, Henry R. 197, 198, 243,
   250
Miller, Jacob 837
Miller, James 150
Miller, James M. 859
Miller, James P. 824
Miller, John 162, 339, 379, 386,
   579, 628, 706, 804, 862
Miller, John A. 300
Miller, John F. 272
Miller, John H. 145, 730
Miller, John P. 730
Miller, Joseph 145, 445, 461, 579,
   866

Miller, Joseph A. 748
Miller, Julius 496
Miller, Lorenzo D. 758
Miller, Louis 711, 758
Miller, Louis W. 166
Miller, Miles D. 502
Miller, Mority 767
Miller, Nicholas 481
Miller, Nicholas C. 846
Miller, Reuben 148, 300
Miller, Robert 531, 561
Miller, Samuel 821
Miller, Samuel D. 357
Miller, Thomas 402, 453, 561
Miller, William 467, 496
Miller, William H. 754
Miller, William M. 614
Miller, Wm. P. 837
Millet, Edgar A. 531
Millett, Densmore 231
Millican, William W. 859
Milligan, Mr. 59
Milligan, John 118
Milligan, John C. 105
Milligan, John H. 540, 550, 561,
   568
Milliman, Silas 726
Milliman, Silas W. 742
Millington, Sherman 809
Mills, Alexander 187, 248
Mills, D.O. 28
Mills, David O. 361
Mills, Edward 255
Mills, Elcanie 614
Mills, George 745, 878
Mills, John 540, 550, 761
Mills, Samuel 838
Mills, Thomas 206
Mills, William G. 438, 769, 783
Mills, Wm. H. 290
Millspaugh, Charles W. 255
Milne, James 95, 140
Milner, Charles 231
Milner, Thomas 740
Milnes, John L. 820
Miltz, Frederick 734, 879
Minard, Alexander 786
Mincke, John 264, 879
Miner, Albert J. 766, 779
Miner, Edwin 562

Personal Name Index

Miner, Smith 609
Minicke, John 481
Minnett, George 730
Minnich, Thomas 402
Minnick, Marvin 631
Minnick, Thomas 689
Minor, Horner 775
Minott, James 248, 769
Minser, Henry 540
Minster, William S. 118
Minton, James 748
Minton, William P. 372
Mirando, Manuel 309
Mirick, Gideon 706
Misener, Isaac N. 638
Misenheimer, William 844
Mitchel, Henry L. 115
Mitchell A. 179
Mitchell, Arthur 179, 281
Mitchell, Charles 804
Mitchell, Charles T. 140
Mitchell, David 789
Mitchell, David P. 657
Mitchell, Delos 281
Mitchell, Digby 745
Mitchell, Francis S. 324, 341, 350
Mitchell, H. S. 357
Mitchell, Henry 445
Mitchell, Henry L. 407, 684
Mitchell, John 290, 562, 822
Mitchell, John E. 758
Mitchell, John T. 859
Mitchell, Lyman E. 695
Mitchell, Myron H. 255
Mitchell, Roland T. 361
Mitchell, Thomas 622
Mitchell, Titus B. 210
Mitchell, William 737
Mitchell, William C. 787
Mitchell, William D. 832
Mitchell, William M. 276, 445, 531, 660
Mitchell, William R. 754
Mitchell, William S. 845
Mitcheltree, Josiah 618
Mitts, Clinton 778
Mix, Hiram 843
Mix, James M. 793
Moate, George 502
Mobley, Fanning P. 223

Moe, Charles N. 769, 783
Moer, Charles B. 742
Moga, Dolph 313
Mohan, James 726, 739
Mohrman, Frederick 655
Moir, William W. 791
Moldt, Peter J. 568
Molina, Ramon 775
Molle, John 134
Molloy, John C. 730
Molloy, Patrick 758
Molloy, Pinkney C. 606
Molloy, William 711
Molton, George 145
Molumby, Michael 264
Monahan, Michael F. 474
Monbilly, Gustavus 660
Monday, James 804
Monea, Charles 248
Mongélaz, Charles 772
Monholland, John 484
Moniear, William C. 614, 878
Monigan, Lawrence 628
Monihon, James D. 359
Monks, Michael M. 601, 663
Monroe, George 348
Monroe, James 128, 461, 489, 496, 869
Monroe, John 862
Monroe, Oscar 115
Monroe, William 562
Montague 28
Montague, Giles E. 638
Montague, James 272
Montgomery, Callin 642
Montgomery, Charles 845
Montgomery, Clark 701
Montgomery, Henry C. 638
Montgomery, J. B. 17
Montgomery, James 178, 206, 255
Montgomery, James S. 600, 642
Montgomery, John 215
Montgomery, John H. 824
Montgomery, Philip H. 223
Montgomery, Samuel 806
Montgomery, William 155, 300
Montgomery, Wm. H. 463
Montlambert, Joseph H. 737
Moody, Charles M. 540
Moody, John 502

Moon, Pvt. 186
Moon, Daniel W. 809
Moon, Hiram B. 775
Moon, John 697
Mooney, James 438, 562, 483
Mooney, John 666
Mooney, Joseph 140, 166
Moonlight, Col. 184
Moor, Patrick 265
Moore, Adam W. 265
Moore, Alexander 568
Moore, Alexander 481
Moore, Alfred N. 660
Moore, Andrew 573
Moore, Andrew D. 281
Moore, Benjamin 463, 660
Moore, Charles 223, 290, 438, 474, 693, 879
Moore, Charles D. 778
Moore, Charles Wisley 740
Moore, David J. 843
Moore, Delevan 859
Moore, Edward 817
Moore, George 726, 783
Moore, George C. 445
Moore, George W. 290, 397, 697
Moore, Hugh 375
Moore, Isaac S. 244
Moore, James E. 562
Moore, James W. 642
Moore, Jeremiah B. 522, 534
Moore, John 281, 300, 438, 540, 693, 866
Moore, John A. 701
Moore, Joseph 255, 740
Moore, Joseph A. 162, 614, 622
Moore, Leo 291
Moore, Louis B. 660
Moore, Louis W. 737
Moore, Mahlon E. 166
Moore, Martin 838
Moore, Milton G. 657
Moore, Peter W. 751
Moore, Robert 817
Moore, Samuel 128
Moore, Stephen 357, 388, 407
Moore, Sydney L. 680
Moore, Thomas 367, 795, 838
Moore, Treadwell 18, 19, 56
Moore, Wesley M. 215

Moore, William 336, 376, 496, 815, 824
Moore, William G. 822
Moore, William H. 397, 697, 859
Moore, William S. 526, 571
Moore, Zachary 481
Moorehead, Samuel C. 782
Moores, William B. 215
Moraga, Augustine 313
Moralles, José 145
Moran, Alexander 502
Moran, James 740
Moran, John 281, 345, 371, 379, 388, 531, 562, 588, 614
Moran, Joseph 628
Morato, Charles 812
Moraz, George G. 793
Morden, Dominic 453
More, John L. 789
Morean, Carlos 316
Morehead, Benjamin 339, 388
Morehead, Samuel C. 481
Morehouse, Charles F. 432, 477, 492
Morehouse, Edward N. 407, 684
Moreland, William 489
Morell, David 531
Moreno, Antonio 313
Moreno, Jesus Maria 319
Moreno, José 316
Moreno, José Maria 319
Moreno, Pio 316
Morey, Cyrus 231
Morey, Rennsalaer D. 140, 145,
Morgan 28
Morgan, Alonzo 248
Morgan, David 105, 110, 339
Morgan, Evan 231
Morgan, Fred A. 470
Morgan, Frederick A. 432, 484, 712
Morgan, George B. 745
Morgan, Green 761
Morgan, Henry 606
Morgan, John 240
Morgan, John S. 801
Morgan, Martin 150
Morgan, Nelson 281
Morgan, Patrick 540, 568
Morgan, Peter 573

Personal Name Index

Morgan, Thomas 622
Morgan, William 166
Morgan, William B. 701
Moriarity, James J. 614, 648
Morin, Alexander 531
Morin, Peter 745
Moritz, Peter W. 155
Morley, George 128
Morn, James 801
Mornington, Charles W. 215
Mornwig, George 755
Morrill, Augustus M. 791
Morrill, David 363, 392
Morrill, Joseph C. 534, 589
Morris, Charles 648
Morris, Frank 453
Morris, George W. 105, 121
Morris, Henry 461
Morris, Hiram 540
Morris, Isador 570
Morris, Isadore 531
Morris, James 240, 272
Morris, John 348, 719, 805
Morris, John B. 606
Morris, John F. 291
Morris, Joseph 772, 869
Morris, Peter 166
Morris, Richard 820
Morris, Samuel N. 869
Morris, William 859
Morris, Wm. D. 265
Morris, Wm. Goveneur 197, 267
Morris, William H. 496
Morrisey, George 628
Morrissey, John 248
Morrison, Alonzo P. 697
Morrison, Angus 371
Morrison, Benjamin F. 754
Morrison, Edwin L. 95
Morrison, George 751
Morrison, Howard 128
Morrison, James 438, 531, 666
Morrison, James H. 361
Morrison, Joseph 339, 388
Morrison, Matthew 719
Morrison, Thomas 255
Morrison, Walter 859
Morrison, William S. 790
Morrow, David 140
Morrow, Francis M. 628

Morrow, Jacob 415
Morrow, William F. 786
Morse, Abner 526, 550, 555, 571
Morse, Benjamin W. 775
Morse, Charles F. 862
Morse, Frank A. 684
Morse, George W. 226, 291
Morse, Hiram G. 758
Morse, William S. 145
Morstadt, Francis A. 281, 562
Mortimer, Harry W. 859
Mortino, Miguel 489
Morton, Alfred 198, 243, 491, 498, 766
Morton, Andrew 453, 562, 579
Morton, Charles A. 779
Morton, Charles B. 219
Morton, Daniel R. 562
Morton, Edward J. 350
Morton, Henry 773
Morton, John 666
Morton, Richard 846
Morvelius, Jacob 778
Moses, Andrew J. 155, 272
Moses, Harrison 689
Moss, Edward 206, 291
Moss, Harrison A. 666
Moss, John 741
Moss, Thomas 693
Moss, Thomas H. 795
Moss, Wiley 231
Mossman, Judson A. 859
Mota, José 313
Mott, Barney 804
Mott, John 795
Moulthrop, William A. 822
Moulton, Harvey 817
Moulton, Theodore 502
Mouze, Joseph H. 474
Mowery, David A. 780
Mowery, Henry 812
Mowry, Sylvester 52, 53, 54, 55, 481
Moxant, Charles 313
Moxim, Henry W. 467, 496
Moylan, James 433, 445, 485
Moynier, Edward 614
Mucke, Francis 812
Mudgett, William H. 95
Muir, Henry 272

Muirhead, James 453, 481
Mulcahy, James 638
Mulcahy, Matthew 291
Mulchaey, Edward P. 467
Muldoon, Patrick 775
Muldowney, Patrick 503
Muleay, Michael A. 502
Mulhare, Frank W. 622
Mullan, John 4, 36
Mullay, James 489
Mullen, Alonzo C. 366
Mullen, Henry 804
Mullen, James 211
Mullen, John 438
Mullen, John M. 95
Mullen, Joseph 223, 272
Mullen, Owen 464
Mullen, William 748
Muller, Adolph 715
Muller, Charles 255
Müller, Fred 109
Muller, Lewis 824
Muller, Martin 741
Mulligan, John F. 642
Mulligan, Michael 240, 754
Mullis, Richard 496
Mulloy, Dominick 438
Mulloy, John 291
Mulloy, Thomas 438
Mulnier, John 678
Multy, John 503
Mulvahill, John 846
Munday, Felix 625, 628
Munday, Henry 525
Munday, James 134
Munday, Patrick 630, 662
Munday, Thomas H. 531, 573
Mundt, Frank W. 276
Munger, Lewis 852, 862
Munholland, Robert 496
Munro, Donald 693
Munshower, Nicholas 568
Munson, Francis M. 776
Murchison, Farquhar 730
Murdock, Robert 824
Murdock, Walter 474
Murphy 28
Murphy, Daniel R. 568
Murphy, Dennis 489, 648
Murphy, Edward 128, 481, 622, 822

Murphy, Edward K. 792
Murphy, Jacob 758
Murphy, James 111, 272, 573, 693
Murphy, James M. 701, 878
Murphy, John 223, 272, 291, 375,
    415, 438, 445, 467, 489, 496,
    503, 554, 562, 573, 628, 666,
    706, 711, 755, 804, 817, 834
Murphy, John H. 461
Murphy, John J. 767
Murphy, Joshua C. 185, 272
Murphy, Matthew P. 642
Murphy, Michael 285, 635, 745
Murphy, Nicholas 345, 392
Murphy, Patrick 379, 461, 467
Murphy, Richard 492
Murphy, Richard A. 210
Murphy, Thomas 140, 265
Murphy, Thomas J. B. 592
Murphy, Timothy 489
Murphy, Timothy B. 453
Murphy, Victor 145
Murphy, William 467
Murray, Charles M. 275
Murray, Charles W. 393
Murray, George 642
Murray, James 95, 160
Murray, James M. 660
Murray, John 145, 272, 481, 492,
    614, 730
Murray, John A. 817
Murray, John N. 648
Murray, Matthew 579
Murray, Michael 95, 711
Murray, Robert 550, 573
Murray, Samuel M. 645
Murray, Thomas 489, 769
Murray, Timothy 666
Murray, Wm. H. 223
Murrh, Mathias 846
Murrow, James 821
Murry, Emery D. 300
Murry, John 846
Murry, John H. 622
Murry, Nelson H. 272
Murry, William 453
Murta, William 741
Murts, Michael 730
Muspratt, George 407, 711
Musselman, Alexander 166

Musser, Christian 736
Musser, John 736
Musson, Frank 474, 562
Mussy, Antoine 795
Mutschler, Henry 461
Myer, Charles 622
Myer, John 730, 815, 878
Myer, Thomas O. 366
Myers, A.H. 335
Myers, Anthony 568, 878
Myers, Augustus A. 255
Myers, Charles F. 281
Myers, Christian 301, 568
Myers, Fidel 281
Myers, George 461
Myers, Henry 353
Myers, Henry A. 345, 393
Myers, Jacob 719
Myers, John 273, 301, 397, 411, 719
Myers, John D. 553-54, 562
Myers, John P. 131
Myers, John S. 554, 810
Myers, Leopold 550, 562, 579
Myers, Louis 658
Myers, Louis A. 588
Myers, Peter 255
Myers, Randolph P. 859
Myers, Reed W. 121
Myers, Silas 150
Myers, Thomas O. 366
Myers, William 523, 566, 772
Myers, William M. 95

N

Nabor, Adam 635
Nagel, Thomas H. 215
Nagle, Charles J.H. 787
Nagle, Ferdinand F. 806
Nagle, John 822
Nagle, Maurice 485
Nail, Samuel D. 481
Namate, Louis 313
Naper, Joy H. 267
Napier, John 467
Nare, Soloman 793
Narry, Richard 749
Nason, Almon W. 821
Nason, Christopher C. 614

Nason, Henry 879
Nason, Horace 481
Nason, Robert P. 656, 660
Naughton, Mark 843
Nauls, George 496, 614
Naval, Richard 155
Navare, Samuel 273
Naylor, Edwin 606
Neal, John 348, 614
Neal, John J. 110
Neal, Johnson W. 95
Neal, Josiah E. 294
Neal, Samuel B. 379
Neale, Patrick 454, 481
Neall, Henry B. 454, 482
Nease, John C. 832
Neaux, Henry 489
Neel, John J. 879
Neeley, Andrew J. 693
Neenan, Edward 751
Neff, William 223
Nefin, Martin P. 824
Neibuhr, Otto 879
Neibur, Henry H. 461
Neil, John 361, 642
Neil, William C. 361
Neinstadt, Frederic 769
Nelligan, Maurice 741
Nellis, Abram R. 236
Nellis, E. 856
Nelson, Charles 535, 642, 671, 715
Nelson, D.S. 845
Nelson, David W. 134
Nelson, H. 856
Nelson, James 804
Nelson, John 301, 569, 751
Nelson, John M. 155
Nelson, Lawrence H. 550
Nelson, Michael J. 648
Nelson, Ole 780
Nelson, Peter 313, 454
Nelson, Rufus H. 281
Nelson, Samuel 134
Nelson, Snyder 879
Nelson, Thomas 730
Nelson, Wellington 366
Nelson, William 336, 359
Nepley, Peter C. 105
Nesbit, William G. 95

Nesmith, George W. 678
Neugent, John 474
Nevarre, John 607
Newbill, Benjamin H. 628
Newbill, Jesse S. 628
Newbill, William L. 628
Newcomb, James 240
Newell, Franklin W. 248
Newell, John B. 244
Newell, Joseph J. J. 311
Newell, Nathan 291
Newell, Silas 115, 397, 701
Newes, Nathaniel F. 579
Newhall 28
Newhall, Samuel W. 522, 573
Newhouse, Samuel L. 273
Newland, Aquilla M. 769
Newland, Aquillon M. 879
Newland, Joel F. 145
Newman, Cpl. 75
Newman, David M. 100, 879
Newman, Edward 407, 711
Newman, Henry 503, 531
Newman, Jacob S. 607, 783
Newman, Miles 801
Newman, Schoolby D. 820
Newsham, Robert V. 699
Newton, George W. 531, 573, 579
Newton, Jackson 775
Newton, James 240
Newton, John 482
Newton, John B. 28
Newton, Loren 166
Newton, William G. 806
Ney, Francis E. 265
Niblock, William 461
Nichol, William 339, 879
Nicholas, Paul 614
Nicholas, William 734
Nichols, Alexander C. 256
Nichols, Charles P. 81, 108-9, 122
Nichols, Nathan T. 792, 795
Nichols, William 573, 869
Nichols, William F. 448
Nicholson, Alexander 715
Nicholson, Andrew 769
Nicholson, James 366
Nicholson, Peter 467
Nicholus, Paul 635
Nickerson, Charles J. 349

Nickerson, Joseph B. 100
Nicklas, John 838
Nicol, James 737
Nicolas, Antonio 734
Nikirk, Daniel 761
Niles, David H. 361
Nillsn, Ole 741
Nimez, Valentin 319
Ningart, John 684
Nininger, Andrew J. 737
Nipley, Peter C. 128
Nix, Frederick H. 812
Nixon, John 856
Nixon, Phineas A. 286
Nixon, William 635, 663, 693
Noah, John G. 734
Noble, Aaron 105
Noble, Aaron, Jr. 128
Noble, Franklin 526, 571
Noble, Herman 200, 234
Noble, John 399, 691
Noble, Samuel J. 775
Nobles, Alexander 845
Nolan, Frank 438
Nolan, James 482
Nolan, John 248, 607
Nolan, Joseph W. 815
Nolan, Thomas 482
Noland, Stephen 820
Nold, Raphael 445
Nolen, Patrick 642
Nolen, Timothy 235
Nolin, John 503
Nolin, Thomas C. 730
Noon, Francis 467
Noonan, Patrick 795
Noquier, John B. 128
Norcross, John C. 849, 857
Norcross, Joseph R. 499
Nordeck, Henry A. 363
Nordyke, Americus T. 206
Nordyke, Caleb 846
Norman, Andrew 445, 454
Norman, Frank 226
Norman, Henry 824
Norman, Saul 281, 291
Norris, George 684
Norris, George S. 153, 155
Norris, Henry H. 132
Norris, James 223

Personal Name Index

Norris, William 28, 281
North, Abram H. 137
North, Henry W. 461
Northcott, Joseph 635
Northcott, Joseph G. 231
Northrop, Lewis B. 820
Northup, Sherman A. 879
Northrup, Sherman M. 353
Norton, Alexander 231, 441
Norton, Alfred W. 157
Norton, Gustavus V. 776
Norton, Harvey 607, 635, 879
Norton, Isaac 628
Norton, James 397, 697
Norton, James M. 179, 265
Norton, John H. 706
Norton, Josiah P. 707
Norton, Michael 345, 375
Norton, Pryor F. 353
Norton, Thomas 550, 769
Norton, Washington 786, 879
Norton, William 666
Norton, William H. 368
Norville, Luderman L. 273
Norwell, Ludiman L. 223
Nottingham, Jerome 123, 215
Novothney, Ernst 445
Nower, Samuel J. 809
Nowlin, John 273
Noyes, Willard W. 265
Noyes, William H. 470, 498, 879
Nubuhr, Otto 445
Nudd, Albert E. 231
Nugent, Edward J. 635
Nugent, James 693
Nugent, William 357, 407, 415, 684
Numan, Morris 489
Nunan, Maurice 463, 496
Nunes, George A. 745
Nuny, John 879
Nutt, Henry W. 438
Nutt, Washington J. 407, 684
Nutt, Washington S. 357
Nutter, David P. 238
Nutting, Albert N. 778
Nuzlee, H. M. 28
Nye, Austin 467
Nye, Austine 445
Nye, George W. 817

Nye, J. W. 41, 849
Nye, Rhudolphus S. 655
Nystrom, Carl P. 474
Nystrom, Charles W. 866

O

Oakley, Daniel 667
Oaks, George W. 375
Oaks, John 656, 731, 735, 738
Oaks, Samuel M. 701
Oardena, Antonio 309
O'Bannon, Yelverton 357, 407, 685, 879
Oberheidt, Frederick 769
Obregue, Pedro 309
O'Brian, James 240
O'Brien 128
O'Brien, Bartley 223
O'Brien, Charles 327
O'Brien, Charles M. 366, 879
O'Brien, David 531, 579
O'Brien, George 340
O'Brien, George G. 843
O'Brien, George P. 91
O'Brien, Henry 265
O'Brien, Jacob 438
O'Brien, James 862
O'Brien, John 454, 562, 569, 607, 635, 739
O'Brien, John J. 776
O'Brien, Michael 178-79, 265, 447, 474, 492, 725, 786, 879
O'Brien, Thomas 489, 749
O'Brien, William 375, 879
O'Brine, John 734
Ocana, Francisco 319
Occampo, Camilo 319
Ockerson, Daniel J. 680
O'Connell, David W. 186, 215, 879
O'Connell, George John 415, 707
O'Connell, Jeremiah 134, 660
O'Connell, John 75, 730, 862
O'Conner, Daniel M. 817
O'Conner, John 105
O'Conner, Wm. H. 115
O'Connor, Bryan 734
O'Connor, George 579
O'Connor, John 231, 445, 468, 730, 738

O'Connor, Michael 155, 438, 635
O'Connor, Thomas 635, 879-80
O'Connor, Thomas M. 580
O'Connor, Timothy 792
O'Connor, William 105, 489
O'Dell, Thomas 635
Odle, Oscar 691
O'Donnel, William 607
O'Donnell, James 207, 301, 635
O'Donnell, James A. 607
O'Donnell, John 128, 223, 454, 879
O'Donnell, John H. 166, 371
O'Donnell, Joseph 719
O'Donnell, Michael 503
O'Donnell, Thomas 105
O'Donnell, William 648
O'Donoughue, Patrick 489
Oechaner, Andrew 232
O'Farrell, John 357, 407, 711
Ofida, Florencio 315
Ogburn, Samuel 131
Ogden, James 648
Ogden, R. L. 23
Ogden, Toleff 454
Ogelvie, Henry 313
O'Grady, Patrick 354, 403-4, 682
O'Halleron, John 407
O'Halloran, John 697
O'Hanley, Henry 667
O'Hara, William 140
O'Hare, John 817
O'Harren, John 489
O'Haver, John 824
O'Hearn, William J. 809
O'Herron, Michael 105
Ohrenshall, Ernest 503
O'Kasson, Hans 207, 291
O'Keefe, Michael 267
O'Keeffe, William 540, 580
Okey, George 660
O'Laughlin, John 454
Oldham, Jesse D. 822
Olds, Norman P. 134
Olds, William 345
Olin, George B. 496
Olinger, John D. 138
Oliot, Jean Baptiste 454
Oliphant, John E. 142, 147, 162
Olivas, Antonio 316, 879

Olivas, Blas 319
Olivas, Felipe 316
Olivas, Jose Victorino 316
Olivas, Pablo 316
Oliver, Charles 215, 715
Oliver, John 474
Oliver, William 379
Olivera, Santiago 316
Ollinger, John P. 215
Olliver, John 562
Olliver, William A. 267
Ollwick, Herman 562
Olmstead, George W. 232
Olmstead, James P. 763, 767, 880
Olmstead, Judson C. 789
Olmstead, Moses 155
Olmsted, Herbert 734
Olney, James N. 418-19, 431
O'Loughlin, John 489
Olson, Joseph 792
Olson, Thomas 749
Olvis, Daniel 845
Oman, John 667
Oman, Moroni 461
Oman, William 384, 403, 677
O'Mara, John 751
Omazta, Joseph 550, 569
O'Meara, Rody 131
O'Mera, Charles 461, 475, 503
Omerd, William H. 734
Ondan, Auguste 313
O'Neal, James 749
O'Neal, Martin 140
O'Neal, Thomas 240
O'Neil, Edward 128
O'Neil, John 628, 786, 879
O'Neil, John M. 196
O'Neil, Patrick 461
O'Neil, Samuel 769
O'Neil, Solomon H. 734
O'Neil, William 397, 689
O'Neill, Chas. 140
Orcutt, William 340
Ordaz, Vicente 315
Ordway, John H. 859
O'Reilly, Michael 602
Orellana, Nicolas 317
Orman, Van 172
Ormsbee, John M. 600, 615
Ormsby, Levi W. 772

Ormsby, William W. 772
Orne, Samuel A. 215, 357
Orona, Antonio 309
O'Rourke, Bernard 574, 825
Orr, Benjamin F. 240
Orr, George 482
Orr, James W. 281
Orr, John 240
Orr, William 106, 256
Orrens, William W. 137
Ortega, José Santos 780
Ortega, Mariano 309
Ortega, Vicente 317
Orton, Richard H. 4, 76-79, 81, 86, 130, 161
Osborn, Archibald P. 843
Osborn, Charles 407, 711
Osborn, Enoch 685
Osborn, Isaac N. 697
Osborn, John D. 628, 880
Osborn, Peter 562
Osburn, John C. 540, 562
Osgood, Charles G. 772
Osgood, Edward W. 106
Osgood, Hoser 240
O'Shaughnessy, Thomas 769
Osier, Charles 215
Osmer, Richard A. 185-86, 256, 258, 275
Osmun, Orson S. 281
Ossenbeck, Henry 786
Osterhaut, Luke H. 562, 574
Ostram, John S. 219
Ostrander, Henry 362
Osts, John 859
O'Sullivan, Dennis 715
O'Sullivan, James 454
Otey, Thomas J. 732
O'Toole, Patrick 468
Ott, Christopher 745
Ott, James 232
Ottan, Peter 817
Otterson, James 484
Otting, Charles 834
Oultzhover, Maliher 745
Oumon, Amery 309
Ourand, John D. 147
Ousley, George W. 827-29, 835
Ousterhoute, Jeremiah D. 121
Overaker, Philip W. 273

Overend, William G. 200, 209, 291
Overlander, Samuel 838, 841
Overmayer, Jacob 163
Overmeyer, Edward H. 786
Overmeyer, Quincy A. 825
Overton, James W. 366
Overton, Samuel W. 393
Oviatt, Patrick 583
Owen, Francis H. 772
Owen, Henry G. 445, 879
Owen, James I. 833
Owen, John W. 764, 781, 856
Owen, William McKay 350, 749, 759
Owen, William W. 775
Owens, David H. 775
Owens, George 475, 482
Owens, George W. 773
Owens, John W. 256
Owens, Peter G. 445
Owens, Richard 468
Owens, Silas E. 751
Owens, Thomas 719
Owens, William 454, 482
Owings, John T. 265, 301
Owtoon, Andrew 115
Oyas, Jesus 319
Ozman, Orson S. 569

P

Pablo, Olivas 880
Pace, John A. 445
Pacheco, Francisco 309
Packwood, Daniel G. 256
Paddock, James L. 628
Paden, John 655
Padilla, John 313
Padilla, José 319
Padilla, Pedro 319
Page, James M. 121
Page, Julius 489
Page, Nathaniel 28
Page, Thomas 809
Paine, Nathan B. 588
Paine, William H. 805
Palacio, Salvador 319
Palm, Adam 445, 496
Palmer, A. S. 179

Palmer, Alonzo R. 281
Palmer, Curtis Z. 813
Palmer, Ezekiel O. 489
Palmer, Frederick 155
Palmer, George W. 846
Palmer, Henry 540, 562
Palmer, John C. 128
Palmer, John D. 703
Palmer, John M. 715
Palmer, John W. 761
Palmer, Jonathan W. 88, 113
Palmer, Joseph 845
Palmer, Joseph C. 273
Palmer, Joseph F. 223
Palmer, Luther H. 550, 583, 588
Palmer, Reuben H. 697
Palmer, William T. 859
Panai, Kirigi 468
Pangburn, James 454, 503
Pape, Christian 366
Pardee, Andrew 838
Pardee, James 438, 562, 590
Parent, Eli 802
Paricella, Stephen 789
Paris, Alexander 310
Paris, Frank 859
Parish, Albert G. 128
Parisse, Eugene J. 562
Park, Charles T. 809
Parker, A. M. 178
Parker, Albert M. 281
Parker, Charles H. 709
Parker, Daniel B. 150
Parker, E. H. 28
Parker, Ernest 475
Parker, Frank 393, 402
Parker, George 804
Parker, George H. 445
Parker, George W. 866, 869
Parker, James C. 841
Parker, James W. 115
Parker, Jeremiah 622, 880
Parker, John 215, 445, 769
Parker, John S. 131
Parker, John T. 767
Parker, R. M. 856
Parker, Robert 599
Parker, Samuel M. 492
Parker, Seth A. 697
Parker, Thomas 562

Parker, Treat H. 345
Parker, William 489
Parker, William E. 866
Parker, William H. 379, 535, 554
Parker, William K. 227, 880
Parker, William W. 148
Parkes, Charles 804
Parkhurst, Daniel W. 661
Parkin, Jedediah 207
Parks, Edwin R. 91
Parks, Jas. H. 160
Parks, Madison R. 759, 770
Parks, Samuel 256
Parkus, Emanuel 357
Parlin, Harlow 628
Parmentier, Jean 812
Parnell, William H. 454, 563, 580
Parquet, John 106, 115
Parr, Daniel 804
Parra, José Anselmo 313
Parrish, Albert S., or G. 880
Parrish, Richard M. 357
Parrisse, Eugene 607
Parrott, William L. 635
Parry, Adam M. 463
Parry, Isaac 431
Parsette, Charles 371
Parsons, Benjamin 313
Parsons, Benjamin F. 232, 371
Parsons, Henry 563
Parsons, James 697
Parsons, James A. 709
Parsons, Milo C. 642
Partridge, Benjamin F. 850, 859
Partridge, William B. 792
Party, August 439, 719
Parvin, Washington L. 359
Paschal, Frank 772
Pascoe, Benjamin F. 147
Pascoe, William C. 148
Paskell, John T. 787
Paso, William 223
Passage, John 863
Passero, Ernest 628
Pastor, Jacob 615
Patch, George W. 555
Patch, Levi 741
Patrick, James 28
Patterson, Aurelius M. 602, 630
Patterson, Charles 841

Patterson, David 106, 145, 345
Patterson, Frank 402, 693
Patterson, George W. 730
Patterson, Hamilton S. 240
Patterson, James 207, 286, 825
Patterson, Martin 150
Patterson, Richard C. 345, 363, 390
Patterson, Washington P. 652
Patterson, William F. 454
Patton, Albert F. 379
Patton, George M. 655
Patton, Harrison 581
Patton, John 215
Patton, Marion 817
Paul, James 615, 622
Paul, William 667
Paul, William W. 592
Paulsen, Charles 503
Paxon, Charles 648
Payet, Joseph 554
Payne, Charles 661
Payne, Henry 563
Payne, John W. 779
Payne, Louis 160
Payne, Norman B. 863
Payne, Sheldon A. 738
Payne, Thomas T. 531, 574
Payson, Edwin G. 128
Payson, Samuel 160, 880
Peabody 28
Peabody, Franklin 775
Peacock, Joseph H. 340, 379, 388
Peacock, William 707
Peaison, Henry C. 822
Pearce, Charles 489
Pearce, George 615, 783
Pearce, Henry S. 115
Pearce, John L. 454, 482
Pearce, William E. 540
Pearsall, Samuel W. 454
Pearse, Almon O. 795
Pearson, Ephraim 223
Pearson, James W. 617, 781
Pearson, John 609
Pearson, John H. 761
Pearson, Richard R. 689
Pearson, Thomas E. 725, 726, 746
Pearson, William 286, 680
Pearson, William W. 801
Pearson, Winfield 574

Pearson, Winfield S. 657
Pease, Henry C. 642
Pease, Jonathan A. 638
Pease, Richmond W. 648
Pease, Sanford O. 795
Pease, Sylvester 362
Peasley, Charles D. 531
Peat, James W. 574
Peavy, James J. 232
Peck, Aaron V. 90, 98
Peck, Andrew J. 301, 880
Peck, George W. 581
Peck, James M. 581
Peck, Joel 128
Peckham, Edward M. 772
Peckham, James D. 801
Pedlar, Rudolph 615, 648
Peebles, James J. 866
Peel, Fernando A. 197, 198, 226
Peine, Julius 281, 301
Peipmire, August 786
Pelham, James W. 856
Pell, John A. 742
Pelton, Aylmer 235
Pelton, Byron 256
Pelton, Simon 715
Pemberton, John 207
Pendergarst, John 707
Pendergrast, Thomas 489
Pendle, Morton M. 863
Pendleton, Benjamin F. 635
Penn, Edmond 454
Pennell, Edward 345
Pennick, Elijah 461
Penny, John C. 115
Penny, Lewis C. 841
Penny, Simeon V. 804
Penrose, John 661
Pensho, Alfred 535, 592
Penter, George 166
Penwell, Henry C. 185, 209, 211, 267, 433
Peoples, George 497
Pepin, Edward 588
Pepler, James 555, 576
Pepper, Hard D. 607
Pepperdine, Trustrum 291
Peppin, George W. 680
Perado, José 301
Percell, John 475

Perceval, Carlos 309
Percey, Robert 754
Percival, Joseph 468
Percival, Thomas 155, 291
Percival, William H. 738
Percy, David J. 805
Percy, James 281
Percy, William 856
Perea, Joseph 635
Peredo, José 281
Perin, Jacques C. 741
Perkey, Felix 825
Perkins, Alfred W. 497
Perkins, Anderson 439, 563, 574, 588
Perkins, Charles E. 820
Perkins, Chas. H. 147
Perkins, Edmund 106
Perkins, Edward F. 522, 531
Perkins, Franklin L. 232
Perkins, George 753
Perkins, Hiram 454, 582, 741
Perkins, John R. 820
Perkins, Lafayette 551, 588
Perkins, Richard 157
Perkins, Samuel 309, 745
Perkins, William 397
Perkins, William J. 243, 767, 838
Perras, Juan 313
Perrault, George O. 162
Perrean, Alexander 815
Perrin, John C. 607
Perrine, Thomas D. 745
Perry, Adam M. 432, 492
Perry, Albert 859
Perry, Albert O. 820
Perry, David 635
Perry, Elijah 89, 880
Perry, Henry 715
Perry, John 215, 635
Perry, John H. 758
Perry, John P. 635
Perry, John W. S. 834
Perry, Jonathan M. 834
Perry, Joseph H. 745
Perry, Ozui S. 846
Perry, William 635
Pervine, Samuel 866
Pervis, Lawrence G. 859
Pesqueira, Ignacio 506

Peterman, Julius 563
Peters, Jacob 661
Peters, John H. 251
Peters, Joseph H. 540, 551
Peters, Yves 786
Peterson, Charles 482, 761, 775
Peterson, Frederick 569, 817
Peterson, Henry 540, 551
Peterson, James A. 821
Peterson, John 783
Peterson, John A. 445
Peterson, Peter 642
Peterson, Westy 701
Peterson, William 265
Peterson, William H. 475
Petray, Jonah A. 772
Pettee, George M. 134
Pettler, Joseph 531, 563
Pettis, George H. 341, 376
Pettis, George M. 76, 327
Pettit, W.H. 235
Petty, John S. 751
Petty, Thomas 146
Pettyman, James 789
Pfeifer, Henry 265
Pfeiffer, Philip 769
Pfeifle, John G. 124
Pfender, John M. 635
Pfiefle, Philip 150
Pfisterer, Julius 755
Pfouts, Robert 207
Pfund, William 812
Pharis, Alfred 775
Pheasant, Harrison 439
Phelan, Jeremiah 47, 324, 335, 341, 376, 609
Phelan, Michael 293
Phelps, Corwin 366
Phelps, Daniel 603
Phelps, Edward 349, 725, 766
Phelps, Edward O. 95
Phelps, Edwards 431
Phelps, George 349
Phelps, William H. 820
Phfay, William 301
Philbrick, Edgar C. 754
Philbrick, Francis 795
Philbrick, Francis A. 880
Philbrook, James M. 615
Philipith, Richard 368

Phillbrook, George S. 439
Phillip, Joseph 631
Philliporske, Lyon 680
Phillips, Alexander 291
Phillips, Charles H. 215
Phillips, Claud 880
Phillips, Edward 207
Phillips, Edward C. 394, 697
Phillips, Edward M. 607
Phillips, Flavel N. 484
Phillips, Franklin M. 155
Phillips, George 134
Phillips, George E. 574, 880
Phillips, George H. 265, 291
Phillips, James S. 379, 880
Phillips, John 667
Phillips, John M. 801
Phillips, John S. 801
Phillips, John Y. 282
Phillips, Levi D. 163
Phillips, Nathan 282
Phillips, Simon R. 789
Phillips, Thomas R. 275
Phillips, William 95
Phillips, William H. 413, 676, 707
Phillips, William N. 715
Picasso, José 307
Pickett, Mr. 26
Pickett, James L. 625
Pico, Andreas 304, 307
Pico, Benigno 307
Pico, José Ramon 305, 307
Pico, Miguel 315
Pico, Rafael 315
Pico, Ramon 315
Picquenot, Napoleon 730
Picquet, Louis 707
Pierce, Abraham L. 531, 574
Pierce, Allen D. 413, 703
Pierce, David B. 566
Pierce, Eben 540, 551
Pierce, Frederick W. 732
Pierce, George 106
Pierce, Ira 379
Pierce, James 635
Pierce, James H. 439
Pierce, James M. 415, 707
Pierce, Joseph 786
Pierce, Nathaniel P. 250
Pierce, Silas S. 806

Pierce, Warren S. 258
Pierre, Jean 313
Pierre, Renoult 313
Pierson, Adam 357
Pierson, John O. 820
Pifer, Daniel 379
Pigeon, Felix 751
Piggott, William C. 491, 818
Pigott, William C. 432
Pike, Eli 642, 707
Pike, Frederick 850
Pike, James M. 795
Pike, John R. 786
Pike, Newell 661
Pilcher, Lewis 628
Pilkinton, Richard 745
Pince, George 745
Pinkham, Charles A. 741
Pinnick, Elijah 503
Pinoche, Gregorio 749
Pinto, Ismael 801
Piper, Eli 90
Piper, Nathaniel S. 642
Piquet, William 866
Pishon, Nathaniel 117
Pishon, Nathaniel J. 72, 73
Pister, Jacob 615
Pitch, Sand 175
Pitner, Berryman 697
Pittman, William 128
Pitts, Benjamin 795
Pitzer, William 792, 795
Pixley, James 776
Pixley, Marshall 822
Pixley, Reuben 563, 574
Place, Warren H. 265
Place, William H. 489
Plana, Barthelamy 734
Plana, Bartholomy 880
Plannett, Charles A. 115
Plass, Frederick 468
Plass, Gustavus W. 223, 880
Plass, Philip 715
Platt, Charles H. 810
Platt, John L. 256
Pleasants, John T. 273
Pliny, Allen 585
Plover, John 207
Plummer, Frederick 569
Plummer, George 856

Plummer, John 602
Plummer, Robert W. 767
Plummer, William 240
Plumridge, Robert 642
Plunket, Thomas 215
Plunkett, James 628
Plunkett, John 734
Plunkett, Thomas 211
Poehler, William 804
Poell, William R. 109, 128
Points, Nathaniel O. 256
Poisal, John S. 397, 697
Polaedee, Thomas 265
Poland, William H. 655
Polk, Charles E. 445
Polk, Richard 805
Pollard, Edward 809
Pollard, John 642
Pollock, Charles 825
Pollock, George W. 815
Pollock, James 393, 730
Pollock, Robert 16, 335, 431, 475, 505, 522
Pollock, Samuel 834
Pollock, Thomas 248
Polmantere, Thomas 155
Pomeroy, Edgar 346, 350
Pomme, John A. 802
Ponce de Leon, Cleopas 317
Pool, Frank M. 775
Pool, John 454, 482
Pool, Joseph B. 795
Pool, Martin M. 793
Pool, Melbourne Z. 856
Pool, Melvin 354, 385
Pool, Waldo 742
Poole, Duff G. 282
Poole, John E. 291
Pooler, Henry 291
Poorman, Giles D. 251
Pope, Daniel 448
Pope, Henry 715, 738
Pope, Wilson 207, 296
Poppe, Henry 340
Porter, Abel G. 497, 574
Porter, Alexander 792
Porter, Ambrose J. 215
Porter, Charles 574, 812
Porter, George F. 368
Porter, John 531

Porter, John J. 775
Porter, John S. 625
Porter, Silas A. 563
Porter, Thornton G. 215
Porter, Vandergiff 775
Porter, William John 273
Porter, Willis 645
Post, Aaron 402, 689
Post, Edward 655
Post, Henry C. 801
Post, Jerome B. 129
Potarf, Andrew J. 131
Potlock, Moses 375
Potter, Duncan C. 265
Potter, Edwin A. 95
Potter, James D. 95
Potter, Joseph 265
Potter, Joseph C. 676
Potter, Jos. E. 123
Potter, Samuel H. 707
Potter, William E. 754
Potter, William K. 256
Potts, Izatus 570
Pound, John S. 340, 377, 388
Pound, Riley 815
Poustian, Henrich 503
Poustion, Henry 685
Powell, Benjamin F. 132
Powell, Colvin 232
Powell, George N. L. 790
Powell, Henry T. 251
Powell, James 240, 265
Powell, John W. 227
Powell, Joseph 532, 615
Powell, Robert 536, 544, 590
Powell, Thomas E. 95
Powelson, Charles 106
Power, William J. 461
Powers, Amos S. 841
Powers, Charles H. 856
Powers, Ebenezer 767
Powers, Ebenezer Z. 349
Powers, Frank W. 256
Powers, George 583
Powers, John 402
Powers, John S. 399
Powers, Nathaniel 635
Powers, Thomas J. 155
Prange, Frederick 446
Pratt, Mr. 513

Pratt, Francis O. 711
Pratt, Lewis B. 569, 880
Pratt, Samuel B. 622, 783
Pratt, William 540
Pratt, William H. 832
Pray, John C. 160
Preble, John H. 301
Preble, William H. 291
Precht, Charles 730
Prentice, Edward S. 282
Prentice, William F. 717
Prentiss, John H. 62, 87
Prescott, Benjamin H. 615
Prescott, W.H. 79
Preston, William 265, 761
Preston, William T. 754
Preston, Wilson 761
Prewett, Elijah 667
Prey, William 441
Price, Alfred 439
Price, Edward 198, 285, 869
Price, George F. 7, 175, 176, 182, 184, 293
Price, Hugh 623
Price, James 223
Price, John 207
Price, John M. 240
Price, John W. 642
Price, Johnson 13
Price, Layman B. 461
Price, Samuel B. 707
Price, William J. 642
Price, William W. 397, 699
Prichard, Daniel 468
Prickett, Jacob 256
Priest, Eber B. 615, 623
Priest, Eli C. 110
Priest, Samuel 783
Prigmore, Ephraim 838
Prigmore, James 838
Pringle, William 825
Pringle, William H. 866
Prior, Robert 223, 240
Pritchard, David 129
Pritchard, William 834, 880
Pritchet, James 834
Pritchett, Reuben 163, 880
Probst, William 202, 207
Proctor, Jonathan F. 532
Proctor, William F. 357

Prole, James M. 834
Prott, Philip 446
Prouty, Calvin R. 259
Provande, Peter H. 497
Provost, Francis 313
Provost, Louis 256
Prow, John 628
Prunty, Hiram 240
Prussing, John 407, 685
Pryor, Jeremiah 454
Pugsley, John I. 711
Puland, Charles 252
Pulgaveen, John 313
Pulis, George E. 244, 880
Pullen, James 199, 244, 265
Pulver, Cassius M. 808
Punk, John 146
Purcell, Charles 754
Purcell, Joseph 792, 795
Purcell, Thomas M. 751
Purdy, George W. 638
Purdy, Grosvenor 649
Purell, Peter J. 454
Purgear, Samuel 719
Pursel, Abner L. 129
Pursell, Henry C. 166
Putman, Jackson 215
Putman, Joseph P. 269
Putnam, Charles E. 820
Putnam, Charles P. 636
Putnam, Newton S. 817
Putney, Henry A. 439
Pyburn, William 54

Q

Quain, David 615, 667
Qualey, John F. 317, 694
Quant, Frederick J. 856
Quarrels, John T. 223
Quayle, Thomas W. 540
Quear, Lewis 834, 880
Queen, Jonathan C. 672, 702, 880
Querloy, Pierre 309
Quick, Robert R. 155
Quigley, John 160
Quigley, Patrick 106, 121
Quim, Patrick 880
Quimby, Elijah D. 251

Quincy, George H. 841
Quinlan, John 693
Quinlan, John (1st) 741
Quinlan, John (2d) 741
Quinlivan, Mark 285
Quinn, John 160, 175-76, 182, 234, 275, 284, 411, 689, 730
Quinn, Michael 415, 707
Quinn, Patrick 523, 580, 685
Quinn, Timothy 623
Quinteros, Dolores 319
Quirk, John 736
Quirk, John J. 863

R

Rabenack, Jacob 583
Raber, Christopher 227
Rabstock, Henry 543
Radcliff, Miles 583
Radcliffe, Thomas 248, 693
Radelfinger, Samuel 468
Rader, William 215, 357
Radford, Robert 629
Radford, William 106
Radigan, Michael 115
Raferty, Hubert L. 745
Rafferty, James 623
Rafferty, John 106, 371
Rafferty, Patrick 563
Rafferty, Thomas 734
Rafter, George 203
Ragan, John 825
Raglan, Pettis G. 353
Rahlert, Frederick 503
Rahn, Thomas C. 477
Rahr, Herman 880
Rain, William A. 265
Rainbow, James P. M. 354
Raines, John P. 615
Rainey, Alexander H. 758
Rainey, Collohan 745
Rainey, John, alias Collohan 745
Rainey, William J. 584
Rains, James M. 661
Rains, John 166
Rajas, Miguel 309
Ralph, Henry 129, 881
Ralph, William H. 147
Ralston 28

Ralston, Abraham W. 822
Rames, Warren 235
Ramey, Stephen B. 397, 697
Ramien, John H. 301
Ramirez, Francisco 320
Ramsdell, A. 179
Ramsdell, Algeray, 590
Ramsdell, Alonzo M. 838
Ramsdell, Roland 838
Ramsey, Joseph 150
Ramsey, Robert T. 770
Ramsey, William 563, 607, 636
Ranch, George 775
Rand, Augustus Y. 349
Rand, Charles R. 880
Rand, George W. 416, 707
Randal, Amos G. 601
Randall, Alpheus W. 845
Randall, Arthur F. H. 179, 593, 825
Randall, James B. 866
Randall, Philip R. 129
Randall, Samuel G. 236, 880
Randall, Samuel T. 783
Randell 28
Randle, Peter W. 335
Randolph, Charles 563, 584
Randolph, George W. 402, 411, 715
Raney, William J. 160
Rank, Amos 375
Rank, William 140, 349
Rankin, Benjamin A. 95
Rankin, Henry E. C. 563
Rankin, John 551
Rankin, John W. 446
Rankin, William 822
Rankin, William H. 497
Ranks, Thomas R. 446
Ranney, Edward 574
Ransford, John 786
Rantz, Adolph 551
Rapely, George W. 286
Rapelye, Abraham W. 88, 143
Raper, Baxton 240
Raphael, Morris 540, 551
Rappley, Jasper 540
Rappley, Jasper S. 593
Rash, Davidson 540
Rass, Levi D. 758

Ratcliff, Aaron 353
Rath, Johann H. W. 780
Rathburn 656
Rathburn, James S. 624, 644
Ratheram, James 569
Rathja, Frank 489
Rau, Henry 585
Ravekes, Henry J. 809
Ravenburgh, William 503
Rawles, Brown 602
Rawles, Moses 607, 636
Rawlings, Thomas G. 800
Raworth, James C. 240
Rawson, Benjamin F. 863
Rawson, Caleb H. 863
Rawson, Meredith 574
Ray, Albert M. 256
Ray, Charles 497
Ray, Charles P. 256
Ray, James 540, 551, 593, 610
Ray, James F. 497
Ray, James J. 200, 282
Ray, James L. 820
Ray, Louis 150
Ray, Major 649
Raymond, George 532
Raymond, Harry M. 725, 726, 736
Raymond, James 475
Raymond, Peter 866
Raymond, William S. 551
Raywood, William A. 615, 649
Rea, James S. 772
Read, Charles W. 115
Read, Milton D. 411, 719
Read, William E. 738
Reader, Samuel W. B. 273
Reagan, William 388, 393
Rearden, Denis 223
Reardon, John 265, 532
Reardon, John R. 256
Reavis, Charles 783
Reavis, Charles H. 607, 667
Reavis, Isham F. 607
Reber, Jacob 795
Reck, Theodore 769
Redd, Patrick R. 629
Redding, Milton 625
Redding, Samuel 580
Redding, Thomas B. 769
Reddy, John 371, 393

Reddy, Martin 91, 106
Redfield, Henry S. 371, 402, 416
Redfoxe, Jonathan 809
Redmond, John E. 805
Redmond, Thomas 761
Redona, Jose 317
Redson, John 446
Reed, Abraham S. 115
Reed, Andrew J. 847
Reed, August 540, 563
Reed, Calvin W. 680
Reed, Edward B. 345, 366, 390
Reed, Emanuel 693
Reed, Etheridge W. 775
Reed, Franklin H. 551, 569
Reed, George W. 866
Reed, Gion 366
Reed, Guion 880
Reed, Hiram M. 772
Reed, J. Sewell 848, 850, 854
Reed, Jesse C. 756
Reed, John 260, 730, 754
Reed, John A. 106, 863
Reed, John K. 863
Reed, John S. 129
Reed, Joseph 95, 623, 880
Reed, Lewis D. 754
Reed, Robert 623
Reed, Shelbourne 178
Reed, Shelbourne C. 282, 880
Reed, Thomas 357
Reed, William 489
Reed, William J. 725
Reed, William P. 223, 273
Reed, Zachariah T. 629
Reeder, Peter 801
Reef, William 265
Reefe, William 301
Reel, John T. 741
Reel, William F. 741
Rees, Daniel 439, 801
Reese, Daniel 432
Reese, DeWitt C. 301
Reese, Jacob J. 686
Reese, James 859
Reese, William 769
Reeves, Joseph 353
Reeves, Joseph M. 134
Reeves, William L. 532, 580
Regan, William 379

Reggio, Arthur 503
Regner, Jacob 340, 377, 388
Rehder, Frederick 240
Reibold, George 642
Reid, Archibald 734
Reid, David 240
Reid, George Francis 551, 563
Reid, Henry 642, 881
Reid, Joseph H. 362
Reid, Myron C. 166
Reid, Robert K. 177-78, 197, 522
Reilly, John 750
Reilly, John O. 232, 607
Reilly, Nicholas 503
Reilly, Patrick 623
Reilly, William 95
Reily, David 454
Reily, James 43, 454
Reily, Patrick 454
Reinecke, Henry 446
Reinhardt, Charles W. 200, 276
Reinhardt, Henry 523, 540, 730
Reise, DeWitt Clinton 265
Reiser, Gustav 758
Reith, Philip 532
Reitinger, Godfrey 655
Reitinger, Jacob 766, 776
Remington, Darius C. 636
Remington, Herbert C. 563
Remmington, Herbert C. 574
Remond, Mott 313
Renfro, John G. 761
Reni, Simon 769, 881
Renicke, John 738
Rennie, William 301
Renshaw, John 109
Rensho, A. 179
Requa, Benjamin F. 136, 140, 157
Rerden, James 223
Resler, Edward 187, 232
Reveia, José Maria 320
Reveia, Ramon 320
Revelles, George 789
Reventlow, Ludwig 379, 388
Revera, Fernando 320
Reuss, Theodore 741
Reyburn, Asa G. 637, 812
Reyes, José Antonio 881
Reyes, Juan 845
Reynaud, Philip 407

Reynolds, Cpl. 184
Reynolds, Abraham 629
Reynolds, Columbus 540
Reynolds, Daniel 216
Reynolds, Edwin S. 551, 569
Reynolds, Frank 134, 407, 685
Reynolds, George W. 663
Reynolds, Horace 95
Reynolds, James 243
Reynolds, James S. 115, 880
Reynolds, John B. 162
Reynolds, Joseph C. 551, 563
Reynolds, Luther C. 282
Reynolds, Richard 166
Reynolds, Richard H. 845
Reynolds, Samuel 649
Reynolds, Thomas B. 801
Reynolds, Titus 234
Reynolds, William 841
Rhea, John 407
Rhegan, John 551
Rhinehart, Jacob B. 301
Rhoades, James H. 282
Rhoades, Jonathan K. 780
Rhoads, Andrew J. 265
Rhodes, Byron J. 806
Rhodes, Daniel 825
Rhodes, Henry C. 324, 363
Rhodes, Isaac 689
Rhodes, James S. 150
Rhodes, Jonas M. 603
Rhodes, Samuel H. 859
Rhodes, William 551, 593
Rhodes, William H. 106, 115
Rhodes, William J. 563
Rhoman, George 267
Rhudolph, Henry 655
Rhuman, Pvt. 187
Rice, Charles 707
Rice, Charles N. 475, 482, 807
Rice, Cyrus S. 409, 713
Rice, Francis C. 754
Rice, George 273, 540
Rice, Hamilton 856
Rice, Harry P. 638
Rice, Henry 544, 563, 588, 761
Rice, Hiram 291
Rice, John 416, 685, 707
Rice, John W. 685
Rice, Joseph C. 219

Rice, Lancious 750
Rice, Otis A. 603
Rich, Edward G. 838
Rich, Isaac M. 651
Richards, Albert 146
Richards, Charles 115, 719
Richards, Daniel 629
Richards, Elgin 772
Richards, Ephraim 817
Richards, Henry R. 256
Richards, James L. 371, 880
Richards, Reuben 416, 707
Richards, Sylvester 711
Richards, Thomas 118, 670
Richards, William 817
Richards, William H. 593
Richardson, Elisha S. 766, 783
Richardson, George 475
Richardson, George G. 313
Richardson, Isaac 541
Richardson, Jackson 730
Richardson, Jackson W. 778
Richardson, John 439, 693
Richardson, John A. 789
Richardson, John C. 362
Richardson, Joseph 825
Richardson, Luke 541, 580
Richardson, Thomas 207, 677, 689, 754
Richardson, Warren 544, 566
Richardson, William P. 147
Richie, Francis H. 129
Richmond, Edward 623
Rickers, Gilbert B. 259
Ricketts, Gilbert R. 809
Rickey, David P. 207, 282
Rickey, Joseph F. 775
Riddle, Samuel 697, 880
Riddle, William 232
Rider, Alexander 475
Rider, Charles 475
Rider, George K. 251
Riding, Henry 273
Riding, Thomas 844
Ridge, Thompson 178, 265, 295
Ridgely, William F. 216
Ridgway, James A. 160
Ridgway, Stephen B. 766, 778
Ridley, Dexter W. 657
Ridley, Mark H. 265, 301

Riehl, Thomas J. 185, 273
Riely, Col. 57
Riely, James 741
Rigans, Thomas 95
Rigby, George E. 95
Rigg, Edwin A. 20, 40, 56, 62, 66, 321, 325, 335-36, 381, 385
Riley 22, 669
Riley, Alexander 817
Riley, Amos 869
Riley, David 642
Riley, Edward 402, 411, 532, 574, 689
Riley, George 563, 588
Riley, Hugh 402, 689
Riley, James 775
Riley, James, alias Frank Kerr 475
Riley, John 134, 187, 216, 357, 375, 807
Riley, Patrick 838
Riley, Philip 475
Riley, Phillis 551
Riley, Thomas 140, 809
Riley, William 155, 340, 388
Rilley, James 615
Rinehart, Charles 775
Ring, Alfred 745, 880-81
Ring, Alfred W. 160
Ring, Joseph 468
Ring, William C. 563
Ringgold, George H. 720, 848
Riordan, James 813
Rios, Miguel 315
Ripley, Albert 589, 593
Ripper, Charles 282
Risdon, Josiah A. 115
Rising, Irving 301
Risoner, John M. 291
Ritchey, Benjamin F. 638, 881
Ritchey, William 482
Ritchie, George 471
Ritchie, James 468
Ritchie, Thomas 810
Ritchie, William 758
Rivas, Francisco 320
Rivera, Felipe 318
Rivers, Frank 265
Rivers, William H. 258
Rivoice, Joseph 349
Roach, John 256, 758

Roach, Michael 134, 751, 881
Roach, Patrick 475
Roach, Richard 129
Roadda, John 738
Robarts, Juan 317
Robb, James B. 379
Robbins, Daniel S. 301
Robbins, Henry 468
Robbins, John M. 223
Robbins, John S. 160
Robbins, Juan G. 607, 636
Robbins, Lawrence S. 804
Robbins, Lorin 294
Robenson, William 584
Roberson, Charles W. 207
Roberson, Jarrett 817
Roberts, Charles 863
Roberts, Claibourn 825
Roberts, Frank 140
Roberts, Henry 825
Roberts, Henry H. 98, 786
Roberts, Hugh 140
Roberts, James 655, 715
Roberts, John 402, 411, 432, 448, 588, 715, 804
Roberts, John C. 623
Roberts, John H. 140
Roberts, Joseph W. 210
Roberts, Pulaski 869
Roberts, Robert W. 357
Roberts, Thaddeus W. 110
Roberts, Theodore 734
Roberts, Thomas B. 574
Roberts, Thomas L. 58, 64–65, 327, 354
Roberts, William 499
Robertson, David 223
Robertson, George 841
Robertson, George W. 291
Robertson, Horatio P. 751
Robertson, James 143, 439, 847
Robertson, John 773
Robertson, William H. 340, 388
Robey, James R. 240
Robin, Gerbard 697
Robins, Charles 869
Robins, L. 178
Robins, Thomas J. 457
Robins, William 143
Robinson, Mr. 54

Robinson, Adolphus 282
Robinson, Elisha H. 793
Robinson, Frederick 141
Robinson, George 809, 822
Robinson, George H. 187, 225, 244
Robinson, George W. 291, 841
Robinson, Harrison G. O. 106
Robinson, Henry 340, 448, 555, 576, 610
Robinson, Horatio 317
Robinson, James 468, 541, 551, 574
Robinson, James H. 291
Robinson, John 95, 631
Robinson, John D. 615
Robinson, Joseph 755, 822
Robinson, Joseph M. 817
Robinson, Joshua C. 809
Robinson, Juan 320
Robinson, Lindsley G. 95
Robinson, Milton J. 218, 223
Robinson, Randolph 362
Robinson, Richard 741
Robinson, Richard L. 734
Robinson, Robert 541, 569
Robinson, Samuel 503, 730
Robinson, Stillman S. 251
Robinson, Stuart L. 258
Robinson, Theodore 734
Robinson, Thomas 21, 22, 30, 31
Robinson, William 150, 569
Robinson, William A. 856
Robinson, William B. 685
Robinson, William H. 150
Robjend, Frederick B. 780
Robjent, Frederick 349
Robran, Louran 667
Robson, John 153
Rocco, Frederick E. 291
Roche, Luis 313
Roche, Thomas 816
Rochester, Richard 711
Rockford, Francis 201
Rockholt, Reuben 625
Rockwell, Porter 177
Rockwell, William H. 603
Rodden, William H. 155
Rodella, José B. 129
Rodemire, Henry 106
Rodgers, Albert 160

Rodgers, Allan 761
Rodgers, Andrew 503
Rodgers, Edward 454
Rodgers, George 842
Rodgers, Geo. W. 468
Rodgers, James F. 541
Rodgers, John 446, 816
Rodgers, Michael 497
Rodgers, Samuel 353
Rodgers, Thomas L. 859
Rodges, Andrew 106
Rodney, George D. 155
Rodrigues, José 309
Rodrigues, José M. 309
Rodrigues, Mariro 309
Rodrigues, Ygnacio 309
Rodriguez, Antonio 315
Rodriguez, Felis 320
Rodriguez, José 314, 315
Rodriguez, José de Jesus 317
Rodriguez, Pedro 317
Roe, Able 780
Roe, Alonzo 807
Roe, David 838
Roe, James 362, 393
Roe, Robert 468
Rogan, John A. 642
Rogers, Augustus 845
Rogers, Charles A. 769
Rogers, Edward 482
Rogers, Ely 655
Rogers, Franklin 95
Rogers, Geo. W. 249
Rogers, James 106
Rogers, John 499
Rogers, John J. 454, 563, 580
Rogers, Joseph 551
Rogers, Lewis 792
Rogers, Louis 629
Rogers, Robt. C. 28
Rogers, Thomas 804
Rogers, William 207, 475
Rogers, William E. 623
Rohr, August 468
Rohr, Herrman 446
Rohr, Jacob 256
Rohrs, Martin 121
Rojas, Juan 320
Roley, Henry M. 795
Roley, James C. 218, 268

Roll, Israel 141
Roll, Jasper P. 775
Roll, Joseph N. 775
Rolland, Antonio 115
Rolland, Patrick 282
Rolland, William 150
Rollins, Ezra D. 735
Rollins, William 276
Rolls, Chester C. 532
Rolson, Samuel T. 615
Roman, William W. 503
Romatka, F.A. 766
Romerez, Antonio M. 318
Romero, H. 75
Romero, José 309
Romero, José Antonio 317
Romero, José M.N. 310
Romero, Pedro 317
Romero, Ylario 320
Romine, John W. 273
Romiro, Navor 781
Ronald, John 801
Ronan, John 813
Ronan, Thomas 416, 707
Ronas, Thomas 881
Rondeville, Charles 216
Rone, Carlos 856
Ronten, Pleasant 563
Roof, Eli 357, 407, 685
Rooney, Chas. L. 249
Rooney, Duke 730
Rooney, Hugh 232, 880
Rooney, John 689, 751
Rooper, Joseph 497, 532
Root, Bolivar 783
Root, James P. 783
Root, Joshua D. 357, 407, 685
Roots, Abram 160
Roper, Edward 157
Ropes, James M. 242, 250
Rose, Alford 825
Rose, Charles 439, 655
Rose, Eugene 636
Rose, James 815
Rose, John 745
Rose, Lewis S. 244
Rose, Luther J. 95
Rose, William 819, 843
Rosea, Antonio 407, 685
Rosemier, John 838

Rosenbaum, Wm. S. 685
Rosenthal, Charles 815
Rosetzky, Charles 588
Rosetzky, Charles H. 804
Ross, Adam S. 784
Ross, Albert 795
Ross, Byron E. 95
Ross, Charles 216
Ross, Daniel 95, 551
Ross, Edward 607
Ross, George A. 745
Ross, Guslavus W. 880
Ross, Ichabod O. 781
Ross, James 745
Ross, James L. 454
Ross, James M. 340
Ross, John 232
Ross, John R. 601
Ross, Joshua C. 856
Ross, Nahan R. 745
Ross, Walter 490, 497
Rosson, Christian 232
Rost, Theodore 695
Roth, Adolph 446
Roth, Conrad 751
Roth, Henry P. 655
Rottone, Otto 563
Roullier, Louis 541, 563
Rountree, George H. 219
Rourk, Henry 454
Rourke, John 655
Rourke, Martin 563
Rourke, Michael 775
Rouse, Lewis 240
Roush, John 623
Routen, Pleasant 544
Routon, Pleasant 569
Rover, Young 207
Rowan, James R. 314
Rowbotham, William 353
Rowe, Adolphus 178, 282, 880
Rowe, Alonzo B. 685
Rowe, Amaziah F. 569
Rowe, Benjamin S. 735
Rowe, Edwin A. 200
Rowe, George W. 265
Rowe, Isaiah K. 249
Rowe, Joseph H. 801
Rowell, C.W.C. 601
Rowen, John 753

Rowland, Henry 130
Rowland, Kemp A. 812
Rowlett, William 366
Rowlette, William J. 881
Rowley, Manoah P. 235
Rowley, Menoah P. 273
Rowling, Andrew C. 730
Roxburgh, John 256
Royal, Benjamin 160
Royce, Alfred 772
Royce, Hiram H. 166
Royer, Samuel Z. 135
Rozel, John 615, 649
Rozmoski, Kasmier 649
Ruault, Eugene 314
Rubarts, James H. 166
Rubie, Henry 393
Rubie, Henry L. 366
Ruble, Joseph 735
Rucker, Hugh G. 91
Rudd, De Courcey J. 282, 291
Rudd, John 786
Ruddell, Frederick M. 454
Rudloff, Christian 761
Rudsell, John 685
Ruegg, Henry 761
Rugg, Charles S. 185, 269
Ruggles, George D. 321
Ruggles, Nathaniel T. 115
Ruggles, Samuel C. 749
Ruggles, Silas 116
Ruhland, George P. 157
Ruhman, Henrich C. 232
Ruis, José 310
Ruis, José Maria 318
Ruiz, Juan de la Cruz 317
Ruland, Charles 446
Ruland, George 600, 623
Ruland, John 588
Rule, Justus 730
Rule, William 667
Rumery, Ezra D. 866
Rumery, Thomas J. 770
Rund, Charles R. 218
Rundell, Francis M. 805
Rundlett, Samuel P. 790
Runyon, Alexander 242
Runyon, Alexander M. 198, 218
Runyon, Alexander N. 258, 284
Runyon, David B. 779

Rupert, Charles 362
Ruperti, Antonio 110
Rush, Critchfield D. 358, 407, 680
Rush, David R. 563
Russell, Alvin H. 860
Russell, Andrew H. 781
Russell, Charles H. 588, 881
Russell, Frank H. 292
Russell, George 216, 783
Russell, Hiram S. 359
Russell, James 433, 615
Russell, James H. 607
Russell, John 141, 772
Russell, John F. 758
Russell, Joseph 735
Russell, Joseph S. 106, 116
Russell, Leonard 610
Russell, Mosier 817
Russell, Philip A. I. 376
Russell, Richard D. 121
Russell, Robert 693
Russell, Robert H. 607, 781
Russell, Rufus C. 359, 390
Russell, William 676, 812
Russell, William A. 148
Russell, William H. 324
Russo, John J. 258
Rutgen, Joseph 216
Rutherford, James F. 353, 393
Ruthnick, George L. F. 607
Ruthstrum, Gustave L. 649
Rutland, John 731
Rutledge, John 735
Rutson, Charles A. 265
Ryan, Andrew 355, 388
Ryan, Edmond 661
Ryan, Edward 216
Ryan, Edward F. 135, 273
Ryan, Edward W. 292
Ryan, Elias D. 680
Ryan, James 232, 345, 497, 532,
   534, 541, 563, 574, 576, 735
Ryan, Jerry 741
Ryan, John 106, 216, 232, 342,
   379, 390, 393, 446, 551, 569
Ryan, John T. 808
Ryan, Lawrence 160
Ryan, Michael 497, 532
Ryan, Patrick 580
Ryan, Timothy 475

Ryan, William 475, 490, 532, 541,
   563, 580
Ryason, Christopher 116
Rychner, Robert 439, 588
Ryder, Abner 251
Ryder, Alonzo F. 569
Ryder, Charles 446
Ryer, Frank 116
Ryer, Henry F. 129
Rynerson, William L. 335, 342, 346

S

Sabowleski, Paul F. H. 745
Sadler, John A. 804
Saenger, Edward L. W. 129
Safford, John 840
Sag, Witch 175
Sager, Henry F. 132
Sager, Louis 439
Sagslatter, Antonio 735
Saintard, Louis 815
St. Clair, David 141, 731
St. Clair, John 753
St. John, Augustus E. 345
St. John, Francis 608
St. John, Marshall 698
St. John, William 179, 593
St. Marie, Michael 731
Salazar, Dolores 320
Salazar, José Maria 96
Salazara, Francisco 314, 882
Sales, Thomas A. 273
Saliceti, Joseph A. 769
Saling, Rumsey 822
Salisbury, Alexander L. 310
Sallu, John 461
Salmon, Francis G. 739
Salmon, Thomas 834
Salter, Faron F. 461
Saltmarsh, John B. 607
Salverson, Gunder 847
Samano, Roman 317
Samburn, Lewis F. 75, 77-78, 97,
   142, 243
Samora, Santiga 314
Sample, David H. 408, 681
Sampson, Philip W. 99
Samuel, Stephen 155
Samuels, Richard C. 856

Sanbanch, Isaac W. 207
Sanburn, Moses K. 243
Sanches, Antonio 75
Sanchez, José Antonio 317
Sand Pitch 175
Sandarts, Higino 310
Sanderbal, Antonio 207
Sanders, Albert P. 240
Sanders, Charles 667, 769
Sanders, Frederick 375
Sanders, George W. 336, 385
Sanders, Henry 667
Sanders, Joseph M. 607
Sanders, Josiah 795
Sanders, Theodore 106
Sanderson, Wm. M. 301
Sandford, William 838
Sandles, Theodore M. 569
Sands, Lloyd A. 629
Sandy, George 661
Sansoni, Anthony J. 816
Santa Cruz, José 838
Santa Cruz, Pablo 320
Saragosa, Francisco 317
Sarchet, Joseph B. 860
Sargeant, James M. 301
Sargent, Asa M. 89
Sargent, Jacob C. 135
Sargent, Roswell R. 607
Sargent, Samuel P. 166, 881
Sarle, Richard N. 702
Sarsfield, John 482
Sasseen, William H. 642
Satchell, George H. 749
Satsu, Henry C. 301
Satterfield, Francis M. 240
Saul, George M. 655
Saunders, Charles 755
Saunders, George 623, 745
Saunders, Haulsey H. 860
Saunders, James F. 732, 802
Saunders, Joseph M. 623
Saunders, Robert 818
Saunders, Theodore 129
Saunders, William M. 155
Sauseda, Feliz 320
Sauvan, August 615
Savage, Ebenezer H. 216
Savage, John B. 379
Savage, Merril 363

Savage, Michael 636, 783
Savage, William N. 636
Savage, William R. 77, 87, 130,
135-36
Savedra, Juan 314
Savery, William G. 241, 349
Savey, Leon 563
Sawtelle, George L. 593
Sawtelle, Howard A. 820
Sawtelle, John E. 116
Sawtelle, Marcus A. 755
Sawyer, James M. 772
Sawyer, Jerome 160
Sawyer, Leroy M. 482
Sawyer, Martin 354, 404, 408,
685
Saxton, Wm. M. 362
Sayers, William 249, 715, 881
Sayles, Mowry 716
Scales, Charles 809
Scaly, James 783
Scannell, Columbus 685
Scannell, Florence 686
Scannell, Sylvester 685
Scantleberry, James 232
Scattergood, Edward 468
Schacht, Frederick 804
Schaefer, Henry 551
Schaeffer, John 282
Schaf, August 301
Schaffer, John 223
Schaik, John B. 461
Scharff, Henry 812
Schatlin, Benjamin 232
Schaub, Philip 258
Schaw, Samuel W. 121
Scheitt, Jacob 822, 881
Schelling, William 815
Schensley, Philip 207
Scheppman, Heinrich 661
Schermerhorn, Nicholas 416, 703
Scheuner, T. 53, 54
Schiesser, Jacob J. 457
Schiffer, Peter 649
Schiller, Henry 433
Schindler, William F.R. 431, 491
Schinsley, Philip 292
Schinthaler, Charles 232
Schirmer, Valentine 758
Schlams, Augustus C. 446

Schlask, Martin 224
Schlasman, John 150
Schlecht, George W. 564
Schmidt, Albert 62, 107, 881
Schmidt, Carl 448
Schmidt, Ernest C. 265
Schmidt, John 135
Schmidt, John C. 431, 440
Schmidt, Ludwig 755
Schmidt, Robert W. 751
Schmidt, William 265, 532
Schmildell, Henry 28, 273
Schmitt, Conrad 448, 477
Schmitt, John H. 532, 574
Schmitt, Michael 454, 482
Schmitzel, Charles 804
Schnabel, Gustavus 551, 588
Schneck, Sebastian 807
Schneeberger, Daniel 141
Schneider, Andrew 121
Schneider, Daniel 745
Schneider, George 358, 388
Schneider, Gottlieb 792
Schneider, Henry 135
Schoepf, Ernst 758
Scholer, Edward 769
Scholes, James 593
Scholle, Jacob 715
Schonheintz, George 416
Schoolcraft, Howard 216
Schoonover, Joseph 661
Schott, Franklin H. 282
Schott, John J. 241
Schout, John 135
Schrader, Charles 265
Schrader, Frederick W. 772
Schrader, George 711
Schram, Frederick 475
Schramm, William 353
Schreve, John 150
Schroder, Henry 866
Schroeder, Cornelius 166
Schrow, Henry 856
Schueler, Charles S. 380
Schult, Fritz 224
Schulte, Bernard 216
Schultz, Carl F. 685
Schultz, Charles 207
Schultz, Frank 155
Schultz, Henry 717

Schultz, Matthew 358
Schultz, Samuel 482
Schumacher, Richard 742
Schupback, Theophilus 141
Schur, John 96
Schurr, Conrad 745
Schussler, John Jacob 446
Schutts, Charles W. 265
Schwab, Charles 778
Schwab, Edward 745
Schwab, Geo. L. 251
Schwartz, Adam 121, 446
Schwartz, August 454
Schwartz, Auguste 441
Schwartz, Frederick 475
Schwartz, Herman 751
Schwartz, James 468
Schwenker, Henry 676
Schwenn, Charles 680
Scobey, Daniel 485
Scobey, Joseph W. 601-2, 609
Scofield, Charles 482
Scofield, George W. 801
Scollan, Eugene 482
Scollard, William 834
Sconheintz, George 707
Sconthal, John 702
Scoons, William C. 91
Scott, Alexander 402, 689
Scott, Alva D. 822
Scott, Bradford R. 155
Scott, David 746
Scott, Edward 818
Scott, Frederick D. 155
Scott, George 146, 565
Scott, George W. 649
Scott, Henry 219, 541
Scott, James 588, 751, 755, 812
Scott, James M. 843, 845
Scott, John 160, 772
Scott, John F. 455, 490, 745
Schott, John H. 116, 416, 448,
   677, 707, 719
Scott, Jonathan 772
Scott, Lyman S. 624
Scott, Lyman W. 615, 623
Scott, Martin M. 96, 881
Scott, Max 371
Scott, Peter C. 786
Scott, Philip W. 446

Scott, Robert 482
Scott, Robert R. 775
Scott, Rufus C. 216
Scott, Sheldon A. 815
Scott, Thomas 99
Scott, William 758, 761
Scott, William W. 751
Scott, Winfield 6, 7, 23, 29
Scovill, Frederick W. 566
Scoville, Austin W. 362
Scranton, William H. B. 642
Scruggs, William 535
Scullin, Soloman A. 793
Seabury, Samuel D. 347
Seago, David 817
Seagrave, Edward F. 866
Seaman, Albert H. 637
Seaman, Frederick 234
Seamonds, Thaddeus C. 241
Searcy, George W. 695
Searle, Richard 475
Searles, Hiram 216
Searls, Hiram 123
Searls, Robert 256
Sears, Francis B. 241
Sears, George C. 821
Sears, Martin 781
Sears, Samuel G. 135
Seaton, William 551
Seaver, Charles B. 258
Seaver, Eben M. 523, 593
Seaver, Samuel R. 276
Seawell, Col. 34, 36
Secin, Joseph 869
See, Thomas J. 256
Seegar, Louis 446, 783
Seeger, David 642
Seeley, David F. 275
Seeley, Frank 468
Seeley, Warren 116
Seely, George 623
Seely, George B. 118
Seely, George H. 265
Segobia, Manuel 311
Segrey, Daniel A. 282
Seguin, Pedro 310
Seibert, Joseph 799
Seide, Solomon 439
Seidle, Francis 256
Seidle, John M. 799, 805

Seidner, William 834
Seiley, Joshua H. 834
Seiman, Jacob 623
Seiner, George A. 116, 712
Selby, Francis 224, 301
Selby, Henry 409, 713, 813
Self, George 107, 116
Sells, David 792, 795
Selmeyer, Henry P. 150
Semmes, Charles 408
Semmilrogge, Pvt. 69
Semmilrogge, William 91
Sennett, John 96
Sentenae, Hippolite 314
Sergeant, James M. 265
Sergeant, William 439
Serles, Quincy V. R. 243
Sesser, Louis 758
Sevalhier, Lewis 825
Severance, Daniel R. 819
Sevier 827
Seward, Horatio L. 207, 292
Seward, Jared 842
Seward, William H. 16, 17, 25, 26
Sexton, George W. 462
Sexton, Michael 786
Sexton, Patrick 789
Sexton, Simon 490
Sexton, Thomas 340
Sexton, Wiley 825
Seymour, Charles 446
Seymour, Charles A. 146
Seymour, Dennis 863
Seymour, Francis 804
Seymour, George 541, 551, 574
Seymour, Wallace B. 273
Shackford, Samuel 131
Shafer, John 265, 881
Shaff, Joseph A. 642
Shaffer, Levi 657
Shaffer, Theodore 397, 697
Shahan, Michael 655
Shale, Charles 755
Shaler, Charles H. 162
Shaller, Frederick C. 534
Shandrew, Charles 89
Shaner, Henry 241
Shankland, Charles H. 532
Shankland, Samuel R. 439

Shanks, George 649
Shanley, John 642
Shannan, Charles C. 411
Shanne, Peter 503
Shannon, Charles 402, 715, 809
Shannon, John 694, 815
Shannon, Patrick C. 249
Shannon, Thomas 770
Sharin, James 623
Sharkey, Daniel 375
Sharp, George R. 109, 152
Sharp, James 758
Sharp, Samuel 789
Sharp, William 834, 881
Sharp, William R. 416, 707
Sharp, William W. 642
Sharples, Abram 599
Sharpless, Benjamin 446, 455
Shattuck 28
Shaub, Peter 178, 301
Shaver, Henry J. 147
Shaw 28
Shaw, Alfred 755
Shaw, Charles 468
Shaw, Charles S. 155
Shaw, Francis A. T. 789
Shaw, George 845
Shaw, Henry 482, 643
Shaw, Isaac 607
Shaw, James E. 475, 783
Shaw, John B. 789
Shaw, Matthew 135, 273
Shaw, Oliver W. 161
Shaw, Samuel R. 207
Shaw, Samuel W. 265
Shaw, Seward H. 649
Shaw, Sylvanus H. 860
Shaw, Thomas 735
Shaw, Thomas D. 789
Shaw, William 860
Shaw, William A. 834, 881
Shawk, William B. 629
Shay, John J. 439
Shea, Daniel 411, 689
Shear, Samuel 129
Shearer, Albert 532
Shearer, Charles 532, 574
Shearer, Edwin S. 216, 353
Shearer, George B. 210
Shearer, John 551, 564

Shearne, Edward 249
Sheay, John 588
Shedd, James F. 649
Sheehan, John 455, 731
Sheehan, Patrick 497
Sheehan, Thomas 745
Sheehan, Timothy 216
Sheela, Conrad 817
Sheen, Timothy 762
Sheeran, Luke 609
Sheerer, John W. 163
Sheets, Daniel 630
Sheffbauer, John T. 220
Shehan, John 564, 580
Shekels, Noah 661
Shelby, George 847
Sheldon, Adelbert 860
Sheldon, Aristarchus C. 198, 216
Sheldon, Aurelius B. 860
Sheldon, Burton 821
Sheldon, Corydon 623
Sheldon, Joseph 860
Sheler, John 388
Shellhorn, John J. 408, 711
Shelling, Jacob D. 593
Shelling, William 497
Shelly, Nathaniel 468
Shelly, Samuel 607
Shelton, Charles 786
Sheny, Henry W. 375
Shepard, Elias B. 793
Shepard, George 738
Shepard, James H. 793
Shepard, James R. 135
Shepard, John 786
Shepard, Joseph W. 843
Shephard, Benjamin F. 755
Shephard, Byron 795
Shephard, Joseph 292
Shepheard, John J. 433, 477, 491
Shepherd, Elias B. 475
Shepherd, John 711, 881
Shepherd, William 266
Sheppard, Daniel C. 282
Sheppard, Isaac B. 100
Sheridan, Gen. 851-52
Sheridan, Daniel 564
Sheridan, Thomas 207
Sheridan, William 804
Sherlock, Eugene 216

Sherman, Gen. 852
Sherman, Aseph B. 397
Sherman, Ephraim 775
Sherman, Frederick 731
Sherman, George R. 781
Sherman, John 393
Sherman, Lucius S. 790
Sherman, Matthew 599, 637, 644, 731
Sherman, Stukely 408, 680
Sherman, Walter 241
Sherman, Zera H. 758
Sherran, Charles 439
Sherrin, William 615
Sherry, David 755
Sherry, Henry W. 116, 353
Sherry, Thomas 755
Sherwin, Henry C. 856
Sherwood, Charles P. 752
Sherwood, Charles T. 267, 725, 759
Sherwood, Thomas 584, 804
Sherwood, William 497
Shibly, Daniel J. 284
Shields, Charles 224
Shields, Isaac W. 719
Shields, James 564, 574, 807
Shields, Joseph 371
Shields, Joseph F. 869
Shields, Joshua C. 623
Shields, Robert 132
Shiffer, James 863
Shiffer, John S. 863
Shilling, Jacob D. 656
Shilto, Richard 541
Shimaell, Valentine 244
Shimer, David 789
Shimer, Moses 602
Shine, Dennis G. 216
Shine, Jeremiah 636
Shine, Thomas 152
Shinn, John B. 47, 62, 66-67
Shipley, Tyler D. 402, 687
Shipway, John 812
Shiririch, Mr. 18
Shirland, Edward D. 64-65, 67, 70-71, 81, 108
Shirley, Hugh 762
Shirley, John 636
Shirley, John W. 795
Shirts, John H. 249

Shissler, John L. 366
Shively, Thomas J. 292
Shoemaker, Conrad 393, 402
Shoemaker, Drury 820
Shoemaker, Francis M. 554, 581, 584-85
Shoemaker, Frank 623
Shoemaker, George W. 462
Shoemaker, Henry 758
Shoemaker, Jesse F. 249
Shoemaker, Washington 769
Shofer, John, Jr. 256
Shomadan, S. 179
Shone, Henrie 784
Shordan, Patrick 490, 497
Shorlig, Augustus F. 835
Short, Elam S. 643
Short, William E. 607
Short, William H. 484, 863
Showalter, Dan 15, 330
Showers, William 636
Shrader, Charles 216
Shrader, John 416, 708
Shrader, John M. 618, 738-39, 752, 759
Shreve, Geo. C. 28
Shrewsbury, William S. 107, 116
Shriber, Daniel 216
Shriver, Aaron P. 107, 116
Shroder, Cornelius 107, 142, 345
Shrontz, Joseph M. 602
Shroth, George 216
Shroyer, John C.W. 790
Shroyer, Louis 107
Shrum, Jacob F. 282
Shuart, William 241
Shuffleton, Charles D. 623
Shuffleton, John H. 623
Shultz, Frederick 482
Shultz, Henry 408, 409
Shultz, John 150
Shultz, Richard 187
Shultz, Sebastian 375
Shultz, Theodore 503
Shulz, Victor 615
Shumacher, Bernard H. 649
Shurleff, Oscar D. 863
Shurtliff, Harrison J. 623
Shuter, Charles H. 532, 544
Shutt, Frederick 282

Shutts, Charles W. 302
Sibley, C.S.A. 22, 31
Sibley, E.J. 37
Sibley, H.H. 43, 48, 49
Sibley, James M. 109
Sickler, Charles H. 96
Sickles, Edward 266
Siedle, Francis 302
Siegler, John F. 820
Siemans, Augustus 629
Sierra, Guadalupe 317
Sierrito 76
Sigert, Xaver 232
Sigwalt, John C. 402, 689
Silales, José Maria 320
Silbereisen, Louis 815
Silvas, José Antonio 318
Silver, Francis 735
Silver, Harry 860
Silverstein, Adolph 482
Silverthorn, John 535, 543, 590
Silverton, Henry 643
Sim, John W. 854
Simcox, Joseph 129, 258
Sime, Jno. 28
Simmonds, George J. 292
Simmonds, George W. 677, 689, 882
Simmonds, John 497
Simmons, Alexander 462, 882
Simmons, Barney E. 302
Simmons, Charles 551, 588, 738
Simmons, George A. 439
Simmons, James L. 161
Simmons, John W. 629
Simmons, William H. 541
Simms, Orrin W. 99
Simon, Jacob 649
Simon, Jules 153
Simon, Theodore 750
Simonds, Carlton B. 244
Simons, Abraham 685
Simons, Emil 439
Simonson, Anthony 869
Simonson, Tompkins 340
Simonson, William 161
Simonton, Charles E. 439
Simpson, Alexander C. 819
Simpson, Andrew J. 337, 386
Simpson, Ebenezer H. 224
Simpson, George 468

Simpson, Henry 146
Simpson, James 463
Simpson, John A. 152
Simpson, John P. 830, 843
Simpson, Joseph W. 155
Sims, Columbus 38–39, 168, 196
Sims, Orrin W. 121
Sinclair, Albert 259
Sinclair, James 694
Sinclair, Jeremiah 689, 881
Singer, William 117
Singleton, James A. 402, 694
Singleton, Mark 96, 455
Sink, Simon P. 150
Sinnott, James H. 256
Sipp, John 497
Sitton, Thomas B. 670, 678
Sivalls, Benson 856
Skelly, William 784
Skerritt, Matthew M. 584
Skiles, Charles F. 786
Skillen, Isaac H. 362
Skillman, Capt. 73
Skinner, Martin B. 623
Skinner, Thomas 135
Skinner, William 541, 552
Skinner, William G. 842
Skinner, William W. 830, 843
Skobel, C.F. Otto 503
Skobel, Charles T.O. 432
Skonby, Ludwick 751
Slane, David 636
Slater, John 381, 399, 686
Slater, Robert 569, 809
Slattery, Patrick 96
Slaughter, Edward 593
Slaughter, Edward J. 825
Slaughter, Samuel C. 224, 232
Slavin, John 815
Slean, Thomas 503
Sleath, Robert 90, 615, 636
Slitz, Philip 273
Sloan, Michael M. 629
Sloane, John L. 209
Sloat, Burget R. 211
Slocum, Alvin H. 697
Slocum, George E. 772
Slocum, Henry E. 143
Slocum, John D. 394, 412, 694,
    703

Slocum, W. M. 178
Slocum, William 179, 282, 881
Smail, Robert 482
Smale, Robert 881
Small, George E. 863
Small, Robert 574
Smalley, Henry 142
Smart, Edwin R. 241
Smart, Emerson L. 359
Smart, John 781, 882
Smart, Sullivan 667
Smart, Sullivan B. 643
Smedley, William W. 866
Smetts, William 603
Smidt, John 745
Smiley, Perry 135, 266
Smith 852
Smith, Cpl. 74, 75
Smith, Pvt. 187
Smith, Abraham B. 440, 457
Smith, Adam 564
Smith, Adam B. 735
Smith, Albert 96, 292, 615
Smith, Albert G. 216
Smith, Albert H. 362, 881
Smith, Albert J. 866
Smith, Albert L. 375, 395, 397
Smith, Albert Y. 107, 276
Smith, Alexander 810, 881
Smith, Allen E. 117
Smith, Amza B. 234
Smith, Andrew 801, 881
Smith, Andrew, 1st 503
Smith, Andrew, 2d 503
Smith, Andrew J. 14, 168, 172–73, 196
Smith, Andrew M. 446
Smith, Benjamin F. 375
Smith, Bryant 455, 564, 580, 615
Smith, Charles 224, 232, 340, 377, 388, 468, 490, 636, 738, 781, 828, 838, 881
Smith, Charles A. 55, 681
Smith, Charles F. 129
Smith, Charles H. 249, 552, 574, 580
Smith, Charles L. 818
Smith, Charles T. 807
Smith, Charles W. 232, 421, 433, 455, 649

Smith, Chauncey G. 162
Smith, Christian 178, 199, 282, 731, 881
Smith, Claremont C. 800
Smith, Clarence C. 731
Smith, David 564
Smith, Edgar C. 260
Smith, Edward 731, 755
Smith, Edward H. 661
Smith, Edwin D. 375
Smith, Edwin J. 822
Smith, Eli F. 345
Smith, Elijah W. 273
Smith, Ferdinand 746, 752
Smith, Frank 446
Smith, Franklin 345, 393
Smith, Frederick 371, 393
Smith, Frederick A. 130
Smith, Frederick W. 615
Smith, George 141, 249, 446, 544, 564, 574, 667, 731, 758, 769, 784
Smith, George A. 416, 702, 715
Smith, George C. 841
Smith, George E. 869
Smith, George P. 349
Smith, George S. 834
Smith, George W. 755, 795
Smith, Gilbert C. 690
Smith, Harvey 179, 266
Smith, Henry 439, 468, 738, 755
Smith, Henry H. 256, 807
Smith, Henry J. 781, 882
Smith, Henry W. 121
Smith, Henry Y. 232
Smith, Horace B. 131
Smith, Isaac B. 580
Smith, Isaac J. 256
Smith, Isaac M. 107
Smith, Isaac W. 795
Smith, Jacob 273, 708, 882
Smith, Jacob F. 784
Smith, James 393, 455, 462, 490, 541, 631, 807, 845
Smith, James J. 615, 719
Smith, James W. 708, 765, 820
Smith, Jesse 758
Smith, John 107, 116, 207, 224, 243, 273, 292, 380, 416, 446, 462, 475, 483, 532, 541, 544,

615, 629, 636, 643, 651, 655, 689, 738, 789, 792, 795, 838, 882
Smith, John (3d) 735
Smith, John B. 464, 643, 881
Smith, John B. (1st) 735
Smith, John C. 446, 535, 593, 804
Smith, John D. 564, 574
Smith, John F. 457, 741, 769
Smith, John G. 110, 601, 661, 786, 882
Smith, John H. 588, 689
Smith, John J. 224, 564
Smith, John O. 96
Smith, John P. 869
Smith, John T. 694
Smith, John W. 340, 388, 655, 787, 807, 860
Smith, Joseph 155, 314, 381, 385, 511, 532, 564, 672, 676–77, 738, 841, 881–82
Smith, Joseph L. 366
Smith, Josiah E. 778
Smith, Lemuel 580, 825
Smith, Leonard F. 694, 860
Smith, Leonard P. 302
Smith, Lewellyn 227
Smith, Louis M. 623
Smith, Luke 232
Smith, Malcom 146
Smith, Martin 276
Smith, Michael 468
Smith, Moses 863
Smith, Napoleon B. 629
Smith, Nathan G. 484
Smith, Nelson C. 362
Smith, Patrick 121, 216
Smith, Peter 292, 784
Smith, Pethnel 588
Smith, Philip 315
Smith, Philip D. 397, 680
Smith, Reiley G. 457
Smith, Reuben P. 142
Smith, Richard P. 661
Smith, Robert 273
Smith, Robert C. 462
Smith, Robert H. 116, 715
Smith, Robert W. 207, 292
Smith, Roswell R. 866
Smith, Rufus W. 851, 861

Smith, Samuel 232, 371, 375, 490, 593, 615, 638, 655
Smith, Samuel, Jr. 856
Smith, Samuel C. 643
Smith, Samuel G. 694
Smith, Samuel P. 171–72, 182, 187, 196, 275
Smith, Samuel W. 601, 617, 630
Smith, Silas 434
Smith, Sydney 772
Smith, Sylvenas 615
Smith, Sylvester 615, 649
Smith, Terrence 655, 697
Smith, Theodore 767
Smith, Thomas 109, 150, 166, 402, 411, 533, 602, 607, 661, 715, 755
Smith, Thomas B. 792
Smith, Thomas D. 786
Smith, Thomas W. 340, 389, 825
Smith, Tip 833
Smith, Walter S. 745
Smith, Whitman B. 363, 372
Smith, William 107, 241, 371, 490, 541, 543, 629, 661, 689, 745, 762, 807
Smith, William F. 778
Smith, William J. 227, 480, 680
Smith, William M. 409, 676, 694, 715
Smith, William R. 541
Smith, William S. 96
Smith, William W. 244
Smithey, Michael 503
Smitzell, Charles 589
Smoke Creek Jim 186
Smythe, Thomas 807
Smythe, William H. 741
Snedden, Joseph 841
Snediker, Thomas 439
Snee, Thomas 292, 533
Snell, Ansel 402
Snell, Ansell 689
Snell, Walter W. 564
Snelly, William 207
Snider, Adam 755
Snider, Henry 832
Snider, John H. 769
Snider, Owen 202, 285
Snodgrass, Benjamin 282

Snodgrass, William 697, 881
Snow, Daniel 416, 708
Snowball, Edwin R. 449
Snowden, Nathaniel R. 266
Snyder, Charles 499
Snyder, Edward W. 617
Snyder, Frederick 273
Snyder, Frederick C. 340
Snyder, George 122, 845
Snyder, George C. 541
Snyder, George W. 266, 302
Snyder, Jacob P. 366
Snyder, James W. 282, 302
Snyder, John 256, 762
Snyder, John P. 772
Snyder, Nelson 207, 232, 881
Snyder, Simon L. 116, 146, 335, 340
Soberanes, Manuel 747
Soles, John 448
Soles, Louis 107
Soligny, Pierre D. 769
Solomon, Marces 371
Somerdyke, Whitfield S. 792
Somerindyke, Whitfield S. 881
Somerville, Peter S. 661
Somerville, Stewart 455
Somes, Thomas 340, 389
Sommers, Charles 292
Sommers, Jas. E. 302
Sommers, Lewis E. 224
Sonders, William 439
Soots, Wm. 124
Soper, Philo 358
Soper, Sylvester 674, 709
Soret, Emil 667
Sortillon, Jesus 320
Soto, Antonio 315
Soto, Crisanto 305, 307
Soto, Jesus 315
Soto, Juan 317
Soto, Miguel 320
Soto, Ysmael 315
Sou, Captain 185
Soule, Charles B. 96
Soule, William H. 202
Southern, Martin 224
Southwick, William O. 630
Southworth, James E. 96
Sowerwine, George 201, 257

Spafford, Edwin T. 155
Spalding, Edward C. 233
Spaniola, John 314
Sparks, Charles W. 340, 389
Sparks, Morris 786
Sparohawk, Jared 866
Sparr, Matthew M. 581
Spaulding, Andrew J. 96
Spaulding, Herbert E. 335, 362
Spaulding, John 860
Spaulding, Jonas 795
Spaulding, Orin 607
Speaight, C. L. S. 856
Spear, Leander 585
Speare, Frederick M. 533, 564
Speedy, James 268
Speegle, Emanuel A. 801
Spence, Abner T. 772
Spence, Daniel F. 282
Spencer, Barton P. 366
Spencer, Charles 416, 708
Spencer, Dennis 273
Spencer, Ebenezer 866
Spencer, Edmund H. 841
Spencer, George W. 789
Spencer, John 292
Spencer, Oscar F. 787
Spencer, Robert C. 441
Spencer, William B. 266, 302
Spencer, William F. 807
Spencer, William S. 266
Sperbeck, Andrew J. 151
Sperry, James W. 224
Sperry, William H. 224
Spiers, Noah 216
Spillane, Jeremiah 207
Spinks, Frank 314
Spiva, Francis M. 636
Spiva, William 636
Splatt, William 233
Spofford, Josiah 121
Spohn, Peter 371
Sponogle, James W. 866
Spoor, George E. 793
Spraggle, Adolph 201
Sprague, Alvah J. 219
Sprague, Bela W. 738
Sprague, James E. 860
Sprague, Joseph 789
Sprague, Oscar W. 789

Sprague, Sylvester 441
Sprague, Thomas 16, 17
Spratt, Joseph 655
Spratt, Thomas 181, 257
Spreggle 179
Spring, Edward E. 282
Spring, Gardiner W. 789
Spring, Henry 129
Spring, James 749
Spring, William 462, 881
Springstein, Everett 552, 574
Sprinkles, William 615, 649
Sproal, James 655
Sproul, James 96, 157
Sprout, Jacob H. 277
Spurger, Jesse 649
Spurr, John J. 340, 389
Squibb, David 468
Squires, Solomon 554, 590
Sry, John L. 834
Staats, George 416, 703
Stack, Edward 207
Stack, John 156
Stack, Julius B. 698
Stack, Maurice 882
Stackam, Matthew 719
Stackem, Matthew 403
Stackpole, Jacob E. 292, 533
Stackpole, William 580
Staddon, Samuel 709, 711
Stadler, Joseph L. 731
Stadtz, Michael 807
Stafford, Alvin 244
Stafford, John 541
Stafford, Thomas 541
Stahl, Francis 393, 403
Stahl, Frederick 446
Stahl, Jacob 554, 810
Staley, Charles 717
Stallard, Thomas E. 585
Stalle, Albert J. 617
Stamey, Wallace 282
Stanberry, Henry A. 584
Stanberry, Nathan 834
Stanbury, Augustus 408, 411, 715
Stancliffe, William 649
Standley, William O. 416, 708
Stanford, Edward V. 825
Stanford, Leland 5, 14, 720, 826
Stanforth, William 469

Stanhope, Frank J. 241
Staniels, John F. 448
Stanley, Frederick 276
Stanley, George T. 210
Stanley, James A. 249
Stanley, James B. 772, 882
Stanley, James F. 822
Stanley, John F. 623
Stanley, Martin 358, 680
Stanley, Ralph B. 766, 778
Stanley, Robert B. 600, 607
Stanley, Walter 242
Stanley, William 818
Stanly, Martin 408
Stanton, Abram 393
Stanton, Abram B. 345
Stanton, James 403, 411
Stanton, John 751
Stanton, William 607
Stapfer, Louis 490
Staples, John F. 420, 506, 524, 589
Staples, Ransom B. 792
Stapleton, Patrick 564, 584
Stapleton, Richard W. 543
Staring, Edwin 455, 462
Stark, Luke 772
Stark, Maurice 694
Starkweather, Eugene 116, 881
Starkweather, Jon. M. 637, 656, 662, 667
Starnes, Oscar 584
Starr, Augustus W. 184, 187, 242, 258
Starr, Charles 208
Starr, Charles P. 208
Starr, Edward T. 601
Starr, Mike 397, 697
Starr, William E. 856
Starritt, James 845
Startlar, Orban D. 792
States, William L. 649
Staton, James M. 781
Staub, Conrad 207
Staub, Joseph 812
Staunton, Michael B. 340
Steadman, Warren 809
Stearer, Augustus 282
Stearnes, William A. 241
Stearns, Edgar C. 758

Stearns, Reuben 129
Stearns, William 541
Stebbins, Edward P. 749
Stebbins, Lucius 815
Stedenfeldt, John 353
Steed, Edward 882
Steede, Edward 224
Steel, W. M. 179
Steel, Walcott 177
Steel, William 43
Steele, George G. 375
Steele, James S. 552, 584
Steele, John H. 340, 389
Steele, Joseph 302
Steele, Leonidos V. 699
Steele, William 57-58, 60-61,
    63-65, 295
Steere, James T. 455
Steger, Augustine 96
Steibert, Joseph 818
Steigle, John 702
Stein, John 541, 564
Steinberger 507
Steinburg, George W. 882
Steinburger, George W. 623
Steiner, Frederick 552, 575
Steinmaker, August 124
Steinman, Julius 441
Steinmetz, Augustus E. 201
Steinmitz, Jean 462
Stemmons, Morton 408, 680
Stephen, Edward 455
Stephens, Alexander 341, 380
Stephens, Bernard 657
Stephens, Geo. W. 166
Stephens, James F. 268
Stephens, James H. 273
Stephens, John W. 649
Stephens, Joshua S. 636
Stephens, Russell 353
Stephens, Thomas A. 455, 462
Stephens, Thomas C. 601, 649
Stephens, Thomas R. 680
Stephenson, Benj. V. 649
Stephenson, Howard B. 284
Stephenson, John 249
Stephenson, Thomas S. 792
Stepp, Jesse 249
Sterling, Edward R. 856
Sterling, F. S. 197

Sterling, George 616
Sterling, John 552
Sterling, William 241
Stern, Louis 533, 580
Sterns, Reuben 224
Stetson, Rodney 655
Steubert, Andrew 107
Stevens 28
Stevens, Sgt. 185
Stevens, Alexander 389
Stevens, Alfred 869
Stevens, Anthony 178-79, 294
Stevens, Benjamin E. 822
Stevens, Charles A. 224, 882
Stevens, Edward 146, 483
Stevens, Eugene A. 249
Stevens, Frederick S. 581
Stevens, Geo. M. 235
Stevens, George S. 141
Stevens, Henry C. 156
Stevens, Henry H. 394, 699, 712
Stevens, Ira 485
Stevens, James D. 593
Stevens, John 178, 273, 295, 302,
    715
Stevens, John R. 469, 735
Stevens, Joseph G. P. 282
Stevens, Peter 569
Stevens, Thomas 869
Stevens, William M. 825
Stevenson, Frank 302
Stevenson, John 781
Stevenson, John H. 860
Stevenson, John L. 201
Stevenson, John P. 825
Stevenson, Joseph S. 156
Stevenson, Robert F. 823
Stevenson, Thomas 146
Stevenson, William 841
Steward, James M. 273
Stewart, Charles 552, 610, 756
Stewart, Daniel 694
Stewart, David D. 821
Stewart, George I. 772
Stewart, Henry H. 800
Stewart, Jacob B. 541
Stewart, Jacob W. 699
Stewart, James H. 447, 484
Stewart, James J. 680
Stewart, James T. 475

Stewart, Jerome B. 689
Stewart, John 497, 680
Stewart, John M. 608
Stewart, Joseph B. 302, 881
Stewart, Robert 455
Stewart, Robert H. 715
Stewart, Royal J. 208
Stewart, Samuel T. 680
Stewart, Thomas 651
Stewart, William 702
Stewart, William A. 881
Stewart, William R. 803
Stibbs, Hezekiah 439
Stickel, George 116
Stickle, George 366
Stickney, Eubray 353, 636
Stier, W. M. 179
Stier, William A. 266, 292
Stiles, Charles W. 845
Stiles, William R. 616
Stilge, Claus 268
Still, Alonzo D. 867
Still, John W. 805
Still, Valentine 504
Stillman, James W. 522, 543, 575
Stillman, Thomas B. 302
Stilson, Henry 341, 389
Stinger, John 809
Stinger, Joseph P. B. 371
Stinson, Benoni 644
Stinson, Joseph W. 362
Stinson, Michael 745
Stitsel, David 397, 411, 702
Stivers, Martin E. L. 715
Stobie, Samuel 434
Stockam, Matthew 411
Stocking, Alanson P. 129
Stocking, Clark B. 680
Stocking, Edwin 869
Stockman, John 216
Stocks, Manuel 310
Stockton, James M. 753
Stockwell, A. Jerome 147
Stockwell, Aaron F. 629
Stockwell, Amricus V. 266
Stockwell, Henry C. 469
Stockwell, Jerome 122, 156
Stockwell, Sylvester D. 302
Stoddard, Henry S. 226
Stoddart, Thomas R. 241

Stoeger, Joseph 715, 881
Stofeet, George W. 702
Stokes, Joshua P. 835
Stoll, Charles 623
Stolzenfels, Rudolph 745
Stombs, Thomas A. 86, 130
Stone 28
Stone, Alvin W. 867
Stone, Elias P. 651
Stone, George 416
Stone, George A. 643
Stone, Harmon E. 823
Stone, Henry 843
Stone, Henry F. 655, 823
Stone, John 708
Stone, John F. 153
Stone, Joseph A. 608
Stone, Lewis B. 809
Stone, Oliver 845
Stone, Paul D. 404, 411, 671, 715
Stone, Richard 266
Stone, Simon F. 462
Stone, William 417, 690
Stoner, David E. 483
Stoner, Isaac 129
Storey, Chauncey H. 702
Storms, John F. 749
Storn, Alonzo W. 711
Story, Chauncey N. 398
Story, Frank 107
Story, Jacob F. 462
Storz, Valentine 483
Stotlar, Theodore 249
Stotts, Clinton 462, 483
Stout, Elijah, Jr. 116
Stoutenberg, Joseph 541, 552, 575
Stovall, John 821
Stover, Capt. 19
Stow, W. W. 28
Stowe, Alonzo W. 643
Stowe, Cyrus E. 122
Strafford, Jacob E. 161
Strate, William 745
Stratton, Henry 769
Straub, August 477
Straub, Edward 860
Straub, Joseph 366
Street, Harlow L. 241, 242, 275
Street, Pennelton 869
Streeter, Franklin 90

Streeter, Philip 678
Streeter, Solon 616
Streeter, Zabina 310, 317
Strickland, Albert 564, 881
Stricler, Jonas 773
Stringfield, Melvin 833
Striper, Charles H. 645
Stroback, John F. 249, 251
Strobel, Charles C. 881
Stroble, Charles C. 268
Stroble, John 446
Strock, Jacob 292
Strohmbe, William 815
Strong, James W. 116
Strong, Jason B. 580
Strong, W.S. 87
Strothman, Henry 497
Strott, Casbar 804
Strowby, William 341
Strubert, Andrew 96
Stryker, James T. 751
Stuart, James 483
Stuart, Peter A. 655
Stuart, Samuel H. 285
Stuart, William 533, 580
Stuart, Wm. A. 121
Stuart, William W. 420, 476
Stubblefield, Arthur 807
Stubbs, Moses R. 199, 227, 283, 564
Stults, Robert C. 818
Stultz, John W. 179, 266, 302
Stultz, William 533, 580
Stupe, William 233
Sturgeon, Henry N. 96
Sturgis, John F. 497
Sturm, Frederick 218
Styles, Charles 224
Suffrene, David 712
Suiter, John 770
Suits, Geo. W. 225
Sullivan, Alfred 804
Sullivan, Daniel 845
Sullivan, Denis 132
Sullivan, Dennis 552, 569, 580
Sullivan, Dennis H. 216, 273
Sullivan, Francis 135
Sullivan, Giles V. 353, 358
Sullivan, James 129, 497, 667, 741, 758

Sullivan, James B. 362
Sullivan, Jeremiah 292
Sullivan, John 75, 166, 358, 371, 440, 469, 616, 741, 881
Sullivan, Joseph L. 784
Sullivan, Martin 135
Sullivan, Michael 216, 749
Sullivan, Patrick W. 784
Sullivan, Philip 475
Sullivan, Thomas 96, 439, 490
Sullivan, Timothy 773
Sullivan, William 552, 589
Sullivan, William C. 302
Sultzer, John W. 792
Sumflith, Peter 490
Summers, Edward 769
Summers, James E. 589
Summers, Philip 575
Summers, Stephen 847
Summers, William 657
Sumner, Charles 778
Sumner, Edwin V. 6, 7, 13, 16-19, 23-25, 27-29, 32, 196, 321, 322
Sumner, Stephen 411, 719
Sumner, William M. 845
Sunderland, Thomas E. 408, 685
Sunol, Juan 310
Susee, Peter 107, 366
Suters, Samuel 712
Sutherland, David 403, 690
Sutherland, George 302
Sutherland, James H. 413, 708
Sutherland, John 845
Sutherlin, William T. 208
Sutterfield, Calvin 462
Sutton, Henry M. 629
Sutton, John D. 789
Sutton, William H. 863
Swab, James G. 795
Swain, John 616, 636
Swain, Joseph B. 399, 690
Swain, R.B. 28
Swallow, Cyril P. 792
Swan, Benjamin 552
Swan, Frederick 217
Swan, G.R. 179
Swan, George K. 201
Swan, George W. 341, 389
Swan, Isaac N. 349
Swan, Robert 310

Swan, William B. 599, 616, 636
Swank, Casper S. 589
Swank, Frederick 199
Swank, Lima 867
Swann, James 608, 778
Swarens, Frank 251
Swarms, William 781
Swartzwalter, Otto W. 795
Swasey, Charles 439
Swasey, Gustavus A. 441
Swasey, William F. 420, 431, 433
Swayzer, John 698
Sweat, James 575
Sweat, Sanford 541
Sweden, William 845
Sweeney, Charles H. 241
Sweeney, Eugene 552
Sweeney, George 497, 812
Sweeney, Henry M. 775
Sweeney, John 804
Sweeney, Peter 483
Sweeney, William 719
Sweeny, William 403, 411, 751
Sweet, Andrew J. 457
Swem, Shepard 795
Swenson, August 208
Swerer, John 504
Swett, Albert 285
Swett, Donald L. 210
Swett, Franklin 483
Swett, Samuel 564
Swier, Abner D. 832
Swift, Armistead 266
Swift, John H. 470
Swinghammer, George 741
Swiss, Henry 446, 881
Switchel, Stephen 116
Switzer, Andrew J. 778
Switzer, George 867
Swoope, Franklin 564
Syan, Moses 490
Sykes, Charles 784
Sykesey, John 146
Sykesy, John 881
Sylva, Manuel 542, 593
Sylvia, Manuel J. 789
Sylvester, Joseph E. 542, 564
Synons, Alexander 457

T

Taber, Alexander C. 807
Taber, Charles 208
Taber, James F. 201, 208
Tackaberry, Benjamin F. 736
Taft, Frank 208
Tagge, Charles 185, 197, 225, 267, 285
Taggerty, James 249
Tait, Edward 845, 882
Tait, Lionel R. 399, 686
Talcott, George 220
Tallman, Wm. D. 123
Tandin, Adolph 663
Tanfer, John 523
Tanfield, James W. 156
Tank, Frederick 656
Tannehill, Jesse J. 787
Tannehill, Uriah 787
Tanner, Charles 166
Tanner, Edmund 398, 698
Tanner, George E. 151
Tant, Samuel J. 552, 569
Tapia, Juan 320
Tappen, William 260
Tarbot, James 680
Tardey, Henry F. 294, 302
Tardi, August 233
Tarrell, John 667
Tascell, Eugene 584, 820
Tate, James A. 715
Tatham, William C. 274
Tatsmier, Frederick 600
Taufer, Edward 812
Taufer, John 533, 564, 575
Tautphast, Charles 208
Tavery, George W. 542
Tay 28
Tayler, Silas M. 116
Taylor 36, 513
Taylor, Adolphus J. 809
Taylor, Amon F. M. 533
Taylor, Amon T. M. 575
Taylor, Amos 96
Taylor, Archibald 251, 869
Taylor, Charles 719
Taylor, Charles W. 233, 455
Taylor, Christopher 838
Taylor, Daniel 815

Taylor, Darius A. 142
Taylor, David 609
Taylor, Edmond 847
Taylor, Edward G. 359
Taylor, Edward M. 812
Taylor, George 636, 698, 784, 869
Taylor, George A. 398
Taylor, George F. 564, 575
Taylor, George H. 815
Taylor, George T. 820
Taylor, George W. 367, 603, 775
Taylor, Henry 266, 552, 564
Taylor, Horace 283, 552, 564
Taylor, Isaiah 266
Taylor, James H. 233
Taylor, James O. 233
Taylor, John 398, 698, 867
Taylor, John A. 217, 266, 789
Taylor, John Boon 657, 742, 746
Taylor, John H. 542, 825
Taylor, John M. 773
Taylor, John W. 564, 818
Taylor, Joseph 129
Taylor, Lewis 241
Taylor, Mannon 834
Taylor, Richard 283
Taylor, Robert 404, 682
Taylor, Rudolph R. 201
Taylor, Samuel 403, 690
Taylor, Samuel M. 484
Taylor, Solomon M. 241
Taylor, Thomas 274
Taylor, Thomas J. 161
Taylor, Thomas P. 631
Taylor, William 146, 616, 731, 762, 784, 841, 882
Taylor, William B. 217
Taylor, William C. 843
Taylor, William F. 99
Taylor, William H. 107
Taylor, William R. 825
Taylor, William S.R. 829, 832
Teal, John W. 217
Teas, George W. 349
Tedford, Charles J. 809
Teegarden, Van Rensaellaer 469
Teeple, Warren D. 789
Teeple, William 661
Teese, Howard 841
Tefft, George 455

Tefft, Perry G. 818
Tefft, William 490
Teinley, Frederick 731
Teller, Tobias 630
Tellier, Edward 738
Temple, John 157, 533, 552
Temple, Rufus A. 781
Tennant, Walter 749
Terdie, Louis 533
Terrill, George W. 649
Terrill, Lorenzo D. 533, 580
Terrulia, Stephen 564
Terry, Abram 758
Terry, David E. 863
Terry, Henry 116, 504, 815
Terry, William 257
Terry, William T. 828, 841, 882
Terwillager, Amos 702
Terwillerger, Jasper 804
Terwilliger, Edmund B. 789
Terwilliger, Levi 367, 398
Teuscher, Daniel 643
Teuscher, Philip 643
Tevalt, Benjamin W. 678
Thackham, James 362
Tharp, Thomas M. 608
Thaw, William M. 580
Thaxton, Richard 542
Thaxton, Richard C. 552
Thayer, Albert 542
Thayer, George F. 863
Thayer, James D. 471, 882
Thayer, John S. 672-73, 686
Thayer, Nelson 156
Thayer, William F. 769
Thayer, William R.B. 233
Theller, Edward R. 491
Therriott, Charles J. 336, 354
Thiery, Wilfred 109
Thinesse, Michel 555
Thistle, James 755
Thistle, James S. 380
Thom, James 755
Thoma, Conrad 116
Thomann, Henry 440
Thomas, Alfred 208
Thomas, Daniel 302
Thomas, Frank 121
Thomas, George 146
Thomas, George G. 226

Thomas, Henry 667, 882
Thomas, Henry R. 661
Thomas, J.B. 28
Thomas, James 151
Thomas, James M. 533, 552
Thomas, Job 762
Thomas, Joel L. 249
Thomas, John 116, 825
Thomas, Lorenzo 12, 20-22, 30, 34-36, 40-43, 46, 304, 322, 419, 421, 506-8, 510, 512, 668-69
Thomas, Mulcay 741
Thomas, Samuel 408, 685
Thomas, Samuel J.W. 178, 593
Thomas, Stephen C. 350
Thomas, Thomas 469
Thomas, Thomas P. 749
Thomas, William 552, 843
Thomas, William B. 863
Thomas, William H. 766, 778
Thomme, Conrad 96
Thompkins, Charles E. 96
Thompson, A.E.W. 657
Thompson, Alexander 208
Thompson, Alfred G. 636
Thompson, Alonzo 778
Thompson, Benjamin J. 349
Thompson, Charles 68, 779, 882
Thompson, Charles A. 792
Thompson, Charles S. 107, 116
Thompson, D.W.C. 510, 848, 853-54
Thompson, David 616
Thompson, Edward 211, 663, 863
Thompson, Edward C. 157
Thompson, George 455, 749, 751, 787, 857
Thompson, Harry 809
Thompson, Henry 257
Thompson, Henry C. 769
Thompson, J.H. 667
Thompson, Jacob 224, 266
Thompson, James 408, 412, 629, 639, 685, 698, 715
Thompson, James H. 219, 224
Thompson, Janes W. 266
Thompson, John 208, 455, 469, 483
Thompson, John G. 224, 446
Thompson, John L. 226

Thompson, Joseph 656, 698
Thompson, Joseph H. 593
Thompson, Joseph W. 869
Thompson, Lawrence 860
Thompson, Marshall D. 257
Thompson, Merandah 702
Thompson, Nathaniel G. 266, 302, 552
Thompson, Oliver E. 542, 593
Thompson, Peter 349
Thompson, Richard A. 208
Thompson, Robert 167, 233, 251, 274
Thompson, Samuel 741
Thompson, Smallwood 838
Thompson, Thaddeus 661
Thompson, Thomas 839
Thompson, Thomas B. 552, 564
Thompson, Uriah 608, 610, 618
Thompson, William 146, 345, 490, 667, 735
Thompson, William A. 325, 350, 354
Thompson, William H. 208, 650
Thompson, William P. 208, 274
Thorington, Samuel K. 839
Thorn, William 233
Thorndike, Daniel W. 243
Thorne, Conrad 107
Thorne, Nathaniel 469
Thornton, John 440
Thornton, Peter T. 616
Thornton, William 156, 735
Thorp, Charles 758
Thorp, George R. 824
Thorpe, Amos 161
Thorpe, Ashbel C. 244
Thorpe, John B. 447
Thorpe, Thomas 490
Thorrieux, Luis 314
Thrasher, Stephen P. 785
Thurston, Elbert N. 636
Thurston, Henry 241
Thurston, Nathaniel G. 241
Tibbetts, Abram 681
Tibbot, Abram 408
Tice, Charles 224
Tice, William S. 745
Ticehurst, George 731
Tickner, Giles W. 565

Tickner, Henry L. 87, 136
Ticknor, Giles W. 179, 593
Tidball, Thomas Theo. 74, 675, 669, 671-72, 716
Tidrow, Joseph 801
Tiedaman, William 584
Tiedamann, Gerhard 758
Tienfer, Andrew 812
Tiernan, Farrel 746
Tiernan, John 380
Tiernay, Joseph 616
Tierney, George B. 292, 681
Tierney, Joseph 624
Tierny, John 823
Tierson, Robert H. 448, 484
Tieufer, Andrew 371
Tiffany, Homer 823
Tilford, Capt. 63
Tighe, Peter 565, 593
Tillapaugh, William A. 141
Tilley, John 657
Tillier, Constant 542
Tillinghast, Allen 218, 224, 225
Tillman, John 661
Tillson, Thomas 535
Tilman, Vestal 802
Tilson, John H. 274
Tilt, Frederick 795
Tilton, George 202, 702
Tilton, Hagen 839
Tilton, Hazen 882
Timberlake, Henry C. 241
Timm, Otto 440
Timmins, Bernard 708
Timmons, Asa 96
Timmons, Bernard 417
Timmons, Thomas O. 117
Timmons, William 257
Timney, John 143
Timson, Robert 257
Tinch, Noah 584
Tinder, William 455
Tingley, John 483
Tinker, Reuben E. 650
Tinney, Albert E. 274
Tinson, William 580
Tipper, George 812
Tipton, Robert M. 151
Tisdale, Lorin 650
Tisdall, William 161

Tittle, David R. 787
Titus, De Witt 617, 630, 656
Titus, De Witt G. 637
Titus, Nathan J. 681
Tobey, Edward A. 349
Tobey, Nathaniel G. 752, 759
Tobias, Charles E. 671, 712
Tobias, James W. 712
Tobin, Henry 497
Tobin, William 751
Tobin, William C. 107
Toby, Edward A. 773
Toby, William 469
Todd 419
Todd, Francis D. 570, 797, 810
Todd, George W. 643
Todd, James 698, 882
Todd, John 129
Todd, Simeon S. 431, 599
Tolan, James 432, 475
Tolan, William J. 650
Toland, Frank 455
Toland, William J. 616
Tolle, Powhattan P. 371
Tolliver, Reuben 650
Tollman, Amos D. 784
Tollman, Blais 146
Tolman, Amos D. 643
Tolman, Danson C. 802
Tolman, George B. 307, 725
Tolman, John M. 802
Tom, Black Rock 186
Tom, Utah 173
Tom, Woeber 173
Tomlinson, Silas 731
Tompkins, Daniel D. 367, 390, 732
Tompkins, E.A. 599
Tompkins, Joseph 815
Tongate, William H. 584, 585
Tonez, Dionissio 882
Tonolla, Henry E.C. 815
Toole, James H. 394, 676, 690, 703
Toole, Martin 504
Toombs, Peter 408, 685
Toothaker, Jeruel 789
Topia, Franszita 314
Toribia, Belardes 310
Torios, Miguel 314
Tornetten, Dedrick 208

Torpy, John M. 809
Torres, Gregorio 320, 882
Torres, Juan 311
Torrey, William 624
Torry, William 611
Totman, Thomas C. 241
Toumey, Michael 274
Toune, Robert W. 274
Tounley, Frank 787
Tournis, Juan 314
Touzet, Julius 314
Tower, George W. 219
Tower, Levi N. 797, 818
Towle, George W. 856
Towle, Walter R. 644
Towle, William E. 616
Town, Chester 163
Town, James 167
Towne, Nathan 860
Towner, Abraham 525
Townsend, Charles A. 749
Townsend, Charles B. 371
Townsend, E.D. 6, 16-19, 23-26, 29, 32, 33, 36
Townsend, Hiram 867
Townsend, John 88, 132
Towsley, Darius 637
Toxopius, John 775
Tracey, Orestes B. 525
Tracey, Patrick 752
Tracy, Garret 735
Tracy, Garrett 475
Tracy, James 483
Tracy, John 475, 490
Tracy, Perry T. 302
Tracy, Samuel H. 156
Tracy, Vernet 804
Tracy, William 476, 584
Trainer, Patrick 802
Trainor, John 569
Trainor, Mellen 241
Trainor, Wm. 266
Trammel, Thomas J. 650
Transue, Levi 358
Trapp, Uriah S. 775
Trask, James W. 795
Trask, John R. 241
Trask, Roswell 650
Travers, John C. 554, 576
Travers, William 217, 447

Travis, Clovis M. 107
Travis, Samuel 656
Tray, John 712
Treadwell 28
Treadwell, Benjamin 752
Treese, Oliver J. 823
Treir, Theodore 497
Treloar, Benjamin 795
Tremblay, Paul 769
Trempf, Henry W. 178, 283, 882
Treston, John W. 731
Trevor, James J. 123
Trewin, Robert 805
Treworgy, Henry E. 241
Trimble, Isaac 499
Trimble, John J. 773
Trinkle, John 117
Triplett, James 208
Tripp, Benjamin F. 208
Trotitz, Edward 882
Trott, Harvey B. 141
Trover, John H. 249
Trowbridge, George 789
Trower, Bashaw 146
Troy, Thomas D. 584
Troy, William H. 217, 609
Truax, Andrew 569
Truax, James C. 752
Truck, Louis N.S. 208
Trudeau, Napoleon 731
True, Frank 629
True, John 608
Truesdell, Lewis 769
Truet, Daniel 882
Truett, Daniel 375
Truett, John 569
Trueworthy, Thomas 504
Trull, John G. 593
Trumbo, David 497
Trumbull, Chas. W. 234
Trumbull, Robert 208, 217
Trunk, Frank 650
Truston, Wentworth 667
Truyllo, Ricordo 314
Trynor, William 455
Tryon, George G. 610
Tubbs 28
Tubbs, Cyrus 358, 389
Tubbs, Henry S.C. 857
Tubbs, Israel P. 208

Tuck, George 476
Tucker, Frank 151
Tucker, John 629
Tucker, Nelson 698
Tucker, Samuel F. 244, 867
Tucker, William 542, 589
Tudsbury, Charles 643, 825
Tuell, Alonzo 569
Tuite, Charles 731
Tully, John 371, 882
Tully, Michael 96, 107
Tully, Patrick H. 483
Tully, Patrick W. 303, 589
Tumey, G. B. 882
Tuohey, John 135
Tuomey, Michael 349
Tupper, Charles 565, 843
Tupper, Roswell 832
Tupper, Samuel 690
Turk, Thomas 117, 719, 882
Turley, John C. 552
Turley, Marshall 584
Turman, Byron J. 823
Turman, Hosea B. 825
Turnbaugh, David 643
Turner, Addison A. 129
Turner, David H. 802, 807
Turner, Franklin 565
Turner, George 152
Turner, Ira 735
Turner, James G. 283
Turner, James H. 469
Turner, James P. 286
Turner, John 151, 863
Turner, John P. 208
Turner, Junius T. 661, 860
Turner, Levi W. 860
Turner, Moses J. 257
Turner, Norman W. 542
Turner, Roland 274
Turner, Thomas 825
Turner, Thomas D. 490, 533
Turner, William H. 775
Turner, William J. 341, 389
Turney, William 685
Turnham, Albert B. 702, 860
Turpin, Dick 226
Turpin, Hamilton C. 847
Turpin, John 629
Turpin, Martin 398

Turpin, Salomon C. 833
Turpin, William 156
Turrell, George 552, 584
Tuskey, John 274
Tuthill, John 375
Tuttle, Edward D. 601, 637, 651
Tuttle, Hiram G. 555, 590
Tuttle, Joseph 675, 669, 712
Tuttle, Leonard 147
Tuttle, Philo G. 844
Tuttle, William H. 470, 476, 490, 755
Tuttle, William N. 841
Tuxford, James 784
Twaddle, Robert 769
Twomey, Michael 497, 882
Tyler, Franklin A. 681
Tyler, Oliver C. 124
Tyler, William W. 616
Tynan, William 584
Tynan, William H. 589, 882
Tyrrel, William B. 781
Tyrrell, Wm. B. 882

U

Uberaker, Frank 341
Ufheil, Mattheus 825
Uhden, Henry J. 802
Ulio, James 422, 430, 725-26, 759
Ullrich, Michael 758
Ulrick, John 219, 224
Umlauff, John F. 781, 883
Underhill, Geo. L. 151
Underhill, Jacob 28
Underhill, William H. 249
Underwood, George S. 469
Underwood, Jacob 839
Underwood, James B. 303, 883
Underwood, James H. 839
Underwood, Jeremiah 839
Underwood, John 353
Underwood, Nathan 161
Unger, McKelvie J. 225, 274, 310
Updyke, Isaac 455
Upham, Charles S. 292
Upham, Frank K. 770
Upper, Nelson A. 97
Upton, John 342

Urbecker, Frank 358, 377, 883
Urmy, John B. 447, 575
Urner, John 616
Urquhart, James 590
Urquhart, S. 179
Urtel, Louis 769
Usher, George F. 847
Usher, Joseph 469
Ustick, Wm. D. 180
Ustick, William L. 522, 524, 534, 575
Utah Tom 173
Utley, Abraham G. 274
Utley, John 584, 815
Utley, William 882
Utter, William H. 787
Uttley, William 712

V

Vagg, James 749
Valdais, see Baldais
Valderamos, see Balderamos
Valdes, see also Baldes
Valdes, José 317
Valencia, see also Balencia
Valencia, Felipe 317
Valencia, Juan Ignacio 317
Valencia, Narcisco 317
Valencia, Pablo 317
Valentine, Charles A. 292
Valentine, Jacob J. 283, 303
Valentine, Michael 800
Valenzuela, Clodoveo 315
Valenzuela, Ignacio 320
Valenzuela, José Maria 317
Valenzuela, Juan 317
Valenzuela, Pablo 314
Valere, Raphael 161
Vallejo, Salvador 304, 307
Vallilly, James 584
Valpey, Charles 241
Valpey, Washington 151
Van Alslyne, David D. 208
Vanalstine, Amen P. 616
Van Alstine, Harrison 412, 716
Van Alter, Charles H. 398, 698
Van Asche, Eugene 719
Van Assche, Eugene 882
Vanatter, Charles H. 883

Van Benscoten H. 867
Van Buskerk, Abraham 141
Vance, Hugh 775
Vance, Joseph J. 117, 719
Vance, Robert H. 490
Vance, William H. 543, 554, 570, 593
Vander, Zwaag Folker 758
Vanderburgh, Liteno C. 569
Vanderburgh, Wm. C. 569
Vanderpool, William 815
Van Dewater, Herman 458, 477
Vandin, Louis 820
Van Dorn, Col. 17
Van Dusen, Peter 233
Vane, George 732
Van Eps, Charles 661
Van Fossen, David A. 283
Van Fossen, Levi 283
Van Gehen, Joseph 156
Van Glahn, Henry 457
Van Hampson, Ira 823
Van Haren, Peter 167
Van Hoosen, Jerome 867
Vanhorn, Franklin W. 244
Van Horn, Jerome B. 735
Van Lavan, Solomon N. 685
Van Mater, John W. 210
Van Meter, John W. 354
Van Metre, John J. 883
Van Metre, John T. 141
Van Meyerhoff, Christian 490
Van Middlesworth, Peter 228
Van Ness, Albert 143
Van Ness, Henry B. 661
Van Order, John H. 337, 386
Van Pelt, Andrew H. 350
Van Ryper, Cornelius 608
Van Scoyk, Jacob 276
Van Sickle, Rensalear 643
Van Slyke, Peter 870
Van Sylke, Delos J. 792
Van Tassel, Silas 274
Van Tassell, Levi 542, 575, 593
Vanthusen, William J. 750
Van Valzah, John M. 283
Van Vleet, DeWitt C. 869
Van Vleet, F. 63
Van Voorhees, Nicolaus 440
Van Wagner, Charles 698

Van Winkle, William 358, 380, 389
Van Zandt, Amos 792
Vargas, Luis 314
Varner, Thomas J. 702, 882
Varnum, Jefferson 770
Varnum, Joseph B. 869
Varsal, Louis 667
Vasques, José 310
Vaugh, George 746
Vaughan, Glendower F. 584
Vaughan, Jeremiah 643, 667
Vaughn, Andrew 667
Vaughn, Anthony W. 784
Vaughn, Daniel 762
Vaughn, James H. 778
Vaughn, John T. 565
Vaughn, Walter W. 820
Veach, Joseph W. 656
Vedder, William A. 303
Veillas, Charles 504
Velardos, see Belardos
Velderrain, see Belderrain
Velie, Orville A. 121
Velser, Stephen 202
Ventras, Francis 759
Ventura, Peraza 314
Venum, Hiram 860
Verbecq, Alfonso 752
Verbecqu, Alphonse 719
Verdel, Charles 787
Verdugo, Andris 320
Verdugo, Feliciano 320, 883
Vergoe, Frank 716
Verick, George W. 857
Vermudes, Pedro 317
Vernal, Dolores 318, 882
Vernal, José Antonio 320
Vernett, Louis H. 371
Vernon, Ronald K. 88, 148
Vernon, Sidney 483
Verrill, Samuel K. 476
Vestal, De Witt C. 330, 350
Vestal, Tilman 802
Vialolos, José de la Luz 320
Vice, David 778
Vickers, Peter J. 825
Vickers, Sylvester 269
Victor, Christian 314
Victor, Michael 708
Vidal, Gregorio 839

Vidal, Guadalupe 314
Vidal, Jean 462
Viebrock, Henry 283
Vierra, Manual Marciel 153
Viles, Henry O. 249
Villa, José Y. 310
Vin Camp, William 823
Vincent, Alfred 616
Vincent, Thomas M. 304, 720
Vinceynes, Pietro A. 314
Vinyard, James R. 91
Vitry, Louis 820
Vitt, Edward F. 808
Vivien, John L. 118
Vleitt, Gershon V. 643
Vogel, Eugene 882
Vogelson, Charles 749
Voght, Henry 314
Vogle, Eugene 274
Vogler, Charles 274
Vojorguez, see Bojorguez
Volekmer, John H. 815
Volker, Jacob 553
Vollum, Harvey 217
Volpillac, Etienne 276
Vondey, Thomas 781
Vondy, Thomas 440
Von Glahn, Henry 533
Von Meyerhoff, Christian 498
Voorhees, James 698
Voorhees, William 616, 650
Voorhees, William C. 776
Vorback, Anthony 249
Vorgues, see Borgues
Voronda, see Boronda
Vose, Rufus C. 97, 142, 162
Vose, Warren 295, 570
Voudy, George 834
Voverdez, see Boverdez
Vreeland, Israel 498
Vrooman, Elias W. 580, 661
Vultee, Francis P. 860

W

Waddams, Caleb 97
Waddams, Wm. H. 97
Waddell, William 542
Waddle, James 283
Wade, Allen 107

Wade, Allen D. 117
Wade, Ephraim H. 269
Wade, James 224
Wade, James R. 233
Wade, John 690
Wade, Joseph 158
Wadsworth, Jacob B. 773
Wagener, George 863
Wagenhals, William 603
Wager, Charles M. 608
Waggle, John P. 156
Waggoner, John H. 867
Wagner, Frederick 211, 303
Wagner, Friend O. 787
Wagner, Henry A. 241
Wagner, John 608
Wagner, Justus B. 883
Wagner, Rufus L. 694
Wagoner, Daniel 637
Wagoner, Justus B. 681
Wagoner, William 746
Wagstaff, Jeremiah 533, 883
Wagy, Albert W. 802
Wahl, Henry 135
Wahler, George 455
Wahlers, George 883
Wainwright, Charles 570
Waistell, Robinson 762
Wait, Daniel D. 736
Wait, Lyon C. 795
Waite, Col. 12, 322
Waite, Isaac 380
Waite, Justice 510-13
Waite, Robert 490
Waite, Samuel 341
Wakefield, Elhana W. 863
Wakefield, Ray 818
Wakely, James T. 107
Wakeman, Alonzo C. 676
Wakeman, Edward 341, 380, 389
Walcott, Charles H. 234, 243, 593
Waldman, Mark 367, 389
Waldriss, Isaac S. 686
Waldron, George 543
Waldron, Robert B. 702
Waldron, Samuel 570
Waldsmith, George 412, 707
Walff, Frederick 883
Walke, Nicholas 533, 553, 565, 575

Walker, Albert P. 97
Walker, Alfred G. 457
Walker, Benjamin F. 349
Walker, Charles H. 376
Walker, Franklin 752
Walker, George 498, 784
Walker, Geo. A. 257
Walker, George W. 91
Walker, Henry 455, 469, 498
Walker, Henry W. 266, 295
Walker, Jackson 490
Walker, James 249, 575, 804
Walker, James W. 266, 303
Walker, Jesse 832
Walker, John 233, 447, 483, 813
Walker, John B. 792
Walker, John D. 713
Walker, John L. 224, 440
Walker, Melvin 393
Walker, Ora 610
Walker, Peter 283
Walker, Philip 808
Walker, Samuel 593
Walker, Samuel H. 823
Walker, Thomas 108, 117
Walker, Thomas B. 178, 553, 593
Walker, William 380, 883
Wall, Frank 694
Wall, James 544, 589
Wall, James P. 842
Wall, John 476, 629
Wall, John F. 218, 224
Wall, John William 208, 883
Wall, Thomas 146
Wall, William 141, 178-79, 883
Wall, William H. 839
Wallace, Charles 575
Wallace, David 834
Wallace, Edward 135, 883
Wallace, Franklin B. 235
Wallace, George 440
Wallace, George T. 746
Wallace, Henry 667
Wallace, Isaac 108, 208
Wallace, Joseph 741
Wallace, Thomas 363
Wallace, William 151
Wallace, William O. 266
Wallack, Frederick 292
Wallcott, John W. 759

Walle, William 462
Wallen, Ezra 462
Wallen, Henry D. 183, 324
Waller, Edward J. 681
Walley, William O. 841
Walling, Lyman H. 455
Wallingford, George S. 652, 810
Walls, John K. 226
Walsh, Henry 818
Walsh, James 117, 153, 341, 565, 732, 741, 752
Walsh, John 464, 667
Walsh, Michael 476
Walsh, Michael J. 498, 616
Walsh, Patrick 469
Walsh, Thomas 73, 90, 109, 643
Walsh, William 217
Walsh, William B. 542, 802
Walshe, Peter 136
Waltemath, John H. 504
Walter, Henry A. 303
Walters, Charles W. 462
Walters, Ezekial 820
Walters, James V. 681
Walters, John 681, 719
Walters, Richard 576
Walther, Jacob 860
Walthour, Christian 498
Walthour, David F. 492
Walton, Francis 141
Walton, James M. 807
Walton, W.M. 179
Walton, William C. 266
Waltz, Alton D. 809
Wandall, James 795
Wandenberg, Wm. C. 812
Wandless, Isaac 266, 303
Wanegoutte, Henry 608
Ward, Alfred D. 624
Ward, Charles D. 694, 815
Ward, Daniel 643, 883
Ward, David 778
Ward, George 151
Ward, George W. 108, 883
Ward, Hiram E. 593
Ward, Hugh 498
Ward, James 469
Ward, John 161
Ward, John L. 341, 389
Ward, John W. 440, 637

Ward, Louis P. 585
Ward, Marcus L. 755
Ward, Thomas 469
Ward, Varner B. 661
Wardell, Rienzi 463
Wardwell, David M. 283
Wardwell, George T. 725, 747
Wardwell, William V.B. 117, 122
Ware, Andrew J. 667
Ware, Edwin 274
Ware, Henry 274, 336
Ware, William 341
Warenken, Ties 398
Warfield, Julius 542, 553, 575
Warfle, George W. 756
Warne, Charles 582, 657
Warneck, William 99
Warner, David C. 681
Warner, George 211, 358
Warner, Henry J. 553, 883
Warner, Hiram J. 249
Warner, Isaac S. 870
Warner, Robert B. 781
Warner, Samuel M. 624
Warner, William 217
Warnken, Ties 716
Warnock, William J. 804
Warrell, Charles 129
Warren, Charles C. 97
Warren, Charles H. 130
Warren, Henry 87, 109
Warren, John C. 380
Warren, Matthew 698
Warren, Oscar F. 600, 608, 637
Warren, Patrick 224, 274
Warren, Richard 372
Warren, Samuel 135, 883
Warren, Thomas 770
Warren, William H. 217
Warthen, William S. 283
Warther, George 542, 553
Washam, William 818
Washam, Albert L. 257
Washburn, Calvin 650
Washburn, Ira A. 161
Washburn, Luman P. 867
Washburn, Lysander 534, 581
Washington, John I. 759
Washington, Orion 656, 841
Wassenberger, Jacob 167

Waterman, James 617
Waterman, James E. 233
Waterman, William H. 650
Waters, James 616, 624
Waters, John 151, 372
Waters, Martin V. 735
Waters, Nathan E. 130
Watkins, Alonzo 167
Watkins, Edward 553, 565, 570, 575, 593
Watkins, James 141, 455, 662, 883
Watkins, James D. 820
Watkins, Luther P. 156
Watkins, William 643, 825
Watrons, William H. 535
Watson, Andrew 97
Watson, David 608, 870
Watson, Edward L. 335
Watson, Frank 136
Watson, Gardner L. 498
Watson, George S. 790
Watson, Grove 424, 441
Watson, Henry 770
Watson, Jacob 274
Watson, James 274, 857
Watson, James D. 795
Watson, John 146
Watson, John A. 712, 839
Watson, Ringrose, O. S. 565
Watson, Samuel 789
Watson, William 167, 553, 570
Watson, William S. 762
Watts, Albert L. 575
Watts, Albion K. 167
Watts, John 810
Watts, John W. 257
Watts, Joseph 303, 476, 883
Watts, William H. 698
Waugh, John 123
Way, James S. 834
Way, John 608
Way, Jonas H. 624
Way, William G. 179, 553, 593
Wayne, Anthony 412, 417, 719
Wear, John H. 643
Wear, Samuel A. 624
Wearen, George 575
Weatherbee, Alfred H. 732
Weaver, Charles A. 789
Weaver, Horace 483

Weaver, Isaac M. 257
Weaver, Joseph 867
Weaver, Leroy B. 834
Weaver, Samuel 476
Weaver, William 867
Webb, Charles H. 217
Webb, Chester 779
Webb, George 283
Webb, James R. 671, 716, 883
Webb, John B. 108, 117
Webb, John S. 770, 883
Webb, Joseph F. 135
Webb, Sheppard 843
Webb, Simon D. 770
Webb, Sydney M. 98, 109, 122
Webb, Thomas I. 161
Webber, Charles F. 818
Webber, Frederick R. 542, 804
Webber, George E. 818
Webber, Henry 372
Webber, Isaac T. 345, 353, 393
Webdell, William H.H. 208
Webele, Williams 447
Weber, Charles J. 738
Weber, Ehler 483
Weber, Henry H. 110, 117
Weber, John 818
Weber, Louis 412, 413, 702
Weber, Philip 690
Weberaker, Frank 389
Webster, Amos 235
Webster, George W. 447, 455, 533
Webster, Hosea 167
Webster, James 367, 643
Webster, Morris C. 810
Webster, Thomas 141
Webster, William 662
Webster, William H. 217
Weed, Frederick 198, 293
Weed, John 752
Weegar, Erastus H. 398
Weeks, Charles H. 209
Weeks, Joseph W. 825
Weeks, Wm. H. 826
Weigel, John 731
Weimemeyer, Valentine 869
Weiner, Harris 787
Weir 28
Weir, Charles 88, 100
Weismuller, Nick 535

Weiss, Joseph N. 117, 376
Weiss, Joseph W. 108
Weiss, William 447
Welch, Asa 663
Welch, Edward 130, 883
Welch, Horace B. 243, 861
Welch, John 178, 209, 492, 608, 823
Welch, John C. 716
Welch, Michael 353
Welch, Robert 883
Welch, Robert T. 678
Welch, Rus 345
Welch, William F. 456, 773
Welde, Gotlick 372
Weldon, Albert 698
Weldon, James 565, 746
Weldon, William E. 241
Weller, Joseph 413, 708
Weller, Samuel M. 749
Weller, William H. 637
Wellington, William 293
Wellman, Chauncey R. 82, 98, 122
Wellman, John 121
Wells, Bezaleel R. 608
Wells, Columbus 812
Wells, Dexter 363
Wells, Edwin J. 362
Wells, Elephalet 91
Wells, Osborne C. 202
Wells, Richard W. 130, 883
Wells, Samuel N. 802
Wells, Thomas 504
Wells, William W. 554
Welsh, Guadelupe 310
Welsh, John 303, 755
Welsh, Robert 492
Welsh, William R. 863
Welton, Benjamin 156
Welton, Walter B. 178, 276
Welty, Jesse 109
Welty, Joseph 608
Wendell, Charles 156
Wendlandt, Theodore 167
Wenner, John 117
Wenstob, Charles J. 504
Wentworth, Ira 702
Wentworth, Thomas B. 698
Wentworth, Truston 883
Wenzel, George 447

Wenzel, William 781
Werneke, Charles 403, 716
Werner, Christian 732
Werner, William H.H. 257
Wescott, William 860
Weske, Alvin 251
Wesley, John 542
Wesley, Samuel 643, 667
Wessa, John 283
West, Benjamin R. 617
West, Courtland 469
West, Darius 759
West, George M. 293
West, James 843
West, Joseph R. 47, 49-51, 54-56, 58, 62, 64, 66-67, 321, 323, 335
West, Merrill E. 257, 651
West, Wells W. 857
West, William 755, 820
Westbrook, Royal L. 200, 293
Westcott, Elliott 130
Westcott, Varnum 802
Westervelt, James H. 108
Westervilt, James H. 130
Westfall, Calvin M. 787
Westfall, Julius 741
Westfield, William 412, 690
Westlake, William 266
Westmore, Henry M. 773
Weston, Benjamin 293
Weston, Frank L. 637
Weston, James 217
Weston, John 779
Wetherwax, Charles H. 276
Wetmore, Theodore 476
Weyant, James A. 807
Weybright, Jacob 823
Whalan, Thomas 802
Whalen, William 589, 804
Whaley, Albert G. 457, 462
Whally, William 624
Whannell, Peter B. 136, 726
Wharton, James P. 823
Whatley, Robert H. 108, 123
Whatley, White 485
Wheat, James L. 857
Wheeler, Alonzo 802
Wheeler, Charles W. 241
Wheeler, Edward B. 163

Wheeler, Egbert F. 367
Wheeler, Frederick L. 201, 202, 249
Wheeler, James 629
Wheeler, John Q. 695
Wheeler, Samuel P. 421, 457
Wheeling, William 57, 359, 883
Wheelock, Samuel C. 795
Wheelock, Samuel O. 749
Wheldon, Marshall 233
Wherly, Samuel 565
Whetstone, Wash'gton T. 820
Whidden, Joseph G. 234
Whipple, Charles B. 249
Whipple, George 589
Whipple, Harvey O. 589
Whipple, Samuel C. 795
Whipple, Stephen G. 827, 832
Whisler, George R. 504
Whitaker, George H. 362
Whitcomb, John 608
Whitcomb, Sylvester J. 867
White, Mr. 61
White, Abner 841
White, Charles 456, 616
White, Charles B. 91, 795
White, Charles J. 818
White, Charles W. 408, 412
White, Daniel 108
White, Enoch I. 712
White, Enoch J. 616
White, Franklin 643
White, George 209, 719
White, George W. 802
White, Henry 593
White, Henry W. 845
White, James 456, 712, 731, 818, 843
White, James A. 235, 860
White, Jeremiah 616
White, John 274, 440, 483, 759, 805
White, John A. 631, 781
White, John C. 762
White, John H. 224
White, John Q. 121
White, John W. 469
White, Joseph G. 818
White, Lemuel 274
White, Leslie 283

White, Luther R. 117, 719
White, Matthew 456
White, Nathan W. 608
White, Nicholas 398
White, Nicholas S. 412, 690
White, Patrick 440
White, Peter E. 857
White, Solomon H. 157
White, Thomas 108, 141, 456, 542
White, Thos. W. 677
White, W. M. 179
White, William 274
White, William H. 800
White, William L. 276
White, William W. 266, 565
Whitehand, William 399
Whitehead, Edward 738
Whitehead, Timothy 283
Whitehead, William E. 773
Whitehouse, George 161
Whiteman, Samuel K. 823
Whitenack, Peter V. 616
Whiteside, John W. 804
Whitfield, William 629
Whitford, Thomas G. 476
Whiting, Charles 593
Whiting, Daniel L. 663, 810
Whiting, George J. 594
Whiting, Henry 610
Whiting, John S. T. 156
Whiting, Joseph H. 663
Whiting, Thomas 244
Whitley, William 490
Whitlock, James 699
Whitlock, James H. 74, 75, 385, 394, 670-72, 674
Whitlock, Wm. H.H. 782
Whitmore, Henry 536, 575, 839
Whitney, Asa W. 662
Whitney, Charles J. 504
Whitney, Charles S. 151, 699
Whitney, Daniel S. 883
Whitney, David 580
Whitney, J., Jr. 28
Whitney, John J. 97
Whitney, Joseph H. 617
Whitney, Nathaniel P. 759
Whitney, Oliver 456, 462
Whitney, Oliver S. 523, 575

Whitney, Robert H. 110
Whitney, Samuel 708, 883
Whitney, Willard 447
Whitney, William 97
Whitney, William A. 380
Whittaker, Nathan 498
Whittall, William C. 625
Whittam, Stephen C. 819
Whittemore, James B. 336, 363
Whittier, Marcellus 209
Whittig, John 792, 883
Whittmore, Moses A. 749
Whitton, James 589
Whitwill, William A. 839
Whyler, John 818
Whyte, John S. G. 88, 97, 108
Whyte, Thomas F. M. 151
Whyte, Thomas M. F. 146
Wickersham, Edward 504
Wicknire, Joseph 770
Wickwire, Joseph 883
Wideman, Antoine M. E. 118
Wideman, Antonie M. E. 88
Wiedman, Charles 741
Wiemeyer, Konrad 731
Wiemeyer, Konrad F. 742
Wiend, John 233
Wiggin, William H. 210
Wiggins, Francis M. 167
Wiggins, Thomas 690, 823
Wight, Orlando 823
Wightman, Joseph H. 293
Wiglesworth, Edward L. 778
Wilber, Fred 504
Wilber, Martin G. 773
Wilbur, Frederick 456
Wilbur, Parker R. 601
Wilburn, James P. 870
Wilcox, Charles H. 741
Wilcox, George 860
Wilcox, Henry A. 738
Wilcox, John W. 818
Wilcox, Jonathan 656
Wilcox, Marvin B. 698
Wilcox, Samuel 440, 883
Wilcox, Willard M. 441
Wilcox, William 690, 870
Wild, Charles H. 274
Wilde, Harry 662
Wilder, Chesterfield 834

Wilder, Frederick A. 283
Wilder, Harvey G. 250, 258
Wilder, Hugh 702
Wilder, Hugh F. 398
Wilderman, John 151
Wildes, Bradstreet R. 867
Wildrick, A. C. 38, 39
Wiley, Charles 249
Wiley, Charles H. 735
Wiley, Gustavus A. 135
Wiley, Hial E. 284
Wiley, Jas. S. 135
Wilgus, David 789
Wilhelm, José 310
Wilkens, Leonard 759
Wilkes, Joseph A. 762
Wilkie, John 708
Wilkins, Andrew F. 624
Wilkins, Henry I. 108
Wilkins, Peter 97
Wilkins, Thomas 266, 295
Wilkinson, George 447, 799, 810, 825
Wilkinson, Isom 274
Wilkinson, William 732, 802
Wilkison, Wallace 476, 498
Wilkson, Michael J. 576
Will, George 314
Willard, Geo. O. 151
Willard, Rushbrook 283, 303
Willard, William 440
Wille, William 225
Willehelm, Frederick 667
Willers, Ludwig 749
Willes, William 776
Willet, John C. 252
Willett, Joseph 349
Willey, George W. 770
Willhalm, Robert 792
Williams 28
Williams, Andrew 863
Williams, Andrew H. 341, 389
Williams, Benjamin N. 359
Williams, Benjamin T. 860
Williams, Charles 111, 130, 225, 870, 883
Williams, Charles F. 179, 590, 844
Williams, Charles H. 108
Williams, Charles W. 422, 440, 463, 491

Williams, David 97
Williams, David J. 580, 616
Williams, David R. 217
Williams, Edward 738, 807
Williams, Elisha A. 161
Williams, Enoch A. 358
Williams, Fountain 417, 708
Williams, Francis M. 883
Williams, Frank 447, 818
Williams, Franklin 694
Williams, Gabriel M. 483
Williams, George 233, 260, 295, 565, 637, 686, 784
Williams, George C. 663
Williams, George D. 483
Williams, George H. 805
Williams, George R. 225
Williams, George W. 249, 883
Williams, Henry 97, 146, 161, 362
Williams, Henry, 1st 476
Williams, Henry, 2d 476
Williams, Henry T. 403, 690
Williams, Henry W. 218
Williams, Isaac 491
Williams, Isaac P. 702, 762
Williams, Isaac S. 121
Williams, Isaiah M. 823
Williams, J.H. 857
Williams, James 219, 233, 345, 393, 469, 643
Williams, James F. 408, 677, 681, 719
Williams, Job 823
Williams, John 117, 135, 209, 225, 257, 349, 380, 390, 393, 403, 469, 477, 533, 631, 746, 870
Williams, John C. 652, 690
Williams, John M. 161
Williams, John S. 233
Williams, Jonah 787
Williams, Joseph 161, 293
Williams, Joseph, alias of John Boyd 286, 619
Williams, Lawrence 807
Williams, Mathias 741
Williams, Matthew 346
Williams, Melvin 283, 303
Williams, Oliver 812
Williams, Perry H. 136
Williams, Richard 818

Williams, Robert H. 863
Williams, Robert N. 167
Williams, Seth 34
Williams, Sexton W. 469
Williams, Stacy 542, 565
Williams, Thaddeus S. 241
Williams, Thomas 219, 476
Williams, Thomas C. 553, 589
Williams, Thomas G.A. 108
Williams, Thomas H. 731
Williams, Thomas M. 130
Williams, William 251, 491, 643, 732
Williams, William C. 565, 581
Williams, William D. 477
Williams, William F. 121, 820
Williams, William H. 752
Williams, William P. 274
Williamson, Andrew S. 341, 417
Williamson, David C. 804
Williamson, David J. 599, 651
Williamson, Jeremiah W. 257
Williamson, Jonathan M. 177, 196
Williamson, William 266
Williamson, Wm. H. 770
Williard, Rushbrook 883
Willie, William 283
Willis, Andrew 731
Willis, Edward B. 54, 74, 78, 123, 325, 335-36
Willis, Isaac 244
Willis, John 456, 462, 485, 662
Willis, Samuel 818
Willis, Thomas 810
Willmott, Carlos V. 523
Willoughby, Nicholas 565
Wills, James 504
Wills, Thomas 834
Willson, Eli 834
Willson, William H. 417
Wilm, John 151
Wilmarth, Barton 257
Wilmot, Carlos V. 589
Wilmot, Lewis A. 210
Wilmot, Richard M. 249
Wilmott, Carlos V. 600, 624
Wilsey, David 249
Wilsey, Jesse 167
Wilson, Abraham 624
Wilson, Andrew J. 629

Wilson, Anthony 211, 504
Wilson, Asher D. 372
Wilson, Charles 179, 259, 283, 643, 694, 825
Wilson, Charles H. 135, 784
Wilson, David 789
Wilson, Edward A. 739
Wilson, Evert C. 762
Wilson, Frank M. 123
Wilson, Frederick 867
Wilson, Gamalid P. 141
Wilson, George 135, 293, 469, 498, 542-43, 778
Wilson, George F. 807, 863
Wilson, George W. 88, 156
Wilson, Henry 202, 209, 227, 285, 762
Wilson, Henry C. 581
Wilson, Horace O. 637, 644, 698
Wilson, Jacob A. 533, 575
Wilson, James 91, 117, 151, 161, 209, 226, 274, 408, 412, 440, 469, 650, 690, 752
Wilson, James B. 657
Wilson, James C. 456, 498
Wilson, James E. 283
Wilson, James H. 456
Wilson, James O. 681
Wilson, James R. 863
Wilson, Japhet 250
Wilson, John 225, 233, 380, 408, 456, 462, 491, 533, 553, 608, 630, 681, 716, 735, 746, 841, 843
Wilson, John F. 841
Wilson, John G. 829, 839
Wilson, John J. 815
Wilson, John L. 570, 594
Wilson, John M. 736
Wilson, John P. 398, 702
Wilson, John W. 217, 784
Wilson, Joseph 770
Wilson, Lucius F. 825
Wilson, Matthew 542, 823
Wilson, Olumpus M. 810
Wilson, Owen 787
Wilson, Peter H. 867
Wilson, Richard 498
Wilson, Robert 200, 211, 217, 358, 755

Wilson, Samuel 778
Wilson, Samuel E. 795, 883
Wilson, Stephen 266
Wilson, Theodore M. 130
Wilson, Thomas 483
Wilson, Thomas J. 484
Wilson, William 135, 274, 447, 542, 556, 565, 608, 656, 662, 712, 746, 770
Wilson, William A. 802
Wilson, William B. 570
Wilson, William E. 870
Wilson, William H. 686
Wilson, William J. 825
Wilson, Zuinglous 815
Wilt, George W. 624
Wilt, William 781
Wiltse, William 823
Wiman, Augustus 667
Wimmer, William R. 778
Winans, George 217
Winant, Jasper 75, 153
Winchell, George 566
Winchell, Theodore C. 422, 431, 457, 499
Winchell, Watson W. 341
Winchell, Woodson W. 386
Winchester, George B. 662, 815
Winckler, Andrew J. 686
Winder 721
Winehall, Edward 376
Wing, Emory 736, 742
Wing, George B. 266
Wing, James 266
Wing, Jesse W. 266
Wing, John 644, 656
Wing, Joseph B. 456, 883
Wingate, J. 179
Wingate, James 476
Wingate, James M. 504
Wingate, William 637
Wingenback, John 694
Winkfield, Robert 752
Winn, James 457
Winn, James M. 217
Winn, Richard 498
Winn, Thomas 135, 250
Winne, Daine P. 807
Winne, James 250
Winnea, John H. 746

Personal Name Index

Winnell, Frederick 367
Winner, Geo. K. 293
Winner, Israel J. 293
Winner, John 286
Winney, Charles 637
Winschel, Paul 695
Winship, Alonzo D. 703
Winship, Jefferson 141
Winship, John 857
Winslow, Henry E. 810
Winslow, John M. 257
Winslow, Julius C. 431, 499
Winslow, Martin C. 146
Wintergust, Charles 447
Winterholder, Joseph 447, 807
Winters, Antoine 97
Winters, Charles E. 845, 883
Winters, John V. 100
Winters, Nathaniel 252, 257
Winters, Peter H. 225
Winters, Robert 151
Wisdom, Andrew T. 662
Wise, Andrew 644
Wisegerber, Stephen 863
Wiseman, George 242
Wiseman, Thomas 130
Wisp, Carl 456
Wissard, Frank 476
Witch, Sag 175
Witham, Benjamin 469
Witham, Gilbert T. 161
Withans, Charles W. 644
Withee, Ezra 566
Witherell, Henry 469
Withers, Edward 209
Witherton, John J. 841
Withey, Alonzo 163
Withrow, Abel A. 870
Witt, George W. 296
Witted, William 376
Witters, George C. 590
Witzel, August 483
Witzell, William 762
Wixson, James 417, 708
Woeber, Tom 173
Woldemar, George 759
Wolf, Frederick 667
Wolf, George 825
Wolf, George W. 251
Wolf, William 447

Wolff, Isaac H. 219
Wolfret, Frederick 746
Wolney, Joseph 731
Wolsey, John L. 483
Wolter, Julius 762
Wolters, Henry 735
Wolverton, Lewis 594
Womeldorf, John R. 553
Womeldorff, Warren W. 773
Wommer, Benjamin F. 283
Wong, William 644
Wood, Aaron 533
Wood, Alfred W. 770
Wood, Arthur 217
Wood, Austin A. 601, 650
Wood, Charles 161
Wood, Charles O. 799
Wood, David 109
Wood, Edward 787
Wood, Edward J. 793
Wood, Edward N. 637
Wood, Erastus W. 36, 54-55, 336, 367, 385
Wood, Eugene H. 735
Wood, George W. 773
Wood, Harvey 398, 716
Wood, Henry 752
Wood, James 600, 662
Wood, John 834
Wood, John A. 349
Wood, John D. 233
Wood, Joseph G. 746
Wood, Palmer G. 767, 773
Wood, Peleg 584
Wood, Van R. 825
Wood, Warren 870
Wood, William 483, 662, 762
Wood, William H. 137
Woodall, William 818
Woodard, Joseph 553
Woodbury, John 462
Wooden, George W. 657
Woodford, Charles W. 735
Woodin, John P. 376
Woodler, Henderson 835
Woodlock, Edward 209
Woodman, Ernest M. 277
Woodman, H.F. 857
Woodman, Samuel 462
Woodruff, Frederick M. 225

Woodruff, Leonard 341
Woodruff, Leonard G. 389
Woodruff, Simeon 795
Woodruff, Thomas A. 773
Woodrum, Henry C. 447, 469
Woods, Amos 847
Woods, Charles 542, 565, 770
Woods, Christopher 109
Woods, David H. 616
Woods, Eugene H. 799
Woods, George 233, 847
Woods, George L. 376
Woods, Henry 476, 698
Woods, Horace 250
Woods, James N. 812
Woods, John 462, 650, 716
Woods, William 311
Woods, Wilson W. 773
Woodward, Charles 594
Woodward, E.W. 857
Woodward, Edward F. 243
Woodward, Francis D. 242
Woodward, Omri 719
Woodworth, Henry M. 867
Woodworth, John 117, 146
Woodworth, Joseph M. 293
Woodworth, Merrick 376
Woodworth, Theodore H. 820
Woolf, Morris 504
Woolfe, Morris 731
Woolsey, John L. 456
Woolworth, Ethan P. 554, 570
Wooster, Arthur J. 860
Wooster, David 62, 676
Worden, Henry 746
Worden, Valentine 752
Worffenden, Richard 835
Work, Alexander 283
World, James 624
Wormley, Henry P. 818
Wornes, Richard C. 773
Worth, David G. 787
Worth, John H. 787
Worth, Thomas G. 787
Wortham, Peter 759
Worthing, James H. 698
Worthington, Charles E. 779
Wray, Edward Hugh 225
Wray, John 498
Wren, John B. 483

Wrenn, Thomas N. 346
Wright, Andrew J. 681
Wright, Anthony 349
Wright, Benjamin F. 242
Wright, Burzilla D. 650
Wright, Charles 97, 225
Wright, Charles S. 616
Wright, Daniel 608
Wright, Fred M. 738
Wright, George 19-25, 30, 32-37, 39-42, 46, 47, 52, 56, 64-67, 180, 304-5, 323, 418, 419, 421, 447, 506-8, 510, 512, 668-69, 720-21, 826-27, 849
Wright, Gustavus A. 779
Wright, James 731, 784
Wright, James B. 209
Wright, John 533, 553, 575, 629, 755
Wright, John P. 792
Wright, John S. 825
Wright, Robert 217
Wright, Romeo 267
Wright, Thomas 476
Wright, Thomas A. 608
Wright, Thomas F. 197, 293, 349, 418, 422, 431, 725
Wright, Truman 469
Wright, Washington 135, 883
Wright, William 841
Wright, William W. 825
Wrightington, James B. 589, 820
Wulff, Frederick 770
Wunder, George 447
Wurster, John 823
Wuth, Eberhardt 141
Wyatt, Edwin 504
Wyatt, Henry C. 485
Wyatt, Henry H. 476, 860
Wyatt, Herbert P. 752
Wykoff, Charles A. 97
Wyles, James 845
Wyman, Caleb E. 499
Wyman, David J. 285
Wyman, Horace L. 682
Wynkoop, John 117
Wynkoop, William F. 656

Y

Yager, George W. 130

Yager, James 618
Yager, Michael 358
Yager, Thomas J. 349, 773
Yancey, Thomas 417
Yancy, Thomas 708
Yandle, George W. 781
Yarborough, Charles T. 283
Yarrington, William H. 610
Yarrow, Michael 741
Yates, Chester 209
Yates, John 662, 883
Yates, John R. 804
Ybano, Francisco 310
Ybarra, Francis 314
Ybarra, Franco 314
Yeable, Joseph 440
Yeamans, Richard 394, 698
Yell, Pilott 317
Yllivaen, Andres 314
Yoacham, James W. 284
Yoder, Ely 741
Yoder, Enoch E. 293
Yokel, Philip 151
Yoray, Louis C. 812
York, George H. 682
Yost, Michael 341, 883
Young, 670
Young, Alonzo 553, 589
Young, Alvin 209
Young, Amos 702
Young, Andrew 565
Young, Brigham 508-13, 515-16
Young, Charles 342, 390, 594
Young, Daniel 841
Young, Dearborn J. 776
Young, Frank 209
Young, George 463, 570
Young, George E. 483, 820
Young, George F. 217
Young, George W. 504
Young, Harvey O. 617
Young, Hiram L. 447, 456
Young, James 553, 565
Young, John 293, 433, 456, 463, 847

Young, Josiah 795
Young, Nathan A. 651
Young, Newland D. 843
Young, Newton 258, 269
Young, Peter 533
Young, Richard W. 839
Young, Robert 543, 565
Young, Robert H. 250
Young, Rufus H. 784
Young, Samuel T. 250, 251
Young, Thomas A. 317, 670, 681, 703, 787
Young, Truman 845
Young, William G. 749
Young, William H. 823
Young, William R. 148
Younger, George 97

Z

Zabriskie, James A. 676
Zahn, Frederick 843
Zanoli, Joseph 820
Zavery, Theophilus 810
Zea, David F. 336, 385
Zeh, John 600
Zeigler, Antone 156
Zeller, George 810
Zenka, Charles 608
Zigler, Edgar J. 781
Zimmerly, Samuel 342
Zimmerman, Anton 146
Zimmerman, Ferdinand 97, 883
Zimmerman, Henry R. 787
Zimmerman, John 712
Zimmermann, August 759
Zink, Zachariah 818
Zinn, William 781
Zissig, Charles 810
Zoeller, William 441
Zollman, J.H. 179
Zopf, Herman 759
Zorkowsky, Nathan 98
Zottman, John H. 565

BLACKS

The following list of blacks is included to assist black genealogists and historians. These names are also listed in the general body of this index.

Allen, Thomas 209
Anderson, George 735
Bloomfield, Martin 805
Crawford, Richard 735
Dean, James H. 267
Edwards, Alexander 209
Ellsworth, Henry A. 815
Francis, Henry C. 735
Gibson, William G. 209
Graffell, Charles 267
Hinsdale, William P. 267
Hutchinson, James 805
Jackson, Josiah C. 233
Jones, Samuel 233
LaJounie, Lewis J. 810

Lambert, William H. 233
Laurence, William H. 825
Lemon, Samuel 815
Lucas, Michael 815
Polk, Richard 805
Pollock, Charles 825
Rhoman, George 267
Ritchie, Thomas 810
Rutledge, John 735
Saintard, Louis 815
Sevalhier, Lewis 825
Smith, Alexander 810
Vickers, Peter J. 825
Williams, George 233
Willis, Samuel 818
Zavery, Theophilus 810